THE BIBLE AND SLAVERY:

IN WHICH

THE ABRAHAMIC AND MOSAIC DISCIPLINE

IS

CONSIDERED IN CONNECTION WITH THE MOST ANCIENT FORMS OF SLAVERY;

AND

THE PAULINE CODE ON SLAVERY

AS

RELATED TO ROMAN SLAVERY AND THE DISCIPLINE OF THE APOSTOLIC CHURCHES.

BY

REV. CHARLES ELLIOTT, D. D.

CINCINNATI:

PUBLISHED BY L. SWORMSTEDT & A. POE,

FOR THE METHODIST EPISCOPAL CHURCH, AT THE WESTERN BOOK CONCERN,

CORNER OF MAIN AND EIGHTH STREETS.

R. P. THOMPSON, PRINTER.

1859.

PREFACE.

During the last twenty-three years, or since 1834, the writer of these pages employed much of his time and attention on the subject of slavery. He commenced editorial life, January 1, 1834, and eighteen and a half years since that time has been occupied as an editor of the religious press. Throughout this period, the discussion of slavery formed a part of his official duties. On this account, he felt himself bound, as far as in him lay, to become professionally acquainted with the subject. He had access to all the leading weeklies, monthlies, and quarterlies of the times, and this subject has all along occupied considerable portions of these publications. The various pamphlets and books issued from the press, during the modern controversies on slavery, have been carefully consulted, whether those in reference to the abolition of the African slave-trade, West India emancipation, or the issues of the last twenty-five years, on American slavery. In prosecuting the subject in reference to the Christian Church, it was indispensable to have recourse to the great law codes of the Roman republic and empire, as contained in the Theodosian code, and the compilation of Justinian, as well as the canon law, as these are the leading standards. The Latin and Greek fathers, too, as well as the classical Greek and Latin writers, furnish very important matter on some portions of the general subject.

When the author of this volume was specially appointed, in 1848, to write the history of the events connected with the secession of a portion of Southern Methodists from the Methodist Episcopal Church, the whole subject of slavery was necessarily in his theme; and after maturely examining the entire ground, his subject naturally was divided into three parts. *First*, the evil nature of slavery; *Second*, slavery as it stands connected with the Church; and, *Third*, as it stood related to the Methodist Episcopal Church, in those difficulties which led to a considerable separation from her fold, in 1845.

The first part of the discussion led to the consideration of slavery in its evil moral character, which is proved from its evil origin, its injustice, its wrongs, its conflict with Christian principles and the Christian spirit, and from its evil effects on all concerned in it. This part of the subject was published six years ago, or in 1851, by Swormstedt & Power, Cincinnati, in two volumes, duodecimo. There is sufficient proof that these volumes have done good service in the Church, in establishing many in the south as to the wrongs of slavery. In the north, it has satisfied thousands, that as this work is in accordance with the teachings of the Methodist Episcopal Church, on the subject on which it treats, the Church herself can not be unsound on this topic. In short, the approbation of all whose suffrage may be deemed valuable, has been given to this part of our subject. The late Dr. Bond, on several occasions, informed the author that the work was unanswerable, and that the writer of it, in consequence, had a decided advantage over his opponents on those points in dispute, between him and them in other parts of the controversy. On review, after the lapse of six years, the writer of these two volumes sees nothing material in them which he would now change. And from all he can infer from the objections of opponents, or the approval of friends, this part of the discussion is sufficiently sustained as far as the author is concerned.

Before the second part of the discussion could be prepared for the press, it was necessary to publish "The History of the Great Secession," which was accordingly printed in one large octavo, in 1855, or two years ago. This involved the principles comprised in the other two parts, and they were used as occasion called for them in the historical narrative. This volume is composed, to some extent, of Church annals, which it was necessary to preserve and arrange, for the future protection of the Church. This work, of course, will never pay the author or the publishers of it, in a pecuniary point of view. But its material is such that it was necessary to be preserved for the benefit of the rising generations.

The present volume—which is entitled, "The Bible and Slavery"—comprises a thorough discussion of the relations of the Bible, historically and theoretically, to the system of slavery. The chapter on patriarchal service, under Abraham, Isaac, and Jacob, will show how their treatment of the slavery of their times led gradually to its destruction. The influence of circumcision on it led to its overthrow. The principles of justice and judgment practiced by these patriarchs warred against it, and the leading element of slavery, that "the child follows the condition of the mother," was overturned in the families of Abraham and Jacob. Ishmael, the son of the slave, Hagar, who became the freed-woman of Abraham, was free, as well as his descendants. The four sons of Jacob's two slave wives, who afterward became freed-women, were patriarchs, or heads of tribes, equally with the other sons of Jacob. And when Jacob descended to Egypt, there were no slaves or servants to go with him.

The cases of Joseph and the Israelites in Egypt, are the proper types of the reigning slave systems of the times.

The chapters on the Mosaic code will show that slavery could not or did not live where, and as long as it was observed. The chapter on Roman slavery, which cost much labor, it is hoped will be acceptable to the reader. The exegesis and application of the Pauline discipline, it is presumed, will satisfy the greater number of unprejudiced persons.

In preparing the chapter on Roman law, there was very little truly available to be found in the English language. What may be culled from the treatises on Greek and Roman antiquities, and the classical dictionaries, will be found very defective indeed, as to any accurate discussion on the merits of the leading topics. The writer was therefore compelled to have recourse to original documents alone as the only reliable source of information. With these solely he prepared the chapter mentioned above, by reading and analyzing all he could find in them on the subject under inquiry. After this chapter was prepared, he found two works which would have aided him much, had he possessed them in time. The one is Blair on Slavery, which is a valuable book, and, as far as it goes, very accurate. This work confirmed fully what had been deduced from the original sources. Another publication of very great merit was obtained, in French, by Mallon. This work is infinitely superior to all in the English language on the subject of the Church and slavery. After perusing every word of it carefully, during the session of the late General conference, while watching over the little daily in Indianapolis, we found these volumes to sustain in full the brief outlines which had been prepared without any aid other than the original authorities themselves. Should any thing further be needed on the subject, the republication of Blair in this country, and the translation of Mallon would satisfy the inquiries of intelligent, candid men.

Though the author has, from the best and most reliable sources, prepared a thorough digest of the discipline of the post-apostolic Church upon the subject of slavery, after mature deliberation, he determined to send out the Biblical discussion as an independent and separate publication. He has not written a word or a sentence that, as he believes, in its connection, can be fairly construed in favor of slavery. The author feels himself relieved of a considerable task, in having completed, although imperfectly, what he has had so long on hand. He would now commit all to the providence of God, and implore him to bless what is good and right, and counteract whatever of error may be found in any of these volumes. He desires also, finally, to render to almighty God his sincere thanks for all his mercies, in sparing life and giving health to complete a service in itself imperfect, as other human performances are.

CHARLES ELLIOTT.

CINCINNATI, O., 1857.

CONTENTS.

CHAPTER I.

INTRODUCTION.

CHAPTER II.

PATRIARCHAL SERVICE.

CHAPTER III.

PATRIARCHAL SLAVERY.

CHAPTER IV.

EGYPTIAN BONDAGE.

CHAPTER V.

MOSAIC CODE—CLASSES OF SERVANTS.

CHAPTER VI.

MOSAIC CODE—CONSTITUTIONAL LAWS.

CHAPTER VII.

MOSAIC CODE—RIGHTS AND PRIVILEGES OF SERVANTS.

CHAPTER VIII.

WORKING OF THE MOSAIC CODE.

CHAPTER IX.

THE ROMAN LAW ON SLAVERY.

CHAPTER X.

THE NEW TESTAMENT.

CHAPTER XI.

THE PAULINE DISCIPLINE.

CHAPTER XII.

PAULINE DISCIPLINE—CASE OF ONESIMUS.

CHAPTER XIII.

PAULINE DISCIPLINE—GENERAL SURVEY.

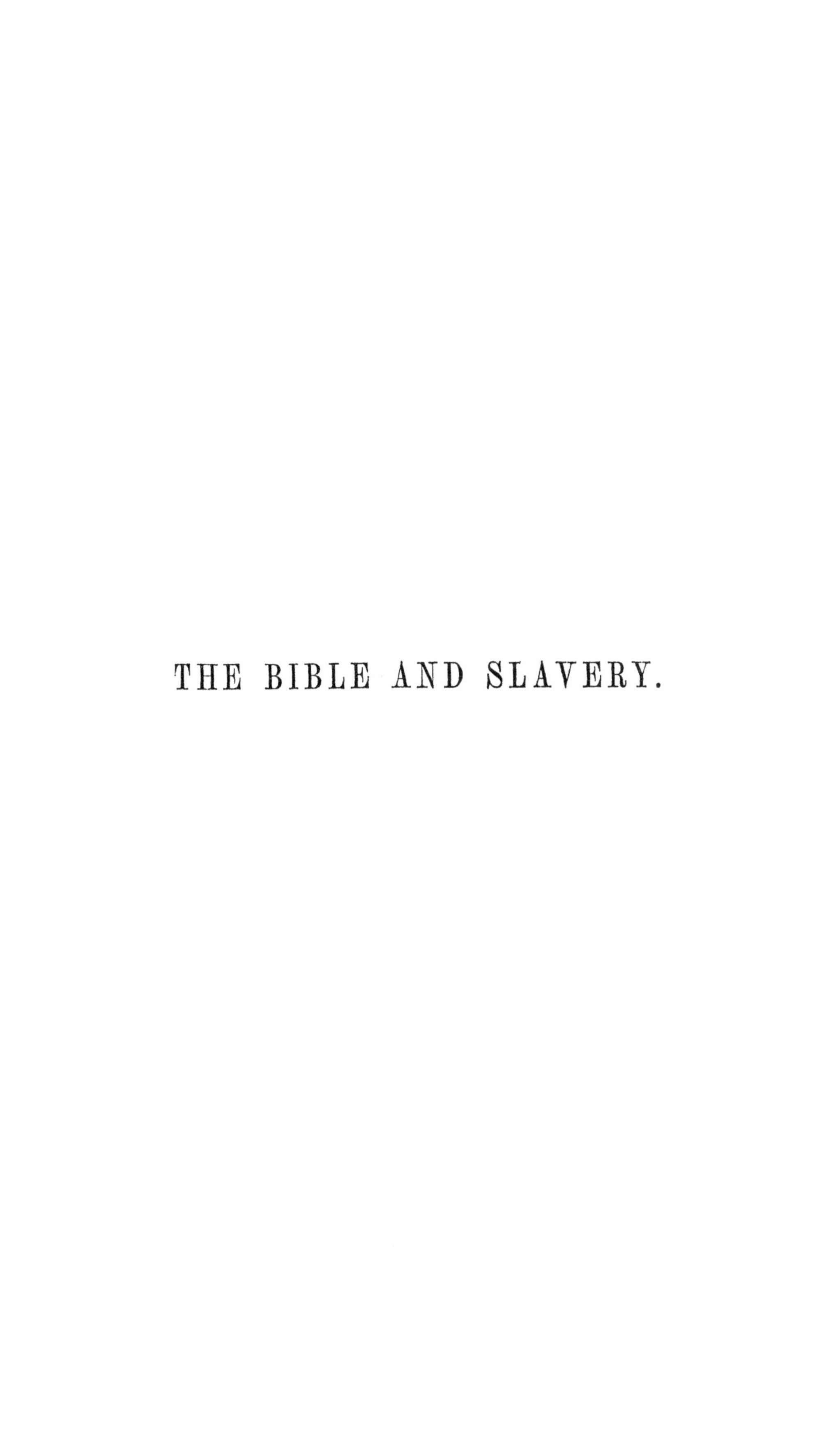

THE BIBLE AND SLAVERY.

THE BIBLE AND SLAVERY.

CHAPTER I.

INTRODUCTION.

1. The Bible is the rule, and only rule, of faith, practice, and institutions for Christians. This Bible has legislated on slavery and service, in many places, and in a great variety of ways, from Genesis to Revelation. This was the case in the days of the patriarchs, before the giving of the law of Moses. The Mosaic code treats on these. So do the prophets, from Moses to Christ. Both Christ and his apostles deliver instructions on these two subjects.

Slavery is condemned in various ways in the history of the patriarchs, in the code of Moses, by the prophets, by Christ and his apostles. Among the patriarchs it is condemned in the case of Joseph, and of the Israelites in Egypt, and in the principles of right delivered in these times in Genesis. The law of Moses makes slavery a capital crime, worthy of death to the enslaver. (Exodus xxi, 16.) The same law regulates service so that it must never, in a single instance, become slavery. The prophets denounce slavery in every case in which the Jews perverted service into slavery. One leading object in Christ's mission was, to proclaim liberty to the captives; and his doctrines of brotherhood, of reciprocal good acts, and of love to others, proscribe slavery as criminal; and man-stealing, by the apostle Paul, is ranked among the most odious vices. The relation of master and slave was never originally instituted by any law of God; and, whenever induced by wrong human laws, it is to be dissolved, with the least possible delay, in consistency with justice and humanity.

Service, not slavery, is an institution of God, and necessary for man. All abuses of it, and all morally-wrong acts in its exercise, are condemned, both on the part of the servant and master; and the regulations respecting it are such, as in the Mosaic code, that it must never run into slavery. In this code there was recognized as lawful the service of the hired man, and the bondman, or bound man. The latter and the purchaser of his services made the contract. It could last only six years, or, by a new contract, during life; and the jubilee terminated all such contracts, and proclaimed liberty to all inhabitants of Hebrew territory. Service was as distinct from slavery among the Jews, as in the United States. The principal difference is, that no slave should tread Hebrew soil; while the laws of the United States admit both service and slavery. No slave could breathe Hebrew air, or tread its soil, without becoming a freeman.

2. Service, as distinguished from slavery, may exist in various relations and circumstances; but the relations of service are essentially different from that existing in slavery. We might mention the services of children, apprentices, minors, hired servants, professional men, servants of government.

The relation of master and slave is very different from that existing between husband and wife, parent and child. The relation of parent and child is a natural relation; that of master and slave is not. The relation of husband and wife is voluntary; that of master and slave is not. In these relations there is no right of sale, or to sunder them for the sake of gain.

The relation of minor is not to be confounded with that of slave. Nature, not force, has made the condition of a minor, and his service is for his own benefit as well as that of his ward.

The service of an apprentice is not like that of a slave. The future good and happiness of the minor is consulted, and a full equivalent is supposed to be rendered for his services. This is not the case with slaves.

The relations of hired servants, professional men, servants of government, are essentially different from that of slavery, as all candid persons will at once concede.

3. The best definition we can think of, and give of slavery, is to be found in the civil law, and is thus expressed in the Institutes of Justinian as well as in the Digest:

"The first general division of persons, in respect to their rights, is into freemen and slaves."

"Freedom, from which we are denominated free, is the natural power of acting as we please, unless prevented by force, or by the law."

"Slavery is, when one man is subjected to the dominion of another, according to the law of nations, though contrary to natural right."

"Slaves are denominated *servi*, from the practice of our generals, to sell them captives, and thus preserve—*servare*—and not slay them. Slaves are also called *mancipia*, in that they are taken from the enemy by hand—*manucapti*." (Instit. Justin. Lib. I, Tit. 3, Sec. 1, 2, 3.)

According to the laws of Louisiana, "a slave is one who is in the power of a master to whom he belongs. The master may sell him, dispose of his person, his industry, and his labor. He can do nothing, possess nothing, nor acquire any thing but what must belong to his master." "The slave is entirely subject to the will of his master, who may correct or chastise him, though not with unusual rigor, or so as to maim or mutilate him to the danger or loss of life, or to cause death." (Stroud, p. 22.)

The laws of South Carolina say, "Slaves shall be deemed, sold, taken, reputed, and adjudged in law to be chattels personal in the hands of their owners and possessors, and their executors, administrators, and assigns, to all intents, constructions, and purposes whatever." (Stroud, p. 23.)

Judge Stroud says, "The cardinal principle of slavery, that the slave is not to be ranked among sentient beings, but among *things*—obtains as undoubted law in all these [slave] states."

A slave is a person divested of the ownership of himself, and conveyed, with all his powers of body and mind, to the proprietorship of another.

Slaveholding is detaining one in this condition, or keeping him subject to the laws of slavery; and the detainer is the slaveholder. Or the slaveholder is one who sustains the legal relation of master or owner of a slave; and *to enslave,* is *to convert a freeman into a slave,* or *to continue him in a state of slavery.* All men are born free; and it amounts to the same thing whether the free person is made a slave, or deprived of freedom by conquest, by kidnapping, or by law. The last mode is that resorted to in the United States, in which, at this time, about one hundred thousand free-born children are annually converted into slaves.

4. On the various ways in which men became slaves in ancient times, we quote the civil law, which is standard on this subject:

"The law of nations is common to all mankind, and all nations have enacted some laws as occasion and necessity required; for wars arose, and the consequences were captivity and slavery, both which are contrary to the law of nature, for by natural law all men are born free." (Inst. Lib. I, Tit. 2, Sec. 2.)

"Slaves are born such, or become so; they are born such of slave mothers. They become so either by the law of nations, that is, by captivity, or by the civil law; as when a free person, above the age of twenty, suffers himself to be sold for the sake of sharing the price given for him."

"In the condition of slaves there is no diversity, but among free persons there are many; thus they are *ingenui*, or free-men; others *libertini*, or freed-men." (Inst. Lib. I, Tit. 3, Sec. 4, 5.)

"A freeman is one who is born free by being born in matrimony, of parents who are both free, or both freed, or of parents, one free the other freed. But one born of a free mother, although the father be a slave, or unknown, is free; notwithstanding he was conceived discreditably. And if the mother is free at the time of the birth, although a bond-woman when she conceived, the infant will be free." (Inst. Lib. I, Tit. 4.)

The various ways in which free persons were made slaves, according to the Roman laws, are the following:

(1.) By making slaves of captives taken in war by force, contrary to the natural law, but according to the laws or usages of nations.

(2.) By the civil law, as when a person allows himself to be sold in order to share in the price.

(3.) By birth, which is the case with all who are born of slave mothers. This mode, too, was incorporated into the civil law, by the common law maxim, *partus sequitur ventrem—the child follows the condition of the mother*.

(4.) Taking into view the whole range of the existence of slavery, writers have enumerated the following modes by which men became slaves: first, by captivity in war;

second, debts; third, thefts; fourth, man-stealing; fifth, children of slave mothers; sixth, by purchase.

5. The following will present some of the leading moral traits of slavery:

As slavery deprives a person of liberty, it deprives him of the possession or control of himself, and of the pursuit of happiness, or it deprives him of personal security, personal liberty, and the right of private property, so much prized by all men.

The person thus deprived of liberty comes under the dominion of his master, to use him according to his will, and he may commit this control over the slave to another person.

The slave thus becomes an article of *property*, and may be bought, sold, transferred, given by will, or used as property is used.

The slave is deprived of the right of marriage, and, of consequence, he is, by law, doomed to *contubernium*—a medium between brutality and concubinage.

The enslaved children are deprived of parental training and control. They are without father or mother, to use the style of slavery. The father is accidental. The mother can not exercise the duties of mother, because the children are bound to obey the master and not the mother.

If slave parents, under moral or religious influence, endeavor to perform the duties of parents, they are prevented from doing so by slave laws. They can not teach their children to read or write, or govern them as parents. They can not put them to trades, prepare them for any business, or control their course for the future. And then their children may be whipped before their eyes, sold from them, and separated from them forever, or hired out to others, etc.

Slaves, in general, are not permitted to learn to read, or go to school.

They are, by slave laws, deprived of the rights of conscience, because the master has the control in this.

They can not be a witness in any case in which white persons are concerned. This is the source of many wrongs.

Slavery visits the sins of the fathers on the children, or it treats innocent children as criminals. A slave, who wrote his own life, says: "The man who stole me as soon as I was born, recorded the births of all the infants whom he claimed to be born his property, in a book which he kept for that purpose." (Life of Brown, p. 13.)

In these United States over a hundred thousand innocent children, born free according to the law of nature and the law of God, are annually *deprived of their liberty*, and from free persons are converted into slaves.

The foregoing moral traits of the system alone are presented. We omit the greater number, as the foregoing will answer the religious object we have in view.

6. Slavery in the United States exists as the creature of the civil law.

Slavery does not exist by the law of nature, but is contrary thereto. The Institutes of Justinian declare this very clearly: "The law of nature is a law not only to man, but likewise to all other animals, whether produced on the earth, in the air, or in the waters. From hence proceeds that conjunction of male and female which we denominate matrimony; hence the procreation and education of children." (Inst. Lib. I, Tit. 2.)

"By the law of nature all men from the first were born free." "*Jure enim naturali omnes homines ab initio liberi nascebantur.*" (Ib. Tit. 2.) "Slavery is contrary to natural right." "*Servitus est contra naturam.*" (Tit. 3, Sec. 2.)

As slavery is contrary to the law of nature, it is also contrary to the Divine law. The principles of Divine truth, given to the pious patriarchs, as well as the case of Joseph, condemn slavery among them. In the bondage of Egypt it is expressly condemned. No slavery existed under the Mosaic code. This code prohibited, condemned, and excluded it. He that stole a man and sold him, or if he was found in his house, was to be put to death. The service between master and servant was by mutual contract—could last only six years, or till death, by a new contract. The foreigners, or strangers, served during their lifetime, by similar contract. The year of jubilee broke up all such contracts among all the inhabitants of the land. None were born slaves; and no such class as Grecian helots ever existed in Judea.

In the New Testament the mission of our Savior confirmed the destruction of slavery, as well as of other forms, in his great mission, for which he was anointed, or consecrated, or appointed by the divine Spirit. (Luke iv, 18.) Paul condemns slavery by condemning traffickers in it, whom he calls man-stealers.

The epistles of Paul and Peter clearly condemn the system by the instructions given and the course laid down in reference to masters and slaves. And, indeed, many Scriptural declarations, threatenings, etc., condemn slavery in no measured terms.

Slavery exists by unjust human laws, at variance with both the law of nature and the law of God. It was introduced among the Romans contrary to the law of nature, as the quotations from the civil law, already given, fully show. It was introduced by *force* and by law, though directly opposed to the best principles of justice and right contained in the Roman law.

So also in the United States, the Declaration of Independence copied the principle of natural law in the civil law, and proclaimed, "All men are created free and equal." The language of Scripture is, "God hath made of one blood all men." The slave laws of the slave states are at variance with the laws of nature, with the laws of God, and with the principles of justice, liberty, and right, embraced in the Constitution of the United States, and of all the states.

Nor does it at all mend the matter to say that this is done by law. The enactment of a law can not make wrong to be right.

7. The purpose of the following pages is to show the relation of the Church to slavery, so as to point out the duties of the Church in the present state of affairs. The code of revelation to the Jews excluded slavery from their territory, as it never could be introduced. Under the Roman Government slavery existed in the state. The Discipline of the Church under these circumstances will be instructive. The result, too, is marked with the best of consequences. In the American republic there exists both the Church and slavery. The several legislatures have more severe laws on slavery than those of the West Indies, or the civil code of heathen and Christian Rome. Emancipation, in various ways, was allowed and encouraged under the Roman code, while emancipation now in the slave states is restrained by the most stringent laws ever enacted on the subject, whether ancient or modern, barbarian, heathen, Mohammedan, or Christian.

CHAPTER II.

PATRIARCHAL SERVICE.

1. SOME preliminary remarks may be necessary before we consider particularly the sort of service in which the patriarchs were concerned, with the approbation of the Almighty.

"God made man upright, but he hath sought out many inventions." In the first human family, the younger son was murdered by his brother. The earth was filled with violence, in consequence of which was the destruction of the flood. In the wars of the nine kings, fighting at once in the vale of Siddim, we have an illustration of the early period of human society. The captives were reserved for bondage. Women were subject to sensual gratification. Servants were bought for money, or were born in the house. Justinian, as we have already shown, maintained that all men were born free; that slavery was contrary to natural law. He describes the origin of slavery in war first, and then by the *power* of civil law, recognizing the children of slave mothers as also slaves. As far as we can trace back the records of nations, we find the existence of slavery in some form. We find it in Egypt, Greece, and Rome. The state of slavery was not *originated* by the patriarchs of the Old Testament, as the system existed around them in some form or other.

Job, who was one of the patriarchs, is said to have had a "very great household"—Job i, 3—of persons employed in his service. Abraham also possessed servants, and so did Isaac and Jacob. Joseph was stolen, sold, and bought—Gen. xxxvii, 27, 28; xxxix, 1—which shows that the stealing, buying, and selling of men was then a common thing. The question before us is, did these devout patriarchs become possessed of servants which they obtained and treated as slaves, or as hired servants; or, in other words, did these patriarchs engage in such thefts, sales, and purchases, as took place in the case of Joseph, or in the bondage of the Israelites? Or did they obtain servants in a different way, in keeping with the principles of right that governed them in other respects, and which we see embraced in the Mosaic code, with the express purpose of preventing the existence of slavery in the Jewish commonwealth?

Our position is, that these devout patriarchs did not obtain or treat servants as Joseph was obtained and treated, nor did they treat servants as Pharoah did the Hebrews. They obtained servants on just and equitable principles, and treated them according to the principles of justice and of equal and reciprocal rights.

2. A survey of the meaning of the Hebrew and Greek words rendered servant, slave, master, etc., may be worth attending to in this place.

The Hebrews used but one word—*ebed* or *abed*—to express all the relations of servitude of every sort. עָבַד, *abad*, the verb, means to *labor*, to *work*. The noun *abed*, derived from the verb, means a *laborer*, a *servant*. It is applied to a person who performs any kind of service.

The Hebrews had two words to denote female servants. The one was *ama*, rendered maid-servant, bond-maid, maid, bond-woman, maid, etc. The other was *shiphcha*, rendered *handmaid*, *bond-maid*, *maiden*, *maid-servant*. As far as the meaning of these words is concerned, there is no countenance for slavery. Indeed, the Hebrew language had no single word to denote a slave. And the context, or peculiar phraseology, must be adduced to show that slavery or slave is intended, as no single word will answer this purpose.

The same remark will apply to the Greek word *doulos*, a servant, and *douleo*, to serve. These words are applied to any sort of service or servants. But there is a Greek word which properly means a slave; this is the word *andrapodon*. The Greeks used the word *doulos* to express a servant in the most general sense; while the word *andrapodon* properly means *slave*.

While the Latins used the word *servus*, to denote any kind of a servant, they had the word *mancipium* in use, which meant a slave only.

The English word *slave* is never applied to a voluntary servant. For such an exclusive word there is no corresponding one in Hebrew. *Abed* may signify a slave, but not exclusively. It properly means a servant, but will equally apply to a bond-servant, or to the most honorable official character. And we may say, in passing, that if the Hebrews held slaves, such as ours, they had no word such as we have, and the Greeks and Latins had, signifying a slave, and nothing else. The foregoing are the bare conclusions on this point, which, we are persuaded, every competent Hebrew, Greek, and Latin scholar will readily assent to.

3. The curse pronounced on Canaan is adduced in order to prove that slavery was instituted of God. "Cursed be Canaan; a servant of servants shall he be unto his brethren." Gen. ix, 25. Calmet, on the word *slaves*, says: "Noah, to punish the affront received from his son, subjected him to slavery." In reply, we remark: It is assumed, without proof, that slavery was prophesied rather than mere service to others, and individual bondage rather than national subjection and tribute.

The curse pronounced neither fell on Canaan nor his wicked father, but upon the Canaanites. These people were exceedingly wicked. (Lev. xviii, xx; Deut. ix, 4; xii, 31.) Their profligacy was great, but it was not the effect of the *curse;* it was the effect of their *conduct.* The *prediction* of crime neither brings crime into being, nor does it justify it. Pharoah might say with our pro-slavery men: "Thy seed shall be a stranger in a land that is not theirs, and they shall afflict them four hundred years." Prophecy is no excuse for slavery, or any other wrong. Our Savior declares, "It must needs be, that offenses come, but woe unto that man by whom they come!"

It is not historically true that the Africans are descended from Canaan. Africa was peopled from Egypt and Ethiopia, and it was settled by Misraim and Cush. (Gen. x, 15–19.) The other sons of Ham settled Egypt and Assyria, and, conjointly with Shem, Persia, and afterward, to some extent, the Grecian and Roman empires.

The history of Canaan's descendants verifies the prophecy. They first became tributary to the Israelites; then to the Medes and Persians; then to the Macedonians, Grecians, and Romans, successively; and, finally, they were subjected to the Ottoman dynasty, under which they yet remain. Thus Canaan has been for ages, mainly, the servant of Shem and Japheth, and secondarily of the other sons of Ham.

As the Africans are not the descendants of Canaan, the assumption that their enslavement fulfills the prophecy is not correct. Besides, only a fraction of the Africans have at any time been the slaves of other nations. If it be objected, however, that a large majority of the Africans have always been slaves in Africa, we answer, this is not true in point of fact, as the greater portion of Africa is not a slave country, as far as we can learn, though represented such by pro-slavery men; and if they were even so, Canaan, in this case, could not be the slaves of Shem and Japheth, as the prophecy says, but the slaves of each other.

4. At the commencement of human society all government was naturally patriarchal. Each family was a little kingdom of itself, relying on its head as the fountain of authority. Abraham seems to have been under the authority of Terah, his father, till he was seventy-five years old. (Genesis xi, 31.) In the year 1921 before Christ, he "took Sarah his wife, and Lot his brother's son, and all their substance that they had gathered, and the souls that they had gotten in Haran; and they went forth to go into the land of Canaan." Genesis xii, 5. He was a prince with regal authority, and his servants were his subjects. He must have been a man of considerable possessions when he had three hundred and eighteen servants born in his house, instructed in the use of arms. He had many not born in his house, and some were given him as a present. These, with the women and children, make a considerable tribe. He possessed many of the rights of sovereignty, in no small degree; and he was even considered as a sovereign prince while dwelling on the territories of others. He was *confederate* with several kings. (Genesis xiv, 13.) He was in alliance with Abimelech and the King of Egypt. It may be proper now to consider how Abraham obtained his servants, and how he employed them.

(1.) The first account we have of Abraham's servants is, when he and Lot removed to Canaan from Haran. They took "the souls that they had gotten in Haran." Genesis xii, 5. As Abraham left Haran on account of its idolatry, the souls that he and Lot had gotten, appear to be persons whom he had been the instrument of converting to the knowledge of the true God, and whom he employed in his service as a religious and civil head. This is confirmed by the Chaldee paraphrase which renders the text, "The souls of those whom they proselyted in Haran." Abraham took these with him from Haran to Canaan, that they might be under his care and government, and that they might be partakers of the promised blessings.

Shortly after, when he was in Egypt, on account of the famine, it is said, "he had sheep and oxen, and he-asses, and men-servants and maid-servants, and she-asses and camels." Genesis xii, 16.

When Abraham and Lot parted, we find their servants were employed principally as *herdsmen.* (Genesis xiii, 7, 8.) Thus far we have no account of the way in which these servants came into the possession of Abraham or Lot. Eight years after, when Abraham went to war with his servants, they were composed of those born in his house. (Genesis xiv, 14.) Twenty-three years after he left Haran, before Christ 1898, we have an account of bought servants: "He that is born in the house, or bought with money of any stranger which is not of thy seed." Genesis xvii, 12, 27. Next year we learn that Abimelech gave Abraham "sheep and oxen, and men-servants and maid-servants." Genesis xx, 14.

(2.) At this stage of our inquiry, it is proper to state that Abraham was a very devout and religious man. When the Lord called him to leave Haran and go to Canaan, it is said of him, that God blessed him, and made his name great; that he should be a blessing to others; and in him all the families of the earth should be blessed. (Genesis xii, 2, 3.) Melchisedek blessed Abraham, and characterized him as a righteous man. (Genesis xiv, 18–20.) God is said to be his "shield and his exceeding great reward." Genesis xv, 1. "He believed God, and he counted it to him for righteousness." In regard to his family government it is said, "For I know him that he will command his children and his household after him, and they shall keep the way of the Lord to do justice and judgment." Genesis.

(3.) We have seen that those who came with Abraham from Haran to Canaan, were proselytes to the true religion, and this is further confirmed twenty-four years after, when God gave to Abraham the covenant of circumcision. The servants were all required to be circumcised. "This is my covenant, which ye shall keep, between me and you, and thy seed after thee; Every man-child among you shall be circumcised. And he that is eight days old shall be circumcised among you, every male child in your generations, he that is born in the house, or bought with money of any stranger, which is not of thy seed. He that is born in thy house, and he that is bought with thy money, must needs be circumcised: and my covenant shall be in your flesh for an everlasting covenant. And all the men of his house, born in his house, and bought with money of the stranger, were circumcised with him." Genesis xvii, 10, 12, 13, 27.

According to the Jewish writers the father was to circumcise his son; and the master, his servant born in his house, or bought with money. If the father or master neglected to do this, the magistrates were required to see that it was done. If the magistrates neglected, then the person himself was obliged, when he came of age, to be circumcised.

There were many adults in Abraham's family bought with money. We can not suppose they were bought without consent from those persons. For as no adults would be compelled to a religious life, the servants of Abraham were voluntary; they were bought with their own consent or from themselves, and none were purchased except those who would renounce idolatry and worship the true God. Their admission, as parties to this covenant, was a recognition that they were not articles of property, but rational, accountable beings, standing before God on an equality with their masters. They were fellow-heirs with him of the promises.

Circumcision establishes the religious element existing in the service which was rendered to Abraham. The original acquisition of servants, by him and Lot, in Haran, was by proselytism, as we have seen. On establishing the covenant with Abraham, on his departure for Canaan, when circumcision was given, twenty-four years after, all these original proselytes were included; so also were all who were afterward purchased by money, as additional proselytes, and their children were all included. It embraced every man-child; every one born in the house, and those bought with money from strangers, not of Abraham's seed. All must be circumcised; they *must needs be circumcised.* The uncircumcised soul shall be cut off from his people; because he "hath broken God's covenant." All uncircumcised servants of Abraham lost their rights of social, civil, and religious privileges, and were therefore separated or driven out from the community of Abraham; and where we have an account of carrying out this institution, in Genesis xxii, 23–27, it embraced Abraham, Ishmael, his son, and all others, as in the words following: "All that were born in the house; all that were bought with money; every male among the men of Abraham's house; all the men of his house, born in the house, and bought with money of the stranger." Hence, all the proselytes and their children that came with Abraham out of Haran, and those under his civil and religious government, eight years after, when he armed his *trained*, or *religiously instructed* subjects or servants, to recover his nephew, Lot, and any others, either bought, or born, were all included in the covenant of circumcision.

And this was to be a permanent institution for the future, in reference to all Abraham's posterity, and any who would become allied to him in religious, civil, or domestic citizenship. The language of the institution of circumcision is, "Thou shalt keep my covenant, therefore, thou and thy seed after thee, in all their generations. Every man-child in your generations, he that is born in the house, or bought with money of any stranger, which is not of thy seed." Genesis xvii, 9–12. Thus the first edition of the Christian brotherhood of man was instituted. It was to be established in the land of Canaan; and indeed all the elements of the Mosaic code or service is embraced in the covenant made with Abraham. And when it was established in Canaan, it provided that no Israelite or stranger who joined them, could be a slave; though temporary service was allowed. But this was so guarded by the right of redemption, and the year of release to all Hebrews, and of the year of jubilee to all strangers as well as Hebrews, that slavery never could, or never did, get any footing among the Jews.

5. We may here notice the various ways in which Abraham came into the possession of his servants. We put them down as follows: 1. By proselytism. 2. By purchase. 3. By birth in his house, or rather under his religious and civil government. 4. By gifts. We will notice each of these.

The first subjects or servants associated with Abraham as their commander and religious instructor, and civil protector, seem plainly to be proselytes to his religion. Those souls which he got in Haran, as the Chaldee has it, were proselytes, who united with him under the covenant, and emigrated with him to Canaan. They are, eight years after, said to be *trained*, or rather *instructed*, servants. The Hebrew word used here means *consecrated*, or *devoted*, meaning those who were devoted to God's service, and *instructed* by him, in the true religion. (Genesis xiv, 14.) These *trained, instructed, religious* subjects, or servants of Abraham, composed his household. The Almighty, constituting Abraham as the person through whom the nations were to be blessed, says: "For I know him, that he will command his children and his household after him, and they shall keep the way of the Lord, to do justice and judgment; that the Lord may do to Abraham that which he hath spoken of him." Genesis xviii, 19. Here Abraham is a *commander*, who commands or governs his children and household, or subjects. The object is that these may keep the way of the Lord, so as to do *justly* in all things, and maintain judgment or religious institutions, both in theory and practice. If we consider also the institution of circumcision, which he and his servants, or subjects, received from God, the religious character is the most prominent one of the service rendered to Abraham. And his receiving them originally as proselytes, and connecting with his institution religion to the very last, the obtaining of proselytes to the true religion was the foundation of the whole. And annexing to this the mode of increasing them by purchase, by gift, or by birth, were all secondary modes of acquisition, to be regulated by the religious element in all things, so that there is no trace of the slave system in the service rendered to Abraham, as it is found in the case of Joseph, in the case of the Hebrews in Egypt, or in Grecian, Roman, or American slavery.

6. Some of the servants of Abraham were "bought with money." There is only one instance of this in the case of Abraham, and it is the following: "He that is born in the house, or bought with money of any stranger, which is not of thy seed; he that is born in thy house, and he that is bought with thy money, must needs be circumcised." Genesis xvii, 12, 13; see also 23, 27.

From this it is inferred by pro-slavery men, that as Abraham bought with money, he might also sell for money; and hence other men may now buy and sell human beings as slaves.

To this we answer, that the mere fact of *purchase* determines nothing as to the nature of the service. It by no means proves that the person purchased must in future be regarded as property, and therefore a slave; or that because a person, or rather his services were purchased or bought, that they could therefore be sold. Abraham may have purchased his servants from themselves, by paying them wages, or securing them protection and support; or he may have bought slaves, in view of emancipating them, and of bringing them to a knowledge of true religion, or to a state which ultimately would be freedom. But Abraham sold no servants. On this important point we furnish the following observations, in order to clear it up fully, and rescue it from the perversions of slaveholders and their expositors.

(1.) The use of the mere words *to buy* does not settle the question. It is commonly used in the sense of purchasing, as applied to land, cattle, or any sort of property. This is a common use, and need not be dwelt on. But its meaning, as applied to real estate or personal property, is very different from what it is, when applied to human beings, as we shall presently show.

(2.) God is represented as having *bought* his people. "Is not he thy father who hath bought thee?" (Deuteronomy xxxii, 6. "Till the people pass over which thou hast purchased." Exodus xv, 16. "Remember thy congregation, which thou hast purchased of old; the rod of thine inheritance, which thou hast redeemed." Psalm lxxiv, 2. "I gave Egypt for thy ransom, Ethiopia and Seba for thee." Isaiah xliii, 3. It is the same word used here, that is used respecting the servants of Abraham; yet those whom God bought, purchased, or redeemed, were not held as *slaves*, or regarded as *property*. Abraham may have purchased his servants to prevent them from being slaves. The mere act of paying a *price* for them no more implies that he continued them slaves, than it does that because God redeemed his people by a price, implies that he regarded them as slaves; or that, because a man may purchase his wife or child, who have been slaves, that he still continues to hold and treat them as slaves.

(3.) Persons were sometimes bought by paying men what they consider a fair compensation for their services, by taking their obligation to serve for a limited time. In this way Jacob was bought, or sold himself, and this was the way contemplated by the law of Moses. "If thy brother wax poor and sell himself." Leviticus xxv, 47. This is a transaction in which the purest minds can engage in and retrospect without guilt. This was a mere purchase of time, or *service*. It gave no right to sell the man again, or retain him beyond the specified time, or to retain him at all, could he or his friends succeed to redeem him. It gave no right of property to the *man*, any more than to an apprentice. In no proper sense of the word could this be slavery.

(4.) The word buy is sometimes applied to the manner in which a *wife* was obtained. Jacob purchased his wives by his labor or service, not by money. And the purchase of a wife by paying a *dowry* was common. (Exodus xxii, 17; 1 Samuel xvii, 25; Judges i, 12, 13.) Boaz bought Ruth to be his wife. So Hosea bought his wife for "fifteen pieces of silver, and for one homer of barley, and one half homer of barley." Hosea iii, 2. The wife among the patriarchs was not a slave, or subject to the laws of property, so that her husband could sell her. She was *his*, to the exclusion of the claim of any other man, but she was his as *his wife*, not as *his slave*. And thus the manner of obtaining a wife by purchase, is the same in which Abraham obtained servants; and this does not certainly imply slavery; but in Abraham's case slavery is out of the question, because he was a just, honest, and pious man.

(5.) Joseph is said to have *bought* the Egyptians. "Behold I have bought you this day, and your land for Pharaoh." Genesis xlvii, 23. The fifth part of the produce was to be Pharaoh's, and the four-fifths were to be theirs. There was a claim on them for produce, the fruit of labor. Farmers who work for shares, are not on that account slaves.

(6.) The case of Joseph will show the difference between the purchase of a slave, and the purchase of a servant for a time, to perform labor or service. He was sold, not by himself, but by third persons. The Ishmaelites paid for him. So did Potiphar. Yet he was *stolen*. Joseph said to the butler, "Indeed, I was stolen." The Ishmaelites paid for him, and so did Potiphar, yet he was stolen. It was theft all over. God does not approve of theft, especially the stealing of a man, and the punishment for it was death. Yet slaveholders are displeased when they are called thieves, though their slaves are all stolen from themselves. The servants whom Abraham bought, he paid for as an honest man, either to themselves or their owners. The objector takes it for granted that Abraham bought from third persons, in the character of owners, as in the case of American slaves. There is no instance in the Bible of any innocent person being sold, with Divine approbation, for a slave. The case of Joseph condemns the slave system, and Abraham can not be supposed to act either like Joseph's brethren, the Ishmaelites, or Potiphar.

(7.) We have many instances of the purchase of

servants for money, without a single element of slavery. In early times many emigrants from Scotland, Ireland, Germany, etc., in order to pay their passage to America, bound themselves to serve in America, a certain number of years, to pay their passage money. These persons, or rather their time and service, were sold in America by the captains of vessels. Many of these servants, by industry and economy, after the expiration of their term of service, became wealthy. Many of their descendants now hold slaves; and were you to remind them that their fathers or grandfathers were bought with money, and, therefore, their children must be slaves, the argument would be as good in this case as it would be to prove that Abraham held slaves.

The mere act of *buying* servants by no means proves that slavery is to be the result. The purchase may amount to nothing else than an act of emancipation. There is not the slightest evidence that either Abraham, Isaac, or Jacob ever sold a slave, or offered one for sale, or regarded servants as justly liable to be sold. There is no evidence that their servants descended by inheritance from father to son. The passage which says that Abraham had "servants bought with money," can not be adduced to justify slavery. He must be little acquainted with the Bible who does not know that buying a man sometimes means securing a right to his services for a limited time by paying him a price; and sometimes it means buying a man of some neighbor, who claims the right to dispose of him as property; or, sometimes, it means buying a servant, or his services, by mutual contract; and sometimes it means buying a slave. The meaning of the word is easily known by inquiring who sold him. We learn that Jacob served, and that Joseph was sold for a slave. They were both bought, and they both served; but Jacob was a free servant, and Joseph was a slave.

Jacob sold himself, and Joseph was sold by others, without his consent. To buy corn of its lawful owners is right, but to buy it from thieves is to partake with them in the guilt of theft. Jacob, by his sons, bought corn in Egypt, not from thieves, but from the proper owner. Abraham bought the services of men and women, either from themselves or from others, in view of their redemption, as the facts in the case show.

7. Some of Abraham's servants were born in his house, or the sons of his house. (Genesis xiv, 14.) As we have already seen, Abraham was a prophet while he lived at Haran. (Genesis xi, 31.) He diligently instructed his neighbors in the truths of religion, and through the Divine blessing *made* disciples or proselytes from idolatry to the true religion. He became a spiritual father to them, and they were dear to him as children. They became so attached to him, that they accompanied him to Canaan. Hence he took all "the souls he had gotten"—all the converts he had made to his religion—along with him. The servants born in Abraham's house—Genesis xvii, 12, 13, 23–27—must have been the children of Abraham's first converts, who raised up families while in his service, and *educated* or *instructed* them in the knowledge and practice of the true religion. They were, therefore, said to be *trained* and *instructed* in the worship of the true God. Abraham governed or *commanded* these, and taught them and their parents to "do justice and judgment." Genesis xviii, 19. This is the only constant interpretation to comport with Abraham's character for *justice*. As he would not take the least plunder taken in war, he certainly would not obtain servants unjustly. (Genesis xiv, 22, 23.) The father of the faithful would certainly not engage in unjust acts. Those, therefore, born in his house were not slaves, as they were all united with him in the brotherhood of the true religion by means

of the sacrament of circumcision, as we have already sufficiently shown.

8. As to the men-servants and maid-servants that Abraham received as a present from Abimelech—Genesis xiv, 14—it is very likely that they had been slaves, but it does not follow that Abraham kept them slaves, nor is it inconsistent with his character as a just and upright man. These servants, too, must be *commanded* by Abraham as a part of his *household*, every individual of whom was required to "keep the way of the Lord—to do justice and judgment." As a part of Abraham's household, these were treated as the other servants were. The others were not treated as slaves—neither were these.

In whichever of these few ways of acquiring servants we consider the subject, the idea of slavery is precluded. The first class of them were disciples, or proselytes, or converts to the true religion, who ranged themselves under the civil, social, and religious superintendence and control of Abraham. Those born in the house were instructed in religion and treated as members of the household of Abraham. Those purchased with money from themselves were under the same regimen; and those received by gift must have fared the same with others.

9. Abraham armed his servants—three hundred and eighteen in number—and led them to battle. This he would never have done had they been slaves. A marauding party came and carried away captive Lot and his family. When Abraham learned this, "he armed his trained servants, born in his own house, three hundred and eighteen, and pursued them unto Dan." Genesis xiv, 14. Had these young men been the children of persons whom Abraham had dragged from their homes, would Abraham have armed them, and drawn them so far from home as Dan—the extremity of Canaan? Would not these servants, while Lot was captive, and his neighbors,

employed in defending themselves, have turned their arms against their master, and recovered their own and their parents' liberty? But Abraham felt himself safe with this band of armed men, though far away from his family and home. Such a company could not have been slaves. Look at our slavery when compared with this. Slaves with us are not allowed to keep arms of any sort, and the severest laws are enacted to keep them from having arms. Hence, slavery in the United States is a very different thing from the service under Abraham. Surely there is no analogy here between American slavery and patriarchal service.

10. The servants of Abraham were such by their own *voluntary* choice. It can not be supposed that Abraham, the pattern of just and righteous dealing, bought or retained any *involuntary* servants. His institution of service was not a system of selfish speculation, but a missionary appointment from God. It is true, that he had some servants born in the house, and some bought with money; but these circumstances do not prove that their service was involuntary. Abraham was a prince, as the children of Heth addressed him—"Thou art a mighty prince among us." Genesis xxiii, 6. His servants were merely his subjects. He had no fixed residence; therefore, he and his subjects dwelt in tents. "By faith he sojourned in the land of promise, as in a strange country, dwelling in tabernacles with Isaac and Jacob." Hebrews xi, 9. His servants must have amounted to over a thousand at one time. It is, therefore, absurd, that a single individual, migrating from place to place, could compel so many persons to involuntary service. Certainly such a number of armed slaves would not submit to compulsory service in a country where emigration was so common and so easy. And as to those bought with money, as he was "very rich in cattle, in silver, and in

gold," and as benevolent as rich, he would be led to *redeem* captives or slaves in view of benefiting them. His whole conduct shows that he considered his subjects as voluntary servants, but not slaves. He exacted an oath from his eldest servant, who was over his house, in obtaining a wife for Isaac. This we might expect of a prince from a subject, but not of a master from a slave.

11. Abraham did not employ *force* to compel service. The servants, therefore, were voluntary both in the commencement and the continuance of their service. They emigrated from place to place with their immense flocks and herds, frequently fifty or sixty miles from home, yet there were no patrols. There was no compact to deliver up fugitive slaves. How easy would it have been for any disposed, to escape; yet there were neither policemen nor military men employed to guard the servants.

12. The social condition of Abraham's servants, their treatment and privileges, are at variance with the consideration that they were regarded as property in view of slavery. In certain circumstances, a servant bought with money, or born in the house, might become heir or ruler in the household. Such, for some years, was Abraham's expectation relative to one of his servants and his own household—Genesis xv, 3—he actually made one of his servants ruler over all that he had several years before his death. (Genesis xxiv, 2.) Indeed, female servants were sometimes taken by their masters as subordinate wives; and this entirely exempted them and their children from vassalage or slavery. This was the case with Hagar and Ishmael, and with the secondary wives of Jacob and their children. When Abraham sent an escort of servants, headed by Eleazar, the oldest servant of his house, to select a wife for Isaac, the reception and treatment of the servant shows there was no slavery in the case. Laban received him courteously into the house. Laban

5

ungirds and feeds the camels, brings water to wash his feet, and food for him and his men. The servant was treated as an equal, or in a manner altogether at variance with the treatment of slaves. Hence, we may infer that Abraham never held any persons as slaves or marketable property. The historical fact is, that he was most assiduous in cultivating the hearts and minds of all under his care, in the ways of wisdom, truth, and righteousness. (Genesis xviii, 19.)

13. The religious patriarchs never *sold* their servants, nor gave them away, nor transferred them to their heirs as slaves; and hence their servants were not slaves.

The patriarchs had servants, bought with money; but no case occurs in which we can infer that any of them sold a servant. They had servants born in their houses, as subjects under their religious, and civil, and social control; but we have no account of any of these being sold or transferred by them to others, or given as an inheritance to their children, as either perpetual or temporary slaves. Wealthy masters sometimes exchanged presents. Abimelech took sheep and oxen, and *men-servants* and *maid-servants*, and gave them unto Abraham. (Genesis xx, 14.) But Abraham, courteous and rich as he was, respected the rights of his servants and subjects, and gave none of them to Abimelech. He *only* "took sheep and oxen and gave them to Abimelech." Abraham gave *gifts* to his sons by Keturah and Hagar, but no servants. (Genesis xxv, 5, 6.) Abraham's servant, who went to seek a wife for Isaac, enumerates the wealth of Abraham thus: "The Lord hath given him flocks and herds, and silver and gold, and men-servants and maid-servants, and camels and asses;" and then adds: "and unto Isaac hath he given all that he hath." Genesis xxiv, 35, 36. As Isaac was the patriarchal successor of Abraham, the servants, or subjects of Abraham continued under his care and protection as a civil and religious head. Hence these servants were employed in keeping these flocks and herds which they had kept for his father. There is no proof that any one ever had any authority over Abraham's servants but himself and Isaac. Certainly Isaac would not give them to Esau, who sold his birthright. Isaac gave no servants to Jacob when he went to Padan Aram to seek his fortune. In the present made by Jacob to Esau, no servants were included. (Exodus xxxii, 13.) In his present sent to the Governor of Egypt, no servants were included. When Jacob went down into Egypt with all that he had, even the servants he had brought with him from Padan Aram did not go with him. All the souls that went with him were seventy—all of whom were his own children and grandchildren. (Genesis xlvi, 27; Exodus i, 5.) The truth of the matter seems to be, as the Rabbins declare, that servants were released, or their term of service had expired, at the death of their masters, and did not descend to their heirs.

14. It is inferred that the servants of the patriarchs were slaves, because they were classed with cattle, asses, and the like. (Genesis xii, 16.) To this we reply, that we may as well conclude that servants were irrational, because they were classed with animals. And if servants are property, because they, in common with cattle and camels, are said to be *owned*, *possessed*, etc., then a wife is property, for she is mentioned in connection with the ox and the ass. (Exodus xx, 17.) In like manner children must be property.

As a general thing, the servants are evidently distinguished from property. "And Abraham took all the substance they had gathered, and the souls that they had gotten in Haran." Genesis xii, 5. The herdsmen of Abraham and Lot are mentioned separately. (Genesis xiii, 7.) When the *wealth* of the patriarchs is spoken of servants are not mentioned, but only when their *greatness* is described. "Abraham was very rich in cattle and gold." Genesis xiii, 2. Servants are not included. The Schechemites say, respecting Jacob and his sons, "Shall not their cattle, and their substance, and every beast of theirs be ours?" Genesis xxxiv, 23. There is no mention here of Jacob's servants. (Compare Genesis xxxi, 16–18; Deuteronomy viii, 12–17; Joshua xxii, 8; 1 Samuel xxv, 2; 2 Chronicles xxxii, 27–29; Job xiii, and xlii, 12, with Genesis xxiv, 35; xxvi, 13, 14; xxx, 43; xxxii, 4, 5; and xxxvi, 6, 7.)

15. We may now consider the case of Isaac. When the servant of Abraham proposed that Rebecca should become the wife of Isaac, he assured the family of Rebecca that Abraham would make Isaac heir to all that he had; and among the possessions he enumerates "flocks and herds, and silver and gold, and men-servants and maid-servants, and camels and asses." Genesis xxiv, 35, 36. And before the death of Abraham, it is said that "he gave all that he had to Isaac." Genesis xxv, 5. But this must be understood as meaning that Isaac, being the son of his first wife, he made him his principal heir. For unto the sons of the concubines "he gave gifts, and sent them away from Isaac, his son, while he yet lived, eastward, toward the east country."

The history goes on to say, that, to some extent, Isaac, as successor of Abraham, exercised civil and religious authority over the servants, or over such of them as remained with Isaac, who was married thirty-five years before Abraham's death. Isaac, during this period, exercised subordinate control over Abraham's servants.

Eighteen years after the death of Abraham, it is said of Isaac that "the man waxed great and went forward, and grew until he became very great; for he had possession of flocks, and possession of herds, and great store of servants. [or *husbandry—margin;*] and the Philistines envied him." Genesis xxvi, 13, 14. Those are called Isaac's *servants* and *herdsmen*, who took care of his herds and flocks, and dug wells. (Verses 19, 20, 32.) We hear no more of Isaac's servants; and he lived eighty-eight years after this account of his servants. (Genesis xxxv, 29.) We can not suppose that Isaac sold any of his servants, or gave them to others. Between Isaac's marriage and Abraham's death—a space of thirty-five years—Isaac probably had the control of many of Abraham's servants, or subjects. For fifty-three years after his marriage we learn that he had servants under his control, or among his dependents.

From the death of Abraham—B. C. 1822—to the death of Isaac—B. C. 1716—a space of one hundred and six years, it is manifest that there was a great decrease of these servants, as we find none of them were given to either Jacob or Esau; at least we have no account of any such thing. For Jacob became a servant himself, in his turn, and served Laban twenty years—fourteen for his two daughters, and six for the cattle—or from 1760 to 1740 before Christ. During this twenty years' service, we can not suppose he would be prepared to have many, or any servants, as he himself had to serve. From the end of this term to the death of Isaac—a space of twenty-two years—we have no account of his having many servants, though he had some.

In brief, we fail entirely, in the case of Isaac, to see any real slavery, although there was a service rendered to him similar to that which was rendered to Abraham, but to a more limited extent.

16. We will next consider the case of Jacob in reference to his servants, in order to ascertain how far his example may be quoted in reference to freedom or slavery.

We find that in 1760 before Christ, or forty-four years before the death of his father, Isaac, he went to Padan Aram to his uncle, Laban's, at the urgent exhortation of his mother, Rebecca. He certainly took no servants with him, as the history shows. By contract with Laban, he agreed to be his servant for seven years, for board and wages. His *wages*, at first contract, was that he should have Rachel for a wife. (Genesis xxix, 15–20.) When deceived by Laban, in substituting Leah for Rachel, he made a new contract, and became the servant of Laban for seven years more, still in order to obtain Rachel for a wife. Thus he served, as a hired servant, for fourteen years, for his two wives. (Genesis xxix, 21–30.) At the end of this period Jacob's large family was unprovided for, as he himself states. He resolves to go to his own country; that he had *served, as a servant*, Laban, but that now he must provide for his family. "And now," says he, "when shall I provide for mine own house also?" Genesis xxx, 30. At the conclusion of this period of twenty years' service, for two wives, and much cattle, Leah and Rachel break out into the following justly-indignant language against their father, who had *counted them strangers*, and had *sold them*, and even devoured their private property. "Are we not counted of him strangers? For he hath sold us, and hath quite devoured also our money." Genesis xxxi, 15.

Laban even acted arbitrarily and unjustly in changing the wages of Jacob. (Genesis xxxi, 7.) Jacob thus states the matter when he had finished his twenty years' hard service, just twenty-four years before Isaac's death. "Thus have I been twenty years in thy house: I served thee fourteen years for thy two daughters, and six years for thy cattle; and thou hast changed my wages ten times." Genesis xxxi, 41. Although Jacob was a servant, who served for wages, partly in wives, and partly in cattle, he was no slave. And although Laban *sold* his two daughters, he did not sell them for slaves, or even menial servants, but only for wives, according to the general custom of the times. In accordance with another custom, he gave to each of his daughters a female servant, or maid, or maid-servant. (Genesis xxix, 24, 29.) These, also, through the urgency of his two wives, became the wives of Jacob. (Genesis xxx, 4, 9.)

Let us now see in what manner, and to what extent, Jacob became the possessor of servants. He certainly brought with him no servants to Padan Aram. At the end of fifteen years' service, or one year after he completed the service for his wives, we find he had servants. "And the man increased exceedingly, and had much cattle, and maid-servants and men-servants, and camels and asses." Genesis xxx, 43. It is not stated how he came in possession of these; but it can not be supposed that he obtained them otherwise than for wages of some sort.

Five years after this—B. C. 1740—when he was on his way to his own country, we learn that he had servants with him, who were employed in taking care of, and driving his cattle, and flocks, and herds, of various kinds. (Genesis xxxii, 16.)

The next and only account we have of Jacob's servants is on his arrival at Luz, or Beth-el. "So Jacob came to Luz, which is in the land of Canaan, that is, Beth-el, he, and all the people that were with him." Genesis xxxv, 6.

We can see nothing of slavery in the service of Jacob to Laban, or among the servants that Jacob afterward obtained. There are other events in the history of Jacob which fully confirm this view of the subject.

The service, or servitude, of Esau to Jacob, will serve to illustrate and support this. Of the two brothers, at their birth, it is prophetically declared, "And the one people shall be stronger than the other people; and the elder shall serve the younger." Genesis xxv, 23. In the prophetic blessing of Isaac on Esau and Jacob, Isaac declares to Esau, "Behold, I have made him thy lord, and all his brethren have I given to him for servants." "By thy sword shalt thou live, and shalt serve thy brother; and it shall come to pass when thou shalt have the dominion, that thou shalt break his yoke from off thy neck." Genesis xxvii, 37, 40.

The nature of the patriarchal government is here indicated. Esau was heir by primogeniture, but Jacob was chosen by the Almighty. The brethren of the proposed sovereign were not given as slaves, but as subjects, as the history shows. Abraham, Isaac, and Jacob, were successive patriarchal rulers of a spiritual and civil government, that was to be continued to the end of the world. They were men of uncommon excellence, and the government they instituted, to promote true religion and good government, is yet but partially developed, though it is destined to fill the world with righteousness.

The Edomites had dukes and kings reigning over them, while the Israelites were slaves in Egypt. Subsequently they became tributary to the Israelites, and were finally absorbed in the Jewish nation. Surely there is no support for slavery here.

If we examine the history of Jacob, after his return from Syria to Canaan, we shall find, that at the time he went down to Egypt, he had no servants, of any sort.

At the time that Joseph was sold—B. C. 1729—eleven years after Jacob came to Canaan, we find that his own sons attended to keeping the flocks and herds—Genesis xl—and we see no account at all of the employ of servants, either hired, or by other contract. All that the history of this period furnishes is, that Judah "had sheepshearers in Timnath." Genesis xxxviii, 12. And the slave-trade seems to have made considerable progress every-where, except in the families of Abraham, Isaac, and Jacob. For Joseph's brethren, being wicked, and unmindful of just patriarchal law, which did not allow of stealing, selling, buying, or using stolen men as slaves, sold their brother Joseph. This was the slavery system as opposed to the legitimate and lawful service under the Abrahamic covenant, whether in his family, and among his descendant patriarchs, or in the Jewish and Christian Churches.

Jacob had no servants, as far as the history testifies, when his sons went down to Egypt to buy corn, either the first or second time. None accompanied his sons in either of the journeys. And we have no account of any servants employed at home with Jacob, at that time, in any kind of service. (Genesis xlii, xliii, xliv.)

When Jacob went down to Egypt he had no servants with him. The number and the name of all are given, and amount to seventy persons. (Genesis xlvi, 5–7; Exodus i, 5.) When presenting the Hebrews to Pharaoh, there was no mention of servants. (Genesis xlvi, 32.)

The case of Jacob stands thus: When he went to Syria—B. C. 1760—he had no servants, but was there himself a servant for twenty years. At the end of fifteen years we find that he had some servants. When he left Syria and came to Canaan, some servants accompanied him. Eight years after we find he had some servants. When Joseph was sold we find no servants in Jacob's possession. When he went to Egypt he had no servants. No one can justly conclude that Jacob ever had a slave, and all the historical facts indeed show the contrary.

17. We will now consider that department of patriarchal life, embraced in, and connected with, their secondary wives, or concubines, which many have made a

principal support of the slave system, though contrary to the leading elements of polygamy, or concubinage; as slavery sinks down into contubernium, which is the condition of the system—ignoring and rejecting marriage first, then concubinage, and becomes brutalized into servile contubernium.

Sarah was barren. She had a "handmaid, an Egyptian, whose name was Hagar." Genesis xvi, 1. In order to obtain children by her handmaid, servant, or slave, Sarah "took her maid and gave her to her husband, Abraham, to be his wife." Verse 2. His connection with Hagar was not proposed by himself, but by Sarah—Abraham yielding in this to her wishes rather than to his own. The custom of more than one wife was common in the east, especially if the first was barren.

Hagar finding herself pregnant, despised her mistress, Sarah. On the complaint of this to Abraham, he permitted Sarah to treat her as she thought fit. Sarah having used her harshly, Hagar fled from the dwelling of Abraham. The angel of the Lord finding her in the wilderness, commanded her to return, and to submit herself to her mistress. She returned to Abraham's house, submitted to Sarah, and was delivered of a son, whom she called Ishmael. (Genesis xvi, 16.) Abraham was then eighty-six years old.

Fourteen years after Isaac was born. When Sarah saw some misconduct in Ishmael, she insisted that Abraham should cast out this bond-woman and her son, "for the son of this bond-woman shall not be heir with my son, even with Isaac." Genesis xxi, 10. Though this was grievous to Abraham, yet he consented; because the Almighty informed him that the succession of religion, and of the covenant, was by Isaac; and that the descendants of Ishmael should be a great people. (Genesis xxi, 12, 13.) The oldest son was the legal heir. For though concubines, or wives of the second class, were legitimate in those times, yet their children did not inherit the principal estate, except in the failure of legal issue.

How Sarah came into the possession of Hagar we know not. All that the history furnishes was, that she was about fifteen years a member of Abraham's family, in a dependent situation, and badly treated by Sarah. It is likely she was of such as were given to wealthy women, when married, to be waiters, but on what terms we know not precisely. Rebecca had her *nurse* and *damsels*, or maids to accompany her when she was married, but we learn nothing more of them. Laban gave a handmaid, or servant, to each of his daughters, Leah and Rachel. (Genesis xxix, 24, 29.) These were also given to Jacob for wives, by Leah and Rachel, for a reason similar to that which led Sarah to give Hagar to Abraham to wife. (Genesis xxx.) These are subsequently mentioned as the wives or woman-servants of Jacob. (Genesis xxxiii, 1, 2, 6; xxxv, 25, 26; xxxvii, 2; xlvi, 18, 25.)

To show that the slave system receives no countenance from the concubinage of the patriarchs, we furnish the following reasons:

First. These maids, maid-servants, handmaids, etc., could not be slaves as members of a circumcised family or community. We allow, that those maid-servants that were given to married women as their servants, may have been given to them as slaves; but they could not remain such in the families of Abraham, Isaac, and Jacob. Their privileges, as disciples, or proselytes, or converts to the true religion, made them members of this great brotherhood. Hence, they could not be continued permanently as slaves. So the history of the patriarchs say, as in the cases of Hagar, Bilhah, and Zilpah. So under the Mosaic code, and in Christianity.

Second. Hagar, Bilhah, and Zilpah were *wives*, and

not slaves. Being concubines, or second or secondary wives, they could not be slaves. The marriage bed was considered as inviolable, in reference to concubines, as to the principal wife, and its violation punished. Concubinage is not the state of slavery. Contubernium is the state of slavery—a state not only below marriage and concubinage, but one bordering on or identical with brutality, or the indiscriminate mixture of the sexes.

Third. The heirship to which the children of the secondary wives were entitled and received, shows they were not slaves. Abraham, it is said, gave all that he had to Isaac. (Genesis xxv, 5, 6.) That is, he made him the principal heir. The oldest son was the legal heir. For though concubines, or wives of the second class, were legitimate in those ancient times, yet their children did not inherit the principal estate, except on failure of the legal issue. The principal right of Isaac was to the land of Canaan, including a confirmation of whatever was contained in the promises of God. To the sons of the concubines Abraham gave gifts. And the sons of Jacob's secondary wives were made partakers of the inheritance of their father, equally with their other brethren; for they became the progenitors of four tribes of Israel, and received their proportion of the land of Canaan, as well as equal religious privileges.

Fourth. Ishmael, Gad, Dan, Asher, Naphthali, the children of these secondary wives, were not slaves. Therefore, their mothers were not slaves, but freed-women. It is a matter of history that none of their sons were slaves. But, according to the established laws of slavery, in every age, it became fixed, *that the child should follow the condition of the mother.* Now, as the children were both born free, as indeed all are, and continued free, the mothers could not have been slaves.

An objection or two may be met here. "When

Hagar ran away from Abraham's family, the angel of God sent her back, and instructed her to submit herself to Sarah." Very true. For as Sarah was the principal wife, and the mistress of the house, it was reasonable that Hagar should submit. But as Hagar was Abraham's wife, and therefore no longer a slave, she was sent back *as a wife,* though a subordinate one. She was not sent back as a slave, nor was she treated as a slave, other than the jealousy of Sarah led to bad treatment.

The departure of Hagar after the birth of Isaac is urged by pro-slavery apologists. But this was a *divorce,* occasioned, too, by the jealousy of Sarah. Yet as God permitted, but did not approve of concubinage and divorce on account of the hardness of men's hearts, he permitted Abraham to divorce his wife Hagar, to gratify his wife Sarah. Yet the overruling providence of God was in this. The reasons given are, that in Isaac and his posterity the world should be blessed in religious descent from Abraham; the son of the bond-woman should be a great nation. The Ishmaelites became a great and powerful people, and were never the slaves of any nation or individuals. (Genesis xxi, 12–21.)

18. It remains to point out the contrast between the service under Abraham, Isaac, and Jacob, and slavery.

Patriarchal service was founded on the conversion of the servants to the true religion. They were also thoroughly instructed in the principles and practice of religion. They were ingrafted by circumcision into the Church of God, and became, equally with their masters, partakers of the blessings of the covenant. Our slavery has no recognition of religion; it forbids mental instruction, makes no provision for religious privileges, and recognizes no brotherhood between master and slave. The maintainers of our slavery, according to the system, have very little regard for moral principle.

The patriarchs employed no *force*, in the exercise of their authority as masters. None became their servants by force of any sort. We hear of no parols; no jails to confine servants; no dogs to hunt them; no chains to bind them. Slavery requires all these, and the strong arm of the civil power to carry them into effect.

The patriarchs did not *sell* their slaves. They did not make merchandise of them. Although they bought servants, either from themselves, or perhaps third persons, in order to free them, they sold none of their servants. In this it differs from slavery, which always furnished for market those whom they held by force.

Patriarchal service could not be slavery, because, after a period of longer or shorter service, it came to an end. Of all the servants once in the possession of Abraham, Isaac, and Jacob, not one of them were in service when Joseph was sold, or when Jacob went down to Egypt, thirteen years after. Something like the year of release, or of the jubilee, must have taken place. The common law maxim of slavery is, that the child follows the condition of the mother. By this means slavery continues its existence; but on the patriarchal scheme it would soon die out.

Indeed, the moral character of the patriarchs forbade them to hold slaves. The act of selling Joseph was repudiated among the patriarchs. The carrying out of the slave system is contrary to the moral sense of all good men.

Patriarchal service threw off entirely the elements of slavery existing around, and established a service antagonistic to slavery. Its principles were justice, moral right, religion, and reciprocal rights. On this account it was directly at variance with the slave system of their times.

Patriarchal service was the forerunner of freedom in

the world, as established in the Mosaic code, and in the Christian system. The foregoing survey of the subject goes to show that the principles of the Mosaic code were only a development of the patriarchal. Circumcision, as among Abraham and his servants, was a necessary part of the Mosaic code. This brotherhood confined service to six years, or to the jubilee, and thus prevented it from running into slavery; while the New Testament principles entirely rooted out the deeply-seated slavery of Rome; as they will yet overturn American slavery.

In conclusion, patriarchal service combined none of the essential features of slavery. Abraham did not hold servants by a tenure which transformed men to mere things, to goods and chattels, or mere property. There is no restriction on mental instruction, no ignoring of religious teaching, or religious privileges. There is no annulling of the fifth and seventh commandments of the decalogue. There is no withholding of the laborers' hire, no pursuit or capture of fugitives, no mercenary trading of human beings, no child bound to perpetual service, on account of the condition of its mother. The application of the leading features of the service rendered to Abraham, Isaac, and Jacob, would, at no distant day, uproot American slavery. Let no slaves be sold on any account; let schools of instruction be established; let religious institutions be maintained and supported by the slave code; let marriage be established; let no children be separated from their parents; let parental authority be respected; let no force of law, or police, or military be resorted to; let any leave their masters who will. These regulations, all of which are imbedded in patriarchal service, would annihilate slavery in America, in about two generations, or even less. It is supremely absurd, then, to quote either the examples or principles of the patriarchs in favor of American or any other system of slavery.

In the cases of Hagar, the damsels of Rebecca, and the maids given to Leah and Rachel, it may be admitted that originally they were slaves; but subsequently they became *freed-women*, though they were never *free persons*, that is, persons born free. But under the patriarchal government of Abraham, Isaac, and Jacob, they became as free as their circumstances would allow. Their children were all free. Ishmael was free, and so were the four sons of the two maids of Leah and Rachel. And they were the heads of tribes equally with the other sons of Jacob. The true slavery maxim is, *the child follows the condition of the mother*. In the families of Abraham and Jacob it was not so—the children followed the condition of the free father. This alone would destroy slavery; and apply it to our slavery, and one generation would annihilate the system in America.

CHAPTER III.

PATRIARCHAL SLAVERY.

We have shown in the previous chapter, that the service rendered to Abraham, Isaac, and Jacob, by their servants, was not slavery. We will now show where slavery may be found among the patriarchs, and will concede to the slaveholders and apologists for slavery, that they have patriarchal examples to produce for the practice of slavery. We allow, nay, we maintain, that there was patriarchal slavery, as well as patriarchal service. We find this service in the example of Abraham, Isaac, and Jacob. We find the example of slavery in the case of Joseph. We will therefore take pains to show the elements of slavery in the case of Joseph, contrast it with the service of the patriarchs, and point out its identity with slavery, whether ancient or modern. In the case of Joseph, let us notice,

1. The evil moral elements that were brought to act, in order to prepare the way for the introduction of slavery.

(1.) The actors in this, before they engaged in the enslavement of Joseph, were, at that time, under the influence of bad principles, and of bad moral conduct. Dan and Naphthali, Gad and Asher, the sons of the secondary wives, seem to have been principals. Joseph gave them offense, because he gave to his father an account of "their evil report." Genesis xxxvii, 2. The readiness in which the nine brothers engaged in the capture of Joseph, in the hatred, conspiracy, and cruel treatment of their brother, show great moral depravity at that time, as well as inhuman conduct.

(2.) They exercised a wicked temper. They *hated* their brother, and *envied* him. "They hated him, and could not speak peaceably unto him." "They hated him yet the more for his dreams and for his words." Genesis xxxvii, 4, 8. "And his brethren envied him"—verse 11—in consequence of his supposed future eminence over them.

(3.) They, therefore, under the influence of these bad dispositions, determined to kill him. Murder, with malice, was their first object, in order to get rid of him whom they *hated* and envied. "They conspired against him to slay him." Genesis xxxvii, 18. Such was the object the Jews had in view, in reference to Paul. They determined to kill him. (Acts xxiii, 14.)

(4.) They entered into a conspiracy to accomplish their object. When Joseph was at a distance, they *determined* to kill him, and *conspired* or combined for that purpose. Their plan of conspiracy was, "Come now, therefore, and let us slay him, and cast him into some pit; and we will say, some evil beast hath devoured him: and we will see what will become of his dreams." Genesis xxxvii, 20. These are the words of the conspiracy. It comprises *murder with malice aforethought*, or with *hatred* and *envy*. A *lie* is invented in carrying it out, and *hypocrisy* in completing the deception on Jacob. The conspiracy consisted in the following: First, murder as the way; second, this was *designed;* third, hatred and envy were the dispositions in exercise; fourth, a lie was resorted to as the means of justification; fifth, and hypocrisy was the closing part of the conspiracy or plan.

(5.) They carried their purposes into effect, without remorse, up to the very last act of putting him to death, but for the sake of gain they did not kill him. "And it came to pass, when Joseph was come unto his brethren, that they stripped Joseph out of his coat, his coat of many colors that was on him; and they took and cast him into a pit: and the pit was empty, there was no water in it. And they sat down to eat bread." Genesis xxxvii, 23–25. Thus, after seizing, by force, their innocent brother, they stripped him of his clothes, cast him into a pit, and then sat down deliberately to eat bread, as if they had done no wrong. Their act was like that of the remorseless transgressor, who "eateth, and wipeth her mouth, and saith, I have done no wickedness." Proverbs xxx, 20. Here we have the *moral picture* of those, in all ages, who are prepared to take the incipient steps in enslaving mankind. First, they are, in general, bad, wicked men. Second, they are under the influence of bad dispositions, as hatred, envy, the love of gain, pride, ambition, or the like. Third, hence their plans, or, if you please, their laws of enslavement, can all be traced to these bad tempers, and can never spring from love, either to God or man. Fourth, murder, or waste of human life, or making it bitter with *service*, whether severe or easy, for gain, or for pleasure, is a part of the system. Fifth, by the acts of enslavement we must judge of these; for by their fruits ye shall know them.

Who, as they contemplate the conduct of Joseph's brethren, can fail to detect all the elements requisite to constitute the system of slavery, or to prepare the way for it?

First. They were, at this time, wicked men. Will not this character apply to all the originators of the slave system, from those who sold Joseph down to the present time? This was the case with the Egyptians. Those who sell their own people in Africa, and elsewhere, are of this character.

Second. The evil tempers of hatred, envy, love of gain in the enslavers, who succeeded Joseph's brethren, are pretty fair patterns for those who are participants in the oppression of their fellows now.

Third. Murder, or sacrifice of human life, is a characteristic of the system, and has been in all ages. Statistics could show this.

Fourth. Look at the plans, conspiracies, and deception in the case of Joseph's brethren. The ambushes of the African slave-trade may be taken as a sample. And the studiously constructed slave-laws of every slave nation in the world present a specimen of this. The laws of the United States possess this characteristic. Its fugitive-slave law, its protection to the system, and its guarantees to support it are of this class. And then the laws of slave states are a complete net-work to surround, entangle, and retain the unwilling bondman in its meshes. The children of slave mothers are slaves. There is no father to protect; no instructor to teach. If the slave attempt to escape, he is an enemy, and must be captured or killed.

Fifth. And then the *practice* of our system is no better than that of Joseph's brethren. The poor slave is stripped of every thing, is chained in ignorance, and bound down by all the laws of the system, in as forcible and cruel a manner as that which took place in the case of Joseph's brethren.

2. The protest of Reuben against the conduct of his brethren, and his grief on account of it.

Of the ten brethren of Joseph only one protested and resisted their course. The narrative goes to say, "And Reuben heard it, and he delivered him out of their hands; and said, Let us not kill him. And Reuben said unto them, Shed no blood, but cast him into this pit that is in the wilderness, and lay no hand upon him; that he might rid him out of their hands, to deliver him to his father again." Genesis xxxvii, 21, 22.

The murderous brethren, however, in the absence of Reuben, sold Joseph; and Reuben expresses himself, on the occasion, in the following mournful strains: "And Reuben returned unto the pit; and, behold, Joseph was not in the pit; and he rent his clothes. And he returned unto his brethren, and said, The child is not: and I, whither shall I go?" Genesis xxxvii, 29, 30.

The following speech, on this occasion, is put into the mouth of Reuben by Josephus, which will show the views he entertained on the subject, as well as point out the great evil of the act by which Joseph was sold to the Midianites.

"It were an abominable wickedness," says Josephus, "to take away the life even of a stranger. But to destroy a kinsman and a brother, and, in that brother, a father too, with grief for the loss of so good and so hopeful a son—bethink yourselves, if any thing can be more diabolical! Consider that there is an all-seeing God, who will be the avenger as well as the witness of this horrid murder. Bethink yourselves, I say, and repent of your barbarous purpose. You must never expect to commit this flagitious villainy, and the divine vengeance not overtake you; for God's providence is every-where, in the wilderness as well as in the city; and the horrors of a guilty conscience will pursue you wherever you go. But put the case, your brother had done you some wrong, yet is it not our duty to pass over the offenses of our friends? When the simplicity of his youth may justly plead his excuse, and make you his friends, rather than his murderers; especially when the ground of all your quarrel is this, that God loves your brother, and your brother loves God." (Josephus, Book II, c. 3.)

Though this speech is put into the mouth of Reuben, it shows the true Jewish views of this transaction by their acknowledged historian.

We have the protests of the best men the world ever saw against the acts of Joseph's brethren, and against slavery. In this are united clergymen and laymen, ancients and moderns. In our work on the "Sinfulness of Slavery"—Vol. II, p. 167–243—we have given an ample list of these protesters; and to this and other such works we must refer our readers, as our space will not allow their insertion. These, too, comprise both slaveholders and non-slaveholders. It is also remarkable that the plea of Judah to sell Joseph for money, and save the imputation or trouble of killing him, is a fair specimen of the best arguments of pro-slavery men. The substance of their pleas is, abolitionism, fanaticism, our property, our institutions, civil law, good feeding, good clothing, good nursing, etc.

3. *The commutation of slavery for death.*

The policy of Reuben was, that they should not kill him, in order that he might deliver him out of their hands and restore him again to his father. This was benevolent and praiseworthy, but was rejected. This was an abolition argument, and could not prevail.

Let us notice the argument of Judah, the sale of Joseph, and the deception on Jacob. Judah adduced a pro-slavery argument, and that succeeded. It is as follows: "And Judah said unto his brethren, What profit is it if we slay our brother, and conceal his blood? Come, and let us sell him to the Ishmaelites, and let not our hand be upon him; for he is our brother and our flesh. And his brethren were content and hearkened." Genesis xxxvii, 26, 27.

Look at Judah's *argument against killing Joseph.* First. It was not expedient to kill him, because this would *shed blood;* and they must lay *violent hands* on him in order to kill him, and this, too, would be either wrong or inexpedient. Second. He is our brother, and our flesh; not only a human being, with the feelings of flesh like ourselves; but he is our natural brother, the son of the same natural father with ourselves. Third. There is *no profit* in killing him.

Next see his reason for making him a slave. 1. They would have *profit* in selling him; though the price was only twenty pieces of silver, or about twelve or fifteen dollars. 2. It would be humane to sell him; because they would not be guilty of murder, so that they would avoid the revolting acts of shedding blood, and using their own hands in doing it.

The argument for sale prevailed. The reasons against the murder were satisfactory, and the arguments for sale conclusive. On the one hand, they could exercise humanity so as not to be reduced to the necessity of becoming the bloody executioners of their own natural brother by their own hands, and at best it was profitless. On the other hand, they could just sell him, and thus avoid all this, and then they would have some price or benefit accruing. The argument prevailed; his brethren were content or satisfied with the profound logic of Judah. And to facilitate the matter, the merchants who then dealt in goods and chattels personal, were just in sight, and presently the bazar was closed in the manner following: "And there passed by Midianites merchantmen; and they drew and lifted up Joseph out of the pit, and sold Joseph to the Ishmaelites for twenty pieces of silver: and they brought Joseph to Egypt." Genesis xxxvii, 28.

Notice now the *deception* practiced on Jacob by this transaction. "And they took Joseph's coat, and killed a kid of the goats, and dipped the coat in the blood: and they sent the coat of many colors, and they brought it to their father; and said, This have we found: know now whether this be thy son's coat or no. And he knew it, and said, It is my son's coat; an evil beast hath devoured him: Joseph is without doubt rent in pieces." Genesis xxxvii, 31–33.

Observe here the *theft* in Joseph's case. Joseph says, "For, indeed, I was stolen out of the land of the Hebrews." Genesis xl, 50. This was *man-stealing*, a capital crime.

The selling of Joseph was a *great sin*. When his brethren saw the act in its true light they confessed, "We are verily guilty concerning our brother, in that we saw the anguish of his soul, when he besought us, and we would not hear; therefore is this distress come upon us." Reuben then said, "Spake I not unto you, saying, Do not sin against the child; and ye would not hear? therefore behold also his blood is required." Genesis xlii, 21, 22. After the death of Jacob, Joseph's brethren were afraid that "Joseph will peradventure hate them, and will certainly requite them all the evil which they did unto him." And they sent a messenger to Joseph to plead for the fulfillment of Jacob's injunction to them. "Forgive, I pray thee now, the trespass of thy brethren, and their sin; for they did unto thee evil; and now, we pray thee, forgive the trespass of the servants of the God of my father." They "thought it for evil against Joseph." Genesis l, 15, 17, 20. Their act was *a sin*, a *trespass* against the principles of right. It was a deliberate act; it was *meant for evil*. In consequence they were *guilty*, and stood in need of *pardon*.

These are the prominent points in the enslavement of Joseph: 1. *The commutation of slavery for death*. The reasons against the murder were, that they would be relieved from shedding the blood of their brother with their own hands; and that there would be no profit in doing so. The reasons for the sale were, they would profit by it, and make money by it; and it would be a humane course. In a word, slavery is the more profitable way; it is the more humane way. 2. His *sale* and his *price*. 3. The *deception* in the affair, and the means of carrying it out. 4. The *theft*, effected by violence of assault and battery. 5. And the *sin*.

All these evil elements in the enslavement of Joseph are to be found in every slave system that ever existed in the world; and they exist in our slave system to an extent equal to, or exceeding, any other. The following observations will present this, we think, in a convincing light:

(1.) The capture of men by theft, violence, or war, and holding men liable to death, has been the principal source of slavery in the world, in all ages. Personal violence and theft in individual cases has always been an element of slavery. Such cases are constantly occurring in our country. Under the covert of slave laws in the United States, multitudes born free, according to law, are re-enslaved in various ways which we have not time to detail. War in olden times, as a national business, gave rise to national slavery, as Justinian declares: "The law of nations is common to all mankind, and all nations have enacted some laws, as occasion and necessity required; for wars arose, and the consequences were captivity and slavery; both which are contrary to the law of nature; for by that law all men are born free." (Inst. Lib. I, Tit. 2, Sec. 2.)

Our mode of enslaving children by law is perfectly identical in principle with the use of violence and theft in the case of Joseph. Violence made Joseph a slave. Our violent laws make children slaves. The work done is precisely the same; namely, a free person is made a slave. The mode is different, as if one would murder a man by slow torture, and another would do it by the easy way of shooting him through the head or heart. Our *Christian* way is different from the pit and the sale, of Joseph's brethren; but the accomplished deed is the same, only our way is the worse way. Our mode is to steal the child as soon as born, and then deny him any instruction or means of moral, religious, or mental improvement during life. But Joseph had seventeen years of good education under his father before he was stolen. If our slaves had seventeen years of paternal instructions their case would be different. But our poor slaves have no fathers; and their mothers have their hands tied, and their mouths sealed; they are themselves in chains.

(2.) The commutation of slavery for death is unjust, and founded on unjust principles.

Blackstone furnishes on this subject the following argument:

"The conqueror, say the civilians, had a right to the life of his captive; and having spared that, has a right to deal with him as he pleases. But it is an untrue position, when taken generally, that by the law of nature or nations a man may kill his enemy: he has only a right to kill him in particular cases—in cases of absolute necessity for self-defense; and it is plain this absolute necessity did not subsist, since the victor did not actually kill him, but made him prisoner. War itself is justifiable only on principles of self-preservation; and, therefore, it gives no other rights over prisoners but merely to disable them from doing harm to us by confining our persons: much less can it give a right to kill, torture, abuse, plunder, or even to enslave an enemy when the war is over. Since, therefore, the right of *making* slaves by captivity depends on a supposed right of slaughter, that foundation failing, the consequence drawn from it must fail likewise." (1 Blackstone's Com., 423.)

(3.) The small profit of Joseph's sale, though only twelve or fifteen dollars, was a consideration. The value of our slaves is far beyond this. By the profits of their sweat and toil their masters and their families are fed, clothed, and maintained. Slaves now sell at from five hundred to one thousand dollars each. Perhaps eight hundred dollars may be an average. This is over fifty times as much as the cost of Joseph. Our slaves, too, if they are religious, are more valuable than others. And almost white, handsome, female slaves sell, especially at private sales, at immense prices. Joseph's brethren, however, had one or two disadvantages in their business. They had to use personal violence to steal and seize Joseph. We raise or breed our slaves, and newly-born babes need no chains; and they are easily raised, as they need no schooling or trades, and therefore can work all the time that other children go to school or are apprentices. The annual *profits* of the slaves is considerable; and the entire value of the chattels of this sort is very great. In 1790 Mr. Gerry valued the slaves at $10,000,000; in 1840 Mr. Clay valued them at $1,200,000,000. At present the value of over 3,000,000 must be about $2,000,000,000. The income of the property at six per cent. would be $3,300,000 annually—a considerable advance from the time of Joseph. What would our slaveholders think of fifteen dollars for a stout boy of seventeen years of age? They could get $1,000 for such.

(4.) On the *sale* of Joseph, as an example, the United States have somewhat improved. With us, fathers sell their own children, and brothers and sisters sell their own brothers and sisters. And if fathers, and brothers, and sisters shrink from this sometimes, as they really do, the law, in its regular course of procedure, does it for them by the sheriff and auctioneer. An entire Church of parents and children, belonging to the late H. R. W. Hill, were recently sold in New Orleans, the narrative of which is given in another place. The United States sometimes goes to market, and makes purchases and sales to save the loss of a bad debt. We know a large family of children sold by a grandfather to his own son, who was the father of the children. Thus the son purchased from his own father his children, and the mother of his children, the grandfather selling coolly his grandchildren, the offspring of his slave. He attempted afterward to repurchase one of the grandchildren, but in vain, as his son needed her for a housekeeper; and this was all according to law. It is believed, as a matter of history, that some descendants of Jefferson are now slaves. Our traders, wholesale and retail, make selling slaves a regular business.

(5.) Joseph was *stolen.* This transaction is represented, in Genesis xlii, 21, 22, as a crime worthy of death, in those guilty of it—as a self-evident and enormous crime against the laws of nature. Joseph says he was *stolen.* (Genesis xl, 15.) The wrong inflicted on him was an act of stealing, or of theft; and as he was a man, that crime was man-stealing—precisely the crime with which our slavery is justly charged. The Larger Westminster Catechism, on the eighth commandment, places among the things forbidden, "theft, robbery, man-stealing, and receiving any thing that is stolen." Bishop Hopkins, of England, in his Exposition, defines theft thus: "Theft is an unjust taking or keeping to ourselves what is lawfully another man's. He is a thief who withholds what ought to be in his neighbor's possession, as well as he who takes from him what he hath formerly possessed." Slaveholders are called by St. Paul—1 Timothy i, 9, 10—*man-stealers,* or the *stealers, venders,* or *holders* of men, as slaves; and that *man-stealer,* or *slave-dealer,* or *possessor* of the property—except a *possessor in trust*—in guilt and sin, is synonymous with thief, is plain, from Exodus xxi, 16, where the *thief,* the *vender,* or *holder* of a stolen man, is equally guilty, and to be punished with death, equally with murderers, or those who strike or revile their parents. The *possession* is principally criminal, because he who possesses the stolen property prevents the true owner from enjoying it.

The moral law makes no difference between the first act of the theft and the willful possession of a stolen article. "Whoso is partner with a thief, hateth his own soul." Proverbs xxix, 24. The crime of theft consists in taking, or having that which the moral law recognizes as the property of another; and this theft is robbery, because it involves fraud and violence without the shadow of justice. While men hold slaves *as property*—except *in trust*, in order to restore it—no other terms will as well designate them as *man-stealer*, *thief*, *slaveholder*, *slave-dealer*, or the like; and such are the very words which the Holy Ghost employs, both in the Old and New Testaments: "And they SOLD Joseph to the Ishmaelites." Genesis xxxvii, 28. "For indeed I was STOLEN away out of the land of the Hebrews." Genesis xl, 15.

These passages show that he who *sells* or *buys* one man from a third person, except to ransom him, is a thief. So, in Deuteronomy xxxiv, 7, it is clear that he who steals, makes merchandise of, or sells a man, is called a THIEF.

(6.) The enslavement of Joseph is, in Scripture, pronounced *sinful*. If the original act of enslavement was sinful, the continuance of this state, by the infliction of wrongs, the deprivation of rights, as well as the great moral principles involved, can not be right. At this time, human beings are deprived of liberty, of education, of the rights of conscience, and are subject to great and cruel wrongs; and of course, as the nature of right and wrong does not change, what was wrong then must be wrong now. It is in vain to evade the charge of moral wrong in our slavery, any more than it was in the case of Joseph.

Take the two following examples of wicked wrong, from Brisbane on "Slaveholding Examined," page 207:

"A slave woman was brought before the Church, for trial, on account of pregnancy. But she escaped censure because she testified that her master met her in the field and forced her. There was no law to protect her."

"Sam, a slave, in consequence of severe treatment, ran away. His master stripped him, cut off one of his ears, whipped him on the bare back till it was laid open in deep gashes from the neck to the hip, and then applied pepper and salt to the wounds. For this there could be no redress by law. His master was in respectable society."

(7.) Nor does the deception practiced in the case of Joseph at all exceed that which is brought into requisition in our own slave system. Jacob, for a time, was deceived, but the issue detected all this. Our system operates *wisely* with the slaves. There is the authority of the United States, assisting the slave states, with the Fugitive-Slave law, as a means, and the army, navy, and Supreme Court of the United States, guaranteeing and upholding, by statute, constitution, and judicial decisions, the system of slavery. Then there are the constitutions and laws of the slave states, which seize every child, as soon as born, and, regardless of the laws of nature, make the innocent a slave for life.

The masters have almost supreme control over the slaves. There are no schools to teach them, and no liberal arts, or respectable pursuits, to elevate them. If they attempt to run away, the blood-hounds are let loose on their scent, or more bloody men become the hunters. There is a conspiracy against them. There is a complete, organized system of oppression; and emancipation is a prohibition, in most cases. The petty conspiracy of Joseph's brethren, in reference to one person, is almost as nothing compared to the legislative, judicial, and executive system, which is brought to bear against three millions of persons, BORN FREE, but now enslaved men, women, and children of the United States.

4. The slave-dealers, in the case of Joseph, and also our own dealers, may now be considered.

Our system of slavery has its model in the seizure and sale of Joseph by his brethren to the Ishmaelites, and by the latter to Potiphar. His brethren stripped him, and sold him to the Ishmaelites. (Genesis xxxvii, 23.) The Ishmaelites, or Midianites, who were *merchants*, and dealt in the purchase and sale of human beings, as well as in spicery, balm, myrrh, etc., bought him from his brethren. (Genesis xxxvii, 25, 28.) The Midianites brought him down to Egypt, and sold him to Potiphar. (Genesis xxxvii, 36 ; xxxix, 1.)

Here is a case described at length, of the forcible seizure, or kidnapping, of one person by others; of his sale as an article of merchandise for money; and a subsequent sale of him as property to another; and all exactly as our slave seizures, and sales, and purchases are now made. The transaction is *theft*, and a *sin*, worthy of death by the law of God.

The seizures and sales, with us, have taken place according to *constitution*, *statutes*, and *judicial decisions*, and with much more deliberation than in the case of Joseph. Our slave laws, too, just in proportion as Christianity has spread in the country by the religious, have continued to become more stringent and severe, to counteract the exercise of moral principle. And the examples in the slave-gangs, and barracoons, have left the case of Joseph in the distance; and, indeed, it will be difficult to say whether the African piratical trade, or our home trade, in breeding, sales, transfers, etc., exceeds in atrocity, considered in themselves. But ours far exceeds theirs in evil, as it is an iniquity *framed by law*, done *deliberately*, by constitution, by statute, by judicial decisions; at the mouth of the cannon, or musket, by the blood-hounds, the auctioneer, the sheriff, and backed by the army and navy, the laws of the United States, the executive, and supreme judiciary.

Some specimens of our home trade, in slaves, will show clearly that our regular legalized traffic is, in no respects, lower than that practiced by Joseph's brethren and their successors in the trade.

The enslavement of brothers and sisters, by brothers and sisters, and even by fathers, is a *lawful* part of our trade, and no *abuse* of it, more or less. Specimens enough could be given. But almost every mulatto in the United States is a proof, not of opinion, but of *fact*, to sustain this; yet we pass it by, leaving it as a subject of reflection, as there are many things in this which we are forbidden to speak out on, through downright shame.

Then there is our practice of slave-growing, that is also a *lawful* business, and no *abuse* of the system. For slavery rejects marriage, and adopts the old heathen maxim, *the child follows the condition of the mother*. If there is any thing in Joseph's case worse than this, we are much mistaken.

And as to seizing persons, and making slaves of them, conveying them from one part of the country to another, in chains, and under escorts, selling families apart, etc., we can scarcely imagine any thing in the case of Joseph which will compare with it. We will here furnish some specimens of the improvements made in the commerce of slavery, which our times may now boast of.

Of the mode of catching slaves by blood-hounds, or

negro dogs, we give the following specimen, from the Lexington Democratic Advocate, a Mississippi journal. We give this without a word of comment:

"NEGRO DOGS.

"I would inform the citizens of Holmes county that I still have my negro dogs, and that they are in good training, and ready to attend to all calls for hunting and catching runaway negroes, at the following rates:

"For hunting per day, five dollars; or if I have to travel any distance, every day will be charged for, in going and returning, as for hunting, and at the same rates. Not less than five dollars will be charged, in any case, where the negroes come in before I reach the place. From fifteen to twenty-five dollars will be charged for catching, according to the trouble. If the negro has weapons, the charge will be made according to the difficulty had in taking him, or in case he kills some of the dogs, the charge will not be governed by the above rates. I am explicit to prevent any misunderstanding. The owner of the slave to pay all expenses in all cases.

"I venture to suggest to any person having a slave runaway, that the better plan is to send for the dogs forthwith, when the negro goes off, if they intend sending at all, and let no other person go in the direction, if they know which way the runaway went; as many persons having other negroes to hunt over the track, and failing of success, send for the dogs, and then perhaps fail in consequence to catch their negro, and thus causelessly fault the dogs. Terms, cash. If the money is not paid at the time the negro hunted for is caught, he will be held bound for the money. I can be found at home at all times, five and a half miles east of Lexington, except when hunting with the dogs. JOHN LONG.

"*February* 14, 1855."

The following is an account of our slave traffic, in one of its most favorable forms, under the best religious and mental culture which the south furnishes; and yet the system turns out to be more at variance with right than even the case of Joseph itself.

Mr. H. R. W. Hill resided long in Nashville, Tennessee; was a zealous, active, and very liberal member of the Methodist Episcopal Church South. He spared no pains or expense to have his slaves instructed and benefited by religion. As he became very wealthy, in the pursuit of commerce, several large plantations, with the slaves on them, near New Orleans, where the family resided, came into his possession. He built churches on the plantations, supported missionaries, and did every thing he thought best to make them intelligent and happy. Last year—1854—he died, and left his vast estate to his son, after having been munificent during life, and at death, to benevolent objects. After his death his negroes were all, or the greatest part of them, sold, at public sale.

The following is the advertisement which appeared in the National Intelligencer, giving notice of the sale:

"Will be sold at auction, at Bank's Arcade, on Magazine-street, in the city of New Orleans, at 12 o'clock, on Tuesday, January 16th, 1855, the slaves at the same hour on Thursday, January 18th, and the following days, for the account of the estate of the late H. R. W. Hill, without reserve, all that extensive and valuable sugar estate, known as the Live-Oak Plantation, etc., including two hundred and sixty choice plantation-slaves, accustomed to the culture of sugar and cotton, and considered to be the best gangs in the south, and comprising all the requisite mechanics, such as sugar-makers, engineers, blacksmiths, coopers, carpenters, bricklayers, choice house-servants, cooks, and field hands, and are to be sold in families and singly, by a descriptive catalogue. The slaves are guaranteed in title only."

The sales took place in New Orleans. Handbills were printed with large black letters, and the words mechanics, seamstresses, cooks, etc., stood out prominent. Advertisements and editorial notices appeared in the papers. Circulars, on fine paper, were printed, giving particulars of each one to be sold, all being duly numbered. The following is the description of the sale, given by a correspondent of the New York Tribune, February 16, 1855:

"On the morning of the sale I wended my way to Bank's Arcade, determined to witness the scene. I found the Arcade to be a very large building, situated in the very center of business, and used as a hall for mass meetings of the various political parties, and it is said will accommodate five thousand people on such occasions. A large bar or counter, about one hundred feet in length, is placed directly opposite the entrance, and some half a dozen tenders are constantly occupied in dealing out poison at a dime a drink. Opposite to the bar the poor negroes were marshaled into line; the men and boys were uniformed with short jackets made of cottonade, pants of the same material, hickory shirts, black brogans, and tarpaulin hats. The women were all clad in common calicoes, and a common handkerchief tied around the head. All the slaves were labeled, a tag or card being tied to the breast of each, giving the name, age, and number of the negro, so as to correspond with the printed catalogue.

"It is impossible for me to give you a faithful description of the scene, as no pen can picture the horrors of it. One hundred and seven poor slaves were there assembled together for the last time in this world. They had for many years all been living on Mr. Hill's plantation, as one family. Most of them were brought up by Hill. They had always been blessed with a kind master. They were all members of one Church, which had been established among themselves. Old men and women, over seventy years of age—some of them blind—were to be separated from their children and grandchildren; husbands about to be torn from their wives; children sold into slavery, never to know a mother's love, or have a father's protection and care. In a few hours the fate of all would be decided. All the slaves were crying; many of them were apparently calm in their sufferings, and had a hope that they might fall into the hands of a kind master; but others exhibited their feelings in violent outbursts of passion. One old woman, who was put down in the catalogue as number 40, Daliah, age sixty-six years, milk-woman, etc., was in great distress, and several of the small children were clinging to her and moaning, half frightened to death, and one of her own sons, about thirty-six years of age, was receiving her farewell blessing. With her left arm clasping him to her bosom, and her right hand placed on his head, she repeated these words, 'Bob, I shall never see you again, never, never! O, God! it will break my heart! Your poor old mother will die!' Other poor slaves were crowding about the poor old woman, all anxious to take leave of one who had been with them from their youth up, and to receive her blessing. She appeared to be regarded as a kind of mother to them all. I noticed among the spectators many northern men who were here on a visit, and many a sympathetic tear was shed by them.

"At twelve o'clock, the auctioneer mounted the stand. On either side of him were placed plans of real estate, and large posters of future sales of slaves and other property. Behind him were two clerks seated at a table, to take down the names of the purchasers. On the table were placed a bottle of brandy and a tumbler, for the use of the auctioneer, who glories in the name of Beard. Before commencing the sale, this Mr. Beard smiled approvingly on the audience, and delivered the following address: 'Gentlemen buyers, I am about to offer you some of the most valuable property ever put up, at auction, and on most favorable terms—a credit of one year. These slaves are very choice, and all brought up by our lamented fellow-citizen, Harry Hill. Most of the women, as you will notice, are pregnant, and of good stock. I must impress it upon your minds that these slaves are exhibited under great disadvantage, as, after being worked very hard, they were hurried on board the steamer, and have had a hard time of it. They will look twenty-five per cent. better after being here a few days. Gentlemen buyers, before I sell this gang of negroes, I will put up three boys, who were sold at the last sale, but the papers of the purchasers were not satisfactory to us. It is, gentlemen, a credit to New Orleans, that, out of the large number of slaves sold on last Friday, only three of the purchasers have been rejected. It speaks well for the prosperity of our state.'"

It is due, however, to Mr. Hill, to state that he made particular request that his slaves should be kept all together, if possible; and in case of their being sold, that husbands and wives should not be separated. On this account the husbands and wives were sold together. There is at least one protest against slavery, in making this arrangement. When Bob and his wife were sold for sixteen hundred and seventy-five dollars, he was about to bid good-by to his mother, but was hurried out of the room, just as his mother was put on the block. The auctioneer praised her as a "good and motherly old wench—good and very useful to take care of children and milk cows." In this way the whole Church was disposed of.

5. The grief of Jacob when Joseph was stolen, and for thirteen years after, is no more than a medium example of what our slavery inflicts on parents and relatives, by tearing their nearest friends from them.

When Jacob heard the deceitful narrative about Joseph, he gave vent to the feelings of a father in the following mournful strains: "And Jacob rent his clothes, and put sackcloth upon his loins, and mourned for his son many days. And all his sons and his daughters rose up to comfort him; but he refused to be comforted; and he said, For I will go down into the grave unto my son mourning. Thus his father wept for him." Genesis xxxvii, 34–36.

The hypocrisy and blunted feelings of Joseph's brethren on this occasion, have their correspondence in the cold-blooded indifference with which some, not all, slaveholders look on when the nearest relatives are separated. So revolting is this law of slavery, that many will never, in their lifetime, allow of such separations. But after their death the law of slavery knows neither justice nor mercy. The revolt of feeling, on such occasions, is a moral protest against the unprincipled atrocity of slavery.

The grief of Jacob when Simeon was detained in Egypt, and when Benjamin was called for to go to Egypt, presents another phase of the slave system. Jacob had lost one child, but now others were in danger of being torn from him. Hear his lamentation: "Me have ye bereaved of my children: Joseph is not, and Simeon is not, and ye will take Benjamin away: all these things are against me. My son shall not go down with you; for his brother is dead, and he is left alone: if mischief befall him in the way in the which ye go, then shall ye bring down my gray hairs with sorrow to the grave." Genesis xlii, 36, 38. When Jacob was urged again to let Benjamin go, he asked, "Wherefore dealt ye so ill with me, as to tell the man whether ye had yet a brother?" Genesis xliii. And when finally persuaded to let Benjamin go to Egypt, he said, after having advised them to take double money, "Take also your brother, and arise, go again unto the man: and God almighty give you mercy before the man, that he may send away your other brother, and Benjamin. If I be bereaved of my children, I am bereaved."

How strikingly does the history of Jacob's sufferings find a counterpart in our slave system! One child is first taken and sold, and then another; and the distracted parents can not tell how soon the last will be taken away. Thus poor slave parents, especially mothers, are left to the mercies of a continued succession of bereavements till their death. The examples of this are so numerous that we are at a loss to select specimens. We give, however, a few.

The following was communicated to us by Rev. H. C. Boyers, of the Methodist Episcopal Church, Maysville, Ky., under date of January 13, 1855, and published in the Western Advocate, of January 31, 1855. It is the experience of a colored woman, taken down as she uttered it in love-feast:

"I have great pleasure in the service of my God, and I've none any whar else. Many years ago I started for heaven, but I had none to take me by the hand to lead me, or teach me the way. Master and mistis was wicked, and nobody near whar I lived loved the Lord Jesus. I lost my child, and God showed me I was a sinner, and had a wicked heart; and something told me I must pray; but I could not pray. I asked Master Jesus to show me how to pray, and then I could pray; and the more I prayed the worse I got, and at last I thought I would die. I was sick of sin, and I went off to a distant neighbor's house, and told an old Methodist sister how I felt; and she knowed what was the matter with me, and told me to look, by faith, to Jesus Christ, and he would save me. And I did; and, thank God! he did save me from all my fears and sins; and I was joyful. But I've had to wade through deep waters and fiery trials since then. Some of my children have died, and some have been sold down south, and my poor, dear husband, too, was sold, and I am almost alone now. I'll never see them on earth any more, but I hope to meet them in heaven. Brethren, pray that my faith fail not."

The lamentation of Daliah, one of Mr. Hill's slaves, as given in the account of the sale, is as touching as any thing uttered by Jacob. Daliah, number 40, of several hundred, with one arm around her son's neck, and the other on his head, despairingly said:

"Bob, I shall never see you again; never, never! O, God! it will break my heart! Your poor old mother will die!"

"Mr. — had a slave of light complexion, whom he took for his wife. She lived in his house as his wife, and had several children by him. The laws of the state—South Carolina—forbid emancipation; she therefore was still legally his slave, although not treated as such. Her master, who in the sight of God was her husband, became involved in debt. His wife and children were levied on and sold to satisfy a claim. A physician, himself a prominent member of a Baptist Church, and a son of a Baptist minister, purchased them, and the husband and father was not allowed to visit them on their master's plantation. The master continued a respected member of the Church." (Brisbane's Slaveholding Examined, p. 217.)

"A prominent southern minister, when invited to the pastoral charge of a leading Church in a northern city, brought with him a slave, and retained her in his service, after selling her children to a planter in Georgia." (Ibid., p. 204.)

6. The distress and sufferings of Joseph are such as slaves are no strangers to.

Joseph was seized violently by his brethren, stripped of his coat, put into a pit, kept there for a time, and then sold to strangers, and, therefore, separated from his father and home, and transformed from being a beloved son to be the slave of such master as might fall to his lot.

The anguish and distress of Joseph are thus described by his brethren when they were convinced of their sin in the presence of Joseph: "We are verily guilty concerning our brother, in that we saw the anguish of his soul, when he besought us, and we would not hear; therefore is this distress come upon us." Genesis xlii, 21. Here is presented, 1. The *anguish* or deep distress of a young man torn from his father and home, and consigned to strangers. 2. His *prayer;* he *besought* his brethren, he pleaded to be sent home. 3. They would not hear, but *sold* him for money. This was the beginning of Joseph's sufferings.

He next served in Egypt, as a slave, his master Potiphar. (Genesis xxxix, 4, 17, 19; xli, 12.) In consequence of his refusal to comply with the wishes of his master's wife, he was put in the dungeon of the prison and bound. (Genesis xxxix, 20.) There he served or waited on the chief butler and baker. (Genesis xl, 4.)

But, although he was well treated in prison, because

the Lord was with him, he was not content as a slave. For having interpreted the dreams, he besought the butler for deliverance with the following entreaty and explanation: "But think on me when it shall be well with thee, and show kindness, I pray thee, unto me, and make mention of me unto Pharaoh, and bring me out of this house. For, indeed, I was stolen away out of the land of the Hebrews; and here also have I done nothing, that they should put me into the dungeon." Genesis xl, 14, 15. Yet the butler forgot Joseph for two full years, which was another aggravation of his sufferings. (Genesis xl, 23.) Joseph was thirteen years a slave. (Genesis xxxvii, 2; xli, 46.)

There are several incidents in the case of Joseph as a slave which will point out clearly characteristics common to him and our slave system. We will present the following: He was deprived of liberty; this was done by force; he pleaded against the wrong, but they would not hear; he was made an article of property and sold; his soul was in anguish on this account; he was torn away from home; suffered much as a slave; was forgotten by those to whom he rendered important services. Thus he mourned after his lost liberty.

As Joseph was deprived of his liberty, so our slaves are deprived of their liberty. "Liberty," according to Justinian—Inst. Lib. I, Tit. 3, Sec. 1—"is the natural power of acting as we please, unless prevented by force or by the law." This is the case with our slaves. They are deprived of the inalienable rights of personal liberty, personal security, and the pursuit of happiness. There is no difference in this respect between the case of Joseph and our slaves. Liberty is denied to the one as well as the other. And liberty is the greatest gift that any one can possess, except religion, and to be deprived of it is to be deprived of what is most prized. And then the enslaved person is placed under the will or dominion of another, who can control him as he pleases, and treat him as a mere thing of convenience.

As Joseph was deprived of liberty by *force*, so it is with our slaves. It is true, there seems to be no apparent force used, when children are born, to place them in the number of slaves; but let the mother of the slave child take her own child, and leave her master, in order to have her child become a freeman, then the power of force will be shown. She and her child will be seized by violent hands, and immediately be arrested and reduced to the submission of the slave. If the slave attempt to run away he is hunted by the dogs, if need be, pursued as a criminal, seized with violence, and punished with stripes. There is the power of law, of courts, of the supreme judiciary, of the army and navy, brought out to compel him to submit to his bondage. He may be shot or killed in almost any way, if he resist his captors. There are three millions of slaves in the country, and about twenty-one millions are in combined federal alliance to keep these slaves under the yoke. These slaves have not one dollar of property, or dollar's worth; they have no arms, they have no learning, they have no press, they have no allies. On the other hand, their oppressors are *seven* times more numerous than they. They have all the property in the country; they have the arms and army of the Union; they have the learning, the press, and powerful allies. The *force* brought to bear against our slaves is greater, in proportion, than that which seized, stripped, and sold Joseph to strangers.

And Joseph did not pray more unavailingly than our slaves. As to signing petitions to legislatures, even by putting down their marks, it could not be entertained for a moment. They could not meet to deliberate, nor send in a petition. They would expect nothing but stripes were they to attempt such a thing. How could three millions of slaves contrive to send in petitions to Congress? It would be impossible. How could the slaves in a state combine in reference to the power that binds them hand and foot? They can make no stump speeches, nor pulpit speeches. They can print nothing, or circulate it, were it printed. If others petition for them, they are rarely heard. Even gag-laws have been passed in Congress both against the petitions in their favor, or any speeches in their behalf. Gag-laws were passed in Congress in 1836, 1837, and 1840. By one hundred and sixty ayes against thirty-five nays, February 11, 1837, the house resolved, "that slaves do not possess the right of petition secured to the people of the United States by the Constitution." The most miserable sinner may pray to God; but slaves among us must not utter any prayer in reference to their case. The powers that be will not receive, respect, or hear their petitions, much less grant them.

Our slaves are as truly reduced to *property* as Joseph was. He was *sold* and *bought*, and so are our slaves. We, too, sell for a price, and a high price at that. Joseph's price was only about twelve or fifteen dollars. Our slaves sell at from five hundred to one thousand dollars, and over. Joseph passed through several hands. The matter of the sale, purchase, conveyance, and securing of slaves has become a great and weighty business. There are the *producers*, who, in the very nature of the system, are the slave-growers. Then there are the *traders*, who buy them by traversing the country, and picking up one here and there till a gang is ready for the southern market. Then there are the great slave merchants, who have the barracoons to keep them safely. Almost every newspaper makes a gain by profitable advertisements of negroes for sale, negroes wanted; the farm-horses, cows.

hogs, furniture, and negroes, are displayed. The hand-bills and circulars, too, increase the business of the country. The auctioneer, the sheriff, and other civil officers, have a share in the merchandise of the souls and bodies of men. The bidders do their work. And if the slave be a Methodist preacher or Baptist preacher, as he is worth much to keep the slaves at work, and keep them from stealing, the bidding becomes often very brisk—the gifts and graces of the man commanding the highest price—as these are valuable qualities on a plantation, so that such a slave becomes an overseer as well as a slave. The *consumers*, properly so called, must not be overlooked; the sugar men and cotton men especially. These purchase hardy males—do not wish to grow slaves—wear them out in about seven years, and by extra profits can afford to buy a new gang. When this *pays*, as it mostly does, it saves the inconvenience and risks of growing the stock. Thus our growers of slaves, our various grades of traders, merchants, and officers, and consumers do a business as far beyond that of Joseph's brethren, the Midianites, and Potiphar, as three millions of slaves exceed one single Joseph.

The *anguish* of our slaves may, in many respects, equal that of Joseph; though, in some cases, it may fall greatly below it. To be torn from parents, and husbands, and wives, and relatives, must always affect any sensitive, intelligent being. And we have instances enough in the history of the slaves' wrongs which inflict wounds on the slave as keen and cutting as Joseph experienced. This will apply, however, to those who, like Joseph, had superior advantages.

But there is a class of slaves, so steeped in ignorance and stupidity by slavery, that some of them seem not to be much alive to their true state. And their masters cherish this, by making them as comfortable as possible, in their way, with food, clothing, and attendance, when sick. Through ignorance and mere animal gratification these often become *contented* slaves, and are *happy*, as they say. This is the darkest and lowest grade of slavery. Here is brutality, induced by the system. The man is unmarried, and the animal rules. And yet the perpetrators of this debauch tell us, "Our slaves are better clothed, fed, and housed, than your free laborers and manufacturers." They seem never to take into the account mental culture, liberty, independence, religion, marriage, elevation of character. They substitute for these, contubernium, ignorance, degradation, servility, irreligion, food and clothing, and thus call these things the chief good of man.

To tear away children from parents is common to the case of Joseph and to our slavery. In one state, we believe, there is a law restraining the separation of children or parents. But, in general, the slave laws pay no regard whatever to this; for, though the benevolence of some masters operates here, the effect is very limited. In the partition of estates it is little regarded. In sheriff's sales it is not known. Those that pass through the trader's hands are liable to separation, with no reference to the wishes of parents or children.

The *changes of masters* are very often attended with untold miseries to the slaves. Even when they fall into the hands of good masters, the evil is not evaded. In such cases there is often the separation of parents and children, and all the grades of relationship. Some are purchased for the sugar and cotton-fields of the south, and from being house-servants in Virginia, now make up a part of the southern gang on the cotton, rice, or sugar plantations. Then young, well-looking females, almost white, are purchased, and treated as God's intelligent creatures ought never to be treated. If there is a curse from heaven, from the conscience, and the result of crime, here it must rest, and adhere like the shirt of Nessus.

The *longing of the slave for liberty*, unless brutality is induced, is keen and undying. He sighs, and groans, and prays for liberty to the very last. This is natural to man. Nothing is so much in accordance with the lawful instincts of man as to enjoy the exercise of going, coming, and staying, as he pleases, or as his judgment directs. It is pleasant to call one's hands, feet, eyes, MINE, not YOURS; to have some property, too, if it is only as much as poor Cadmus had, is worth something, as it is a man's all; to wear a chain, only occasionally—to anticipate a sale—to be placed in the very lowest grade of humanity, must prey on human feelings, and produce anxiety. Justinian describes this well where he says, in the civil law, that, "in the condition of slaves, there is no diversity, but among free persons there is many, as ingenui—freemen, or libertini—freed-men." (Inst. Lib. I, Tit. 3, Sec. 5.) A slave is the lowest state, and none can be lower or higher, as all are *andrapoda*, that is, *men underfoot*, who can sink no lower. And no human being can inflict this on another without doing a great moral wrong. The sorrows of the slave, and his longings for liberty, show that slavery is both inhuman and unjust.

And yet all these evils, to which the slave is subject, seem to be overlooked and forgotten. His services and trials are not kept in view. Like Joseph and the butler, the slave is forgotten by his master, except to reap the fruit of his labor. This, at least, is the genuine operation of the system. When benevolence interferes, by its kind offices, it is like the good Samaritan doing the work which the slaveholding priest and Levite knew nothing of. Slaveholders ride in their carriages, eat at their sumptuous tables, possess property, enjoy their homes, and all by the toils of the slaves. Surely here is as great a forgetfulness as the two years' forgetfulness of the butler. There is this difference, however, that the slaveholder's forgetfulness lasts always.

7. The care and providence of God over Joseph will enable us to notice the care, protection, and deliverance which the Almighty exercises toward slaves, and all that are oppressed.

The Lord was with Joseph and prospered him. His new master, Potiphar, discovered this. This brought Joseph into favor. He was made overseer in the house of his master, and all his concerns were intrusted in his hands. (Genesis xxxix, 2–6.)

The singular piety of Joseph was remarkable in fidelity to every trust, and his resisting the overtures of his mistress. (Genesis xxxix, 7, 20.)

When put in prison, and even in its dungeon, for a crime of which he was not guilty, the Lord was with him, showed him mercy, and gave him favor in the sight of the keeper of the prison. He was even here intrusted with the care of every thing. (Genesis xxxix, 21–23.)

After interpreting the dreams of the butler and baker, and then of Pharoah, he was not only set at liberty, but promoted to the highest distinction in Egypt, the particulars of which we need not here detail. (Genesis xl, xli.)

And after all the evils which Joseph suffered from his brethren, he generously forgave them, when they came to a proper sense of their crimes. (Genesis xlv, 3–8; l, 15–21.)

Two lessons, connected with our subject, we learn from this part of the history. The first is, that the Lord will hear and protect the poor, the needy, the slave, and the oppressed. The second is, that he will punish their oppressors, and deliver the oppressed in his own good time.

8. The reverse of circumstances in the case of Joseph's brethren will furnish a specimen of what has occurred, in the history of mankind, to the oppressors of their fellow-men.

An unexpected famine rendered it necessary for Joseph's brethren to go to Egypt to purchase corn to prevent starvation. There the recollection of their past evil conduct came up fresh in their minds. They were harassed with the conditions of their case, in the detention of Simeon as a hostage for bringing down Benjamin.

The reverse of circumstances brought them to a sense of their guilt. They confessed to each other their guilt; they were *distressed* on account of it, and they acknowledged now that their course was a murderous one. "We are verily guilty concerning our brother, in that we saw the anguish of his soul, when he besought us, and we would not hear; therefore is this distress come upon us." Reuben said to them, "Spake I not unto you, saying, Do not sin against the child; and ye would not hear? therefore, behold also his blood is required." Genesis xlii, 21, 22. Thus they expressed themselves when they were before Joseph the first time. At the second interview they say, "What shall we say unto my Lord? what shall we speak? or how shall we clear ourselves? God hath found out the iniquity of thy servants." Genesis xliv, 16.

They were haunted with fears even to the very last. After the death of their father, Jacob, they feared that their former evil deeds would be visited on them. They approached Joseph with trembling, and entreated him to forgive their *trespass*, their sin.

The adverse reverse of circumstances of the supporters of the slave system, if variously examined, will be found to exist in it in all ages. In Greece, and in Rome, it was found to produce the greatest disasters, and often broke out in insurrections and bloodshed. It reduced the West Indies to the greatest distress, financially and socially; and, although the blame has been laid at the door of emancipation, it properly belongs to slavery. The horrors of St. Domingo were nothing else than the convulsive throes of slavery.

In our country the low morals, in connection with the system, are manifest to all men. The majority of the whites, in the slave states, are but poorly educated, and have even obtained the name of "white negroes." Landed property in slave states, is, perhaps, only one-half, or two-thirds the price it is in the free states. The money pressures, too, have a greater effect on them than on others. The overt efforts of the slave power, in forcing pro-slavery measures on the General Government, as in the Fugitive-Slave law, the Nebraska bill, and other acts of like sort, are now producing an opposition to the whole system that will never be settled while slavery exists. The civilized world looks now with horror at our system, and we are forced to be dumb, having no argument or reason to meet their just reproaches. If prices of cotton and sugar are greatly reduced, by the cultivation of these staples, in other countries, the result will be to humble and depress the slave power. In short, the moral sense of the world has now solemnly uttered its condemnation of the entire system. What reverses may be in the future, none can tell, but, according to the fixed laws of God's government, these reverses will come.

Sober reflection has brought the most devoted friends of slavery to the conviction of its wrongs, and distress of mind in consequence. In 1832, just after the insurrection in Virginia, this conviction became very general throughout the south. After some respite, this conviction died away, and elaborate essays have been published to defend the system. The issues of the press, from the north, since that time, have shown up, pretty clearly, the great moral evils of the system. And, however numerous they are who now plead for the system, the conscience of the south, to some extent, is greatly disturbed, if not convinced.

9. We may here inquire how far our confession and repentance, for the sin of our slavery, may correspond with the confession and repentance of Joseph's brethren.

By the wonderful change of circumstances, and the providence of God, there is much conviction in the minds of men in regard to the moral, social, and political wrongs of slavery. The discussions in the north, though mixed up with some extravagant sentiments, have greatly convinced the public of the evils of the system. The conscience of the south, after all the denunciations of abolitionists, has been greatly awakened. It is true, that many now in the south contend for the system on Scriptural grounds; but this we must consider similar with pleading and arguing for heterodoxy, or false doctrines, and bad morals from the Scriptures. The exercise of natural conscience, and sounder teachings, will, in time, do away these errors from the minds of men. But, if men are deaf to the convictions of justice, the adverse providences of God, by judgments, will plead the cause of right, as in the case of Joseph's brethren. We need not stay to portray this—the history of God's righteous government proves it to every reflecting mind.

10. If we contrast the service of Joseph with that under the patriarchs, Abraham, Isaac, and Jacob, nothing can be more different. Abraham, Isaac, and Jacob were eminently good men, and were governed by the principles of justice. Joseph's brethren were bad men, at the time they sold their brother.

No force was used in procuring the servants of Abraham. They became his servants, or subjects, from religious considerations, and for the sake of protection and support. Those bought with money, by Abraham, were bought for their benefit. The servants of Abraham were never *sold*, or transferred to others, and it gradually became extinct, by voluntary agreement, as we see in the servants of Abraham, Isaac, and Jacob. No cruel treatment can be found toward the servants of Abraham, Isaac, and Jacob. In short, the two systems are as opposite as freedom and slavery—as right and wrong.

11. On survey of the subject, we find that there is a perfect identity between the slavery of Joseph and our slave system; at least, it has all the parts that can be common to the case of an individual, compared with a general system.

The brethren of Joseph, when they seized him, were wicked men, under the control of bad tempers, such as hatred and envy. Enslavers, in general, are wicked men; and if envy, hatred, and malice, be not uppermost, the love of gain, of power, gratification, or the like, govern them. They are not under the influence of *love*, which worketh no ill to his neighbor, nor do they observe the golden rule, "Do as you would wish to be done by."

The commutation of slavery for murder, has nothing to recommend it; because the murderous temper still remains, and is now, and always has been, an element in every slave system. Such unworthy motives as *gain*, *pleasure*, *convenience*, govern in this. So, while our system has disavowed murder, it includes it, nevertheless, and alleges for it the argument of gain, pleasure, or custom.

In their case Joseph's brethren used force. We use it in originating, continuing, and practicing our slavery, with no less a force than the army and navy, the treasure and police of the whole Union, in *compelling* our slaves to lie quiescent *under our feet*, as the word *andrapodon*, or *slave*, properly means. And we are *andrapodistae*, *those who stand upon the slave*, in this downtrodden condition.

Our *theft*, or stealing of men, is as palpable as that of Joseph, and the charge is as applicable to us as to his brethren. The *sin* of it, too, is nothing less; and no evasion can clear us of the guilt and shame which are incurred by our acts.

Our slave-dealers are certainly more competent, and greater adepts in their profession, than those who bought and sold Joseph. We employ dogs to catch them, hunters to hunt them, and marshals to seize them. And our stripes and stars float proudly over a poor Burns, and we carry him back in triumph to receive his quota of stripes, minister as he was.

In Joseph's case there seems to be no mourner but one; that is, the father. The bereavements of our system reaches father and mother, brothers and sisters, and all relatives. Look at the picture found in the case of Mr. Hill's slaves.

As to the distress of the slaves themselves, in their bondage, while some, through the mere ignorance and degradation inseparable from the system, seem content, the greater number carry with them the miseries of the system, both bodily and mental, down to the grave, in which at last they find a resting-place.

The remorse and confession of slaveholders, among us, are sufficiently exhibited to declare our guilt. Of late, especially since 1832, some have boldly disavowed all sense of guilt. But this disavowal is no proof that it does not exist. Almost all culprits, like Joseph's brethren, deny, to the last extremity, their sin, even were it murder. Joseph's brethren did so. Our slaveholders do so. It is a part of their sin, after doing their evil deed, to *eat bread,* like Joseph's brethren, and then cry out, "*Abolitionist!*"—"*Fanatic North!*" while inward guilt preys on their conscience. But we have hosts of slaveholders, who now, like honest men, denounce it all over, as Jefferson did.

While we earnestly hope, we would humbly pray that all our slaveholders might be led, by God's grace and providence, to forsake their sins, and turn their attention to the slave system, so as to do it away as soon as possible, in consistency with the principles of the New Testament, under the influence of the great law of love, which works no ill to his neighbor, and does to all as he would desire that they should do to him. Whenever love of God and man shall govern, slavery will die out.

CHAPTER IV.

EGYPTIAN BONDAGE.

THE inquiry here is, whether there is such a just analogy between the bondage of the Hebrews, in Egypt, and our slavery, as to justify us to argue from the one to the other. There were certainly some points in which the service of the Hebrews, in Egypt, differed from our slavery; but there are many points on which they agree. It is not always safe to argue from mere analogy, between two cases, so as to infer from the one the same conclusions which we may infer from the other. But in forming the comparison here, we have great moral principles so clearly pointed out, in both cases, that we are saved from mere conjecture. Besides, the law of Moses, in drawing instructions from the bondage of Egypt, expressly declares to the Hebrews, that this bondage conveys the lessons, that they should not enslave one another, nor enslave strangers.

1. The Hebrews in Egypt were held by the government, and were employed in the service of the government, without particular reference to the will of individuals. They were held to service, enslaved, or oppressed, as a *people*, or *nation*, rather than as individuals, to the service of others. They were not claimed, or owned, or required to serve individuals, or distributed on farms, as the property of individuals.

Our slavery, like that of Egypt, is established by the authority of law and Government; and it is as much the *creature* of law and Government as Egyptian slavery. Both were created by the sovereign civil power. Our

Government does not, however, either own slaves, or require the service of our slaves. It disavows these, except in case of debt to the Government, in which case the slaves are sold to pay the debt. Our Government authorizes individuals to own slaves, and maintains the full exercise of this to the utmost power of the civil arm. And this seems to give bad eminence to our system, as the civil power gives to the master the complete dominion over the services of the slave; and also such power over his life and limb as no just civil power ever granted to one human being over another. Our slavery originated in private individuals taking possession of men as slaves. Subsequently this theft, robbery, violence, or assault and battery were sanctioned by law; hence, our slavery differs from the Egyptian, and is worse on that account. The Egyptians, however, appear to have had domestic servants or slaves in their families. (Exodus ix, 14, 20, 21.)

2. On many accounts the servitude of Egypt was more mild than our slavery. Although it was *hard, oppressive, grievous*, a *furnace*, yet in several of the features it was much more lenient than our slavery. The following are the principal points of lenience in the bondage of Egypt. (See Barnes on Slavery, pp. 83–86. Weld's Bible Argument, pp. 43, 44.)

The Israelites were not dispersed among the families of Egypt, but formed a separate community of their own in the land of Goshen, of which they had exclusive possession. (Genesis xlvi, 35; xlvii, 6, 11, 27; Exodus ix, 26; x, 23; xi, 7.)

The Israelites lived in permanent dwellings. These were houses and not tents; because the doors, side posts, and lintels are mentioned. (Exodus xii, 6, 22.) And each family seems to have occupied a house with several apartments. (Exodus ii, 2, 3; Acts vii, 20.)

They were the *owners* of vast herds of cattle; "a mixed

multitude of flocks and herds," and "much cattle." Exodus xii, 32, 37, 38. They were, therefore, the possessors of much property, as the history shows.

They had their own form of government, as their tribes, their elders, their family divisions, though a sort of province of Egypt and tributary to it. (Exodus ii, 1; iii, 16, 18; vi, 14, 25; xii, 19, 21.)

They seemed to have had, to a considerable degree, the disposal of their own time. (Exodus ii, 9; iii, 16, 18; xii, 6; Exodus xxiii, 4.)

They possessed the use of arms. (Exodus xxxii, 27.)

None but adult males seem to have rendered service. There is no account of the bond service of females. The mother of Moses had him three months; and afterward she contracted to nurse him for wages. (Exodus xii, 29.) The great body of the people seem not to be in the service of the Egyptians at any one time.

None of these privileges belong to our slaves. On this account the bondage of Egypt had several meliorating traits which do not belong to our slavery. Our slaves do not dwell in separate communities, in their own houses, do not possess much property, assemble when they choose, or make contracts, etc.

3. As to the proper character of the service rendered by the Hebrews, by the exaction of the Egyptians, it is thus described by the inspired penman: "They did set over them taskmasters, to afflict them with their burdens. And they built for Pharoah treasure cities—Pithon and Raamses. And the Egyptians made them serve with rigor. And they made their lives bitter with hard bondage, in mortar and in brick, and in all manner of service in the field: all their service wherein they made them serve was with rigor." Exodus i, 11, 13, 14. "They sighed by reason of their bondage, and they cried; and their cry came up unto God, by reason of the bondage."

Exodus ii, 23. "I have surely seen the affliction of my people which are in Egypt, and have heard their cry by reason of their taskmasters, for I know their sorrows. I have also seen the oppression wherewith the Egyptians oppress them." Exodus iii, 7, 9. "But they hearkened not unto Moses for anguish of spirit, and for cruel bondage." Exodus vi, 9.

The Israelites were employed in severe labor, of the lowest and most laborious kind. They worked *in mortar and brick*, in digging the clay, kneading and preparing it, and then forming it into bricks, and drying and burning them. They also served in the field by carrying these materials to the places where they were to be put into buildings for the public.

Josephus says: "The Egyptians contrived a variety of ways to afflict the Israelites; for they enjoined them to cut a great number of channels for the river, and to build walls for the cities and ramparts, that they might restrain the river, and hinder its waters from stagnating upon its own banks. They set them also to build pyramids, and wore them out, and forced them to learn all sorts of mechanic arts, and to accustom themselves to hard labor." Antiq., B. II., cap. ix, Sec. 1. Philo tells us they were employed to carry burdens beyond their strength. They were forced to be workers and servers.

The service was with *rigor*, with cruelty, and oppression. They served with *hard bondage*, with *grievous servitude*. Their life was one of laborious service; oppressive enough in itself, but made more severe by the treatment they received.

This service was *compulsory* by the supreme law of the land, which they could neither gainsay nor resist. "They MADE THEM SERVE with rigor." It was compulsory on the part of the Egyptians, and involuntary on the part of the Hebrews.

There were TASKMASTERS, שׂרי מסים—*sawray missim,* princes of burdens, works, or tribute. The Septuagint calls them *overseers of the works.* *Tax-gatherers* is the most exact meaning, perhaps. These appointed them their work, and exacted from them the performance of it.

This service was attended with both bodily and mental affliction. The strongest words are used to express this. It is called *oppression,* because it crushed the man. It is called *affliction,* because of the constant uneasiness experienced. Their very lives were *made bitter,* so that the comforts of life were greatly lessened or allayed. The very spirit was in anguish, so that they sighed by reason of their miseries.

Add to all this, that their burdens were increased in refusing to give them straw to make the brick, in order thoroughly to subdue them and preserve them in subjection. (Exodus v, 5–19.)

The foregoing presents a tolerably faithful picture of slavery in several of its leading characteristics. Our slaves are employed in the most laborious drudgery, of the lowest sort, with no opportunities of mental culture; so that it may be said, in general terms, to be hard, rigorous, constant, and degrading. The Egyptian taskmasters and officers correspond to our overseers and drivers with a good degree of coincidence. The overseer is the taskmaster, and the officer is the black driver, who urges on the gang in their toil. The anguish, bitterness, and affliction of the one are well represented by those of the other. We have also a very fair specimen of the excessive exaction of Egypt, in the demands made on multitudes of slaves in the cotton-fields and sugar plantations, in order to exact the most possible service at the least expenditure. The points of agreement are very marked between our slavery and their bondage—in the nature and degree of labor exacted, in the compulsion used, in the oversight employed, in the mental and bodily sufferings endured, and the immeasurable and unjust exactions demanded.

4. Egyptian bondage is said to have commenced at a time when there was a king "who KNEW NOT Joseph." Exodus i, 8. The word to *know* often signifies to *acknowledge*, to *approve*, as all allow. We may, therefore, understand by the new king's *not knowing* Joseph, his *disapproving* of that system of government which Joseph had established, as well as his haughtily refusing to *acknowledge* the obligations under which the whole country was laid to Joseph. The entire period that the descendants of Abraham were in Canaan and in Egypt, was four hundred and thirty years, being about two hundred and fifteen in the one and two hundred and fifteen in the other. (Exodus xii, 40.) The enslavement of the Hebrews, when the new king arose, occurred about B. C. 1604, or one hundred and three years after the descent of Jacob to Egypt. They were one hundred and thirteen years in bondage, or from B. C. 1604 to 1491. The Hebrews were treated on the basis of equal rights over one hundred years in Egypt; then the policy changed, and the reign of oppression continued for one hundred and thirteen years.

It was a dark day in Christendom when the Christian nations of Europe entered on the extinguished system of slavery. The Christian nations of Spain and Portugal took the lead. England soon followed. These Governments did *not know;* they forgot, or did not acknowledge the antislavery practice of the patriarchs Abraham, Isaac, and Jacob. They either forgot, or they did not acknowledge or approve the unbending antislavery laws given by God to Moses, so that no slave could touch Hebrew soil, or breathe its air. They did not study the antislavery principles of the New Testament. They overlooked the victories of Christianity in destroying slavery wherever it existed.

Worse yet, the Biblical interpreters, from Cornelius a Lapide, down to our times, have blindly taught, or conceded, that slavery existed in the families of Abraham, Isaac, and Jacob; that the Mosaic code allowed it, and so did Christ and his apostles. From the Spanish commentators, as far as we can learn, the teaching has passed to all the Protestant commentators, Wesley, Clarke, and Coke not excepted, strong antislavery men as they were. They have not shown that the true slavery was found in the case of Joseph, among the Egyptians, and the heathen nations, and received its support from unjust human laws, and not from the word of God.

Our slave system finds its type in this new king of Egypt, who ignored the just principles of Joseph's government. The Roman code, in establishing slavery, rejected the law of nature, and counteracted its own definition of justice, and right, and liberty. The American constitutions and laws, establishing the system, reject the sound principles of the Declaration of Independence, of the constitutions of the land, of holy Scripture, and natural law. And by such barbarous principles as that *the child follows the condition of the mother*, our system of slavery has grown up, maintained by the army, navy, treasure, judiciary, and laws of the states and United States. And now, most recent pleaders for the system treat with sneer and contempt the antislavery principles which the fathers of American liberty held, professed, and practiced to the end of their lives.

5. There are many strong points of resemblance between the servitude of the Hebrews in Egypt and our slavery.

There are some respects in which, as we have seen, there was a great dissimilarity between the two systems. The Israelites were not dispersed among the families of Egypt, but formed a community by themselves. They owned much property, they had a limited government of their own, and the females were not held to service, but the adult males only. They were not liable to be sold for debt, they were not held strictly as chattels, nor were they under the constraint, or in the service, of individual owners, but of the government only. They were held to involuntary service by compulsion of law. They were oppressed men, but not reduced to all the conditions of property, as our slaves are.

Yet there are, as stated, strong points of resemblance between their servitude and our slavery, that give the same moral character to the one and the other.

They were a different race, as the African with us. We can not call our slaves a *foreign* race, as distinguished from our whites; because both, as to America, are foreign; the Indians alone being the original people of the country. The difference of race, say *color*, is the leading badge by which to mark out, in this country, the slave. And if difference of race be a reason for enslavement, then any one race may enslave another race which is different from it.

The service, in both institutions, is one of *force* or mere *power*. It was the work of oppression and wrong. There was no right but power alone. They were *made* to serve. This is the case with our slavery—it is compulsory and involuntary.

The bondage of Egypt had all the essential features of our slavery, being a state of compulsory, involuntary, unremunerated toil. It was *hard bondage*. They had taskmasters to afflict them with their burdens. They had also their *officers* or drivers, to see that the work was done. The tale of bricks is demanded, while no straw is given. There is no voluntary labor. "And they made their lives bitter with hard bondage in mortar, and in bricks, and in all manner of service in the field; all their service wherein they made them serve was with rigor." Exodus i, 14. "I am the Lord thy God which brought thee out of the land of Egypt, out of the house of bondage." Exodus xx, 2. Thus, many of the leading qualities of slavery are identical with Egyptian bondage.

6. The Egyptians did not wish to lose the services of the Hebrews. They did not wish them "to get them up out of the land." Exodus i, 10. It is not to be supposed that the Egyptians were ignorant of the Israelites' intention to return and settle in Canaan. Sensible, therefore, of the advantages arising from such a body of people, yet fearful of their numbers and power, they determined to prevent their increase, and so weaken their power. Hence the recourse to very severe labor, and the sacrifice of life.

In the estimation of our slaveholders, who are unaccustomed to labor, and who make large demands for personal services from their slaves, the services of our three millions and a half of slaves can not be dispensed with. The climate, and culture of rice, cotton, and sugar, they say, does not suit the constitutions of white men, and therefore slaves are necessary. And yet white people reside wherever the slaves labor. Though they can not go into the cornfield, and toil in the production of sugar, cotton, and rice, they can ride in carriages, and live in luxury, notwithstanding the climate. Slaveholders want the slaves to *work* for them, to *wait* on them, and to administer to their pleasures, conveniences, and luxuries. Here is the secret of the whole system. There is the *profit, pleasure,* and *ease* of the system; therefore, they will not let the people go. Even after the ten plagues had destroyed Egypt, and the Israelites had left, Pharaoh and the Egyptians repented of their course, and resolved to overtake them and bring them back. "And it was told the king of Egypt that the people fled; and the heart of Pharaoh and of his servants was turned against the people, and they said, Why have we done this, that we have let Israel go from SERVING US?" Exodus xiv, 5. We hear loud complaints of the worthlessness, expense, and vexations of slavery; yet when the proposal of emancipation is presented, it is scouted with abhorrence. And our Fugitive-Slave law, with its officers, and the army of the Union, and the President of the United States, commander-in-chief, furnishes a pretty good imitation of Pharaoh and his army pursuing the Israelites.

7. The increasing number and power of the oppressed always gave uneasiness to their oppressors, and the most rigorous means have been resorted to, to keep numbers within due bounds, and subdue the rising and dangerous power.

The Israelites were *fruitful* as *fruit-trees*, and increased with the fecundity of *fishes*, as the Hebrew words imply. Hence they are said to *multiply*, and wax exceedingly mighty, so that the land was filled with them. They were more numerous and strong than the Egyptians. They grew and were multiplied under afflictions. They multiplied and waxed very mighty. (Exodus i, 7, 9, 12, 20.) Their number and power were a source of alarm to the Egyptians. Two expedients were resorted to, to counteract the number and the power of the slaves. The one was to destroy the male children; or a certain proportion of them. (Exodus i, 16–21.) The other was to increase their labor, and refuse them the necessary means of performing their tasks, by withholding straw. (Exodus v, 7–14.) They had *more work* to perform, and the material was diminished.

The increase of the number and power of slaves, is no small cause of alarm and precaution in our country. There is no resort, however, to direct murder, because the slaves are too valuable for this. The slave-growing states are, by natural increase, constantly swelling the number. And as they cost high prices in the south, and then the profit is considerable, to kill them would be bad policy; indeed, ruinous. Hence, *more territory* is constantly wanted, sought, and obtained, so as to make room for their numbers; and severe protective laws are enacted, to guard against their growing and formidable power.

The entire number of slaves in the United States, in 1850, was 3,204,313; of free colored people, 434,495; total colored people, of slaves and free persons, 3,638,808; or over three and a half millions of colored persons; who about this time—April, 1855—are about four millions, or nearly one-sixth of the population of the United States.

The proportion of free colored and slave population, to the free white population, was,

As 1	slave or	colored to	4.1	whites	in	1790.
1	"	"	4.2	"		1800.
1	"	"	4.2	"		1810.
1	"	"	4.4	"		1820.
1	"	"	4.5	"		1830.
1	"	"	4.9	"		1840.
1	"	"	5.3	"		1850.

Louisiana, Mississippi, and South Carolina, have each more colored population than white. The states of Alabama, Florida, and Georgia, have nearly as many colored as white persons; while the states of Maryland, North Carolina, Texas, and Virginia, have about one-third colored. Maryland has about one-seventh of her population free colored persons, and about one-eighth slaves, which shows that free colored persons there find a home and protection.

There are now—1855—about four millions of colored people in the United States, and about twenty-six millions of whites, making nearly one-sixth of the whole colored. Then there are about ten millions of colored people, as some state, on the American continent and islands, making the colored force about fourteen millions. The population of Mexico and South America, may be set down now at about nineteen millions; so that the colored population make up a numerous body of men, who may form, yet, pretty formidable enemies; especially as their race is treated *as enemies*, in enslaving so many of them. Add to this, that the civilized world, Britain and France especially, are arrayed against the whole system of slavery. Besides, the *conscience*, wherever it is a *good* one, is against the system, and for freedom. And what is greater than all, God is against it, and it must come to an end. The fears of Pharaoh, and of the Egyptians, are the type of the fears of our slaveholders, in reference to the number and power of the colored people; and the strong political movements of the south, within the last few years, aided by northern sympathizers, in passing the Fugitive-Slave law, and the Nebraska bill, indicate a purpose to continue and extend the system. The plan is not to kill, or even overwork the slaves; but perhaps it is even worse in its results, as it is to establish firmly, and extend greatly, the system, and make the whole Union the allies in this huge work of oppression.

8. The Israelites were oppressed, lest they should join the enemies of the Egyptians. "Come on, let us deal wisely with them, lest they multiply, and it come to pass that, when there falleth out any war, they join also our enemies, and fight against us, and so get them out of the land."

The fear of insurrection is one that has haunted slaveholders from the days of Pharaoh down to this day. Pharaoh undertook to meet the difficulty by killing off in due time the dangerous excess of the Hebrews, by murder, and then subduing the rest by excessive labor, and a most vigilant police of taskmasters, and under officers. This was dealing wisely with them.

Among the Greeks various methods were employed, when necessary to diminish the power and number of the slaves. We can not enlarge here, but refer to the well-known authorities.

The Romans, too, found the same difficulty pressing upon them. Here, too, we must, for want of space, refer to the authentic histories on this subject.

An *insurrection* of the slaves strikes terror to all hearts, especially the guilty, and those who are exposed to the danger. The little insurrection in Southampton, Virginia, above twenty years ago, moved the whole Union ; and the project of emancipation was discussed, remembered for a while, and then forgotten. Presently the old measures of subjecting the slaves were considered and revised, and new measures of vigilance and restraint were resorted to. The Sunday schools, and other schools, that had, through the tolerance of the times, been established, were now shut up, and the laws favoring emancipation have been done away, so as to make it almost impossible. The southern slaveholders, in their generation, have acted wisely, and have fortified themselves pretty firmly against the colored people, whom they consider their enemies ; as the colored people view slaveholders, in general, as their enemies. Hatred, envy, love of gain, began slavery ; and these inhere to it as parts of its very life blood. There is no *love* in the system. The slaves and masters never can be brothers, according to the slave code. They are natural, traditional, and practical enemies, and ever will be so, on the principles of the system. We will barely mention a few of the methods employed to preserve the dominion over the slaves, as effectual, for the time being, as the wise plans of Pharaoh.

It is rather an ungracious work to single out the substitutes which our system of slavery has selected to do the work which the Egyptians did, by the murder of the male children, the increase of burdens, and the refusal of the material necessary for the work required.

The brand of *color* is a pretty formidable one, so that wherever there is the African tinge, however slight, the strong *presumption* is, there is the slave. And even when the African is absorbed by the Saxon, *genealogy* comes in, and the *descent*, by the mother, answers the same end of pronouncing the man a slave.

Then, *the child follows the condition of the mother*. This becomes the source of the new generations of slaves, after the thefts from Africa had furnished the original stock of mothers.

Next, these generations of slaves must be raised *without education*, so that they should forever remain *ignorant* of the proper modes of redress, and of asserting their rights. Hence, they can never use the press in any form in their behalf.

They are disfranchised of all political or civil powers as citizens. They can neither vote nor hold any office. They can not even *petition*, in order to have any wrong redressed.

They can not *assemble* together, or deliberate, or confer with one another, for any purpose whatever. They can have no primary meeting, in which to complain of their wrongs, nor utter any opinions about them, nor assert any principles to support their cause. They can not stand up as orators, nor plead before any power on earth that can relieve them. They can have neither *hearing* nor *redress* for any real or supposed wrongs; as any acts by them, on these points, are pronounced and treated as treasonable, insurrectionary, or rebellious.

Even their *religious worship* is at the will of their masters, and under the control of severe and unjust laws. All their churches may be shut up, if the state sees fit. Masters may prevent all their slaves from ever attending any place of public worship.

The southern *police*, or patrols, are organized, and on constant duty, as an armed force to preserve the peace of the town or vicinity. This may be necessary, because there is slavery; but, because such a thing is necessary, the cause which produces it ought to be discontinued.

And then the slaves can have no *arms* to protect themselves, or assert their own rights. This, too, of course, is as necessary for the maintenance of the system, as the murder of infants, the increase of burdens, and the refusal of straw, was to the Hebrews in Egypt. But the system is radically wrong that needs the support of such means.

And even when a poor *fugitive*, not from justice nor service, but from slavery, sets out to obtain freedom, the whole United States, from the President to the constable, with the army, navy, and police at their backs, are in motion to catch the poor runaway, as if he were the common enemy of mankind, or the safety of the United States, and of the world, depended on his capture, his enchainment, and the stripes he receives on his unwilling return.

It would make a long list of means and ways, indeed, to trace out, in detail, all the various processes of the United States Government and of the slave states, of the masters and their ends, in order to accomplish what the original Egyptian slave power attempted by three simple and direct instrumentalities—murder, more hard work, and the denial of the proper material for this work. The wisdom of Pharaoh, and of his wise counselors, in our day, would be mere bungling, compared with our well-adjusted scheme of enslavement. Our southern slaveholders have studied the subject, and have done a master-work of legislation and diplomacy. There is no part of the old British code so much improved, as the part relating to slavery, in making it the completest despotism the world ever saw. As it excels the Egyptian and British codes, so does it the Roman code, in the complication of its wrongs.

9. The oppressed Israelites prayed to God for relief, in consequence of their distress. "And the children of Israel sighed by reason of the bondage, and they cried; and their cry came up unto God by reason of the bondage." Exodus ii, 23. "And the Egyptians vexed us, and our fathers; and when we cried unto the Lord, he heard our voice." Numbers xx, 15.

Petitions to men are frequently unavailing, because men often want power to hear the request. The humblest of God's creatures are authorized and encouraged to ask God for redress. "Ask, and ye shall receive; seek, and ye shall find; knock, and it shall be opened unto you." The poor and the needy, the stranger and the fatherless, are especially privileged to ask God for deliverance.

Our slaves have prayed, sighed, and groaned, in vain, as it respects human aid. By stern law, they are not permitted to assemble in order to petition; they are not allowed to draw up one, or set their mark to it. They can not present it to congress, legislature, judge, jury, or any power on earth to which they have access. Their private prayers, and sighs, and tears, can speak only in silence, with closed lips, to the SUPREME RULER of the world. They have now *appealed* their unprotected, unheeded, unredressed cause to the TRIBUNAL ABOVE. The four millions of colored people in the Union have done this. The more than three hundred thousand of Christian slaves in bonds, have prayed, night and day for liberty. They are praying for it now. They will continue to pray for it till death. Millions of free white Christians are praying for them. Will the cry of all this host of oppressed ones and those who saw them, reach the ears of the Lord of armies? Will God avenge his elect who cry to him day and night? Have these poor ones no Redeemer? Does Jesus Christ intercede only for white people? Are the tears of all these little ones entirely forgotten by God, that made them, by Jesus Christ, who died for them, and by the Holy Ghost, who sanctified them? Are slaveholders the only persons who will find favor with God?

10. The Almighty had respect to their prayers, and answered them, by a great deliverance from their bondage. "And their cry came up unto God, by reason of the bondage. And God heard their groaning, and God remembered the covenant with Abraham, with Isaac, and with Jacob. And God looked upon the children of Israel, and God had respect unto them." Exodus ii, 23–25. "And I have also heard the groanings of the children of Israel, whom the Egyptians keep in bondage; and I have remembered my covenant. Wherefore, say unto the children of Israel, I am the Lord, and I will bring you out from under the burdens of the Egyptians, and I will rid you of their bondage, and I will redeem you with a stretched-out arm, and with great judgments." Exodus vi, 5, 6.

These passages of Scripture apply particularly to the case of the Hebrews; but the same great principles here laid down, are every-where declared in Scripture as the standard according to which the Almighty will deal in all like cases. Observe here,

(1.) Bondage, oppression, and the like, are abhorrent to God. He abhorred it in the case of the Egyptians, and he does in reference to all. It is as hateful in his sight now as it was then; and as he changes not, he must always hate it. American slavery can claim no exemption from this, any more than Egyptian, Roman, or Grecian slavery. The righteous God hateth the wrong, and can never approve of it.

(2.) The oppressed always had, have now, and ever will have, the ear of the Almighty, who hates oppression. No edicts of man can shut out their petitions from before the mercy-seat, and God's justice. No privileged class can exclude them from the compassion of the most merciful God.

(3.) Indeed, God has made a covenant with man in this matter. He says, in reference to this bondage, "I have remembered my covenant." This is the covenant of grace and mercy, made with Abraham, but to be extended to the whole human family; for in Abraham all the families of the earth were to be blessed. This covenant recognizes the brotherhood of man, and was completely established under the Gospel dispensation. There was no slavery under it in the days of Abraham; as all his servants, whether bought with money, or born in his house, were circumcised, and this broke up the slave system, which even then was in process of formation. There was no slavery connected with this covenant under the Mosaic code, because this code made every enslaving act a capital crime, punishable by death. No slavery existed according to this covenant under Christ and his apostles. Christ's mission was to proclaim the Gospel; and the sequence of that was, *liberty* to the *captives*. This brotherhood existed under the *apostles*.

In the primitive Church, slavery died out under its influence. Our Christian slavery never was in accordance with God's covenant, whether the African slave-trade—the parent, or the American commerce—the offspring; for both are of the same birth and kin; and if the one be wrong, they must both be wrong. The one is piracy, and the other can not belong to godliness.

(4.) God has no attribute in favor of slavery. In reference to it, he says: "I am the Lord, and I will bring you out from under the burdens of the Egyptians." Here, we presume, Jefferson found the sentiment, that "no attribute of God was in favor of slavery." The God of love can not love slavery. The God of all grace can not favor the wrong. Mercy itself must arm itself against its cruelty. Justice weighs it in the balance and finds it wanting. God's omnipotence, in the exercise of judgments, are at war with the whole system. And as Omnipotence has destroyed the slavery of Egypt, Greece, and Rome, it will destroy our slavery, unless we repent, and reform, and voluntarily, like the primitive Christians, and all truly good and enlightened Christians, have done with it.

11. The commission of God to Moses to deliver the Hebrews from being involuntary laborers, or slaves to the Egyptians, runs in this wise: "Now, therefore, behold the cry of the children of Israel is come unto me; and I have also seen the oppression wherewith the Egyptians oppress them. Come now, therefore, and I will send thee unto Pharaoh, that thou mayest bring forth my people, the children of Israel, out of Egypt." Exodus iii, 9, 10.

Under the leadership of Moses, all this was accomplished, as the history shows. The *oppression* was hateful to God, and it therefore could not be endured. The *prayer*, too, of the oppressed had reached the ear of the Almighty. Hence, deliverance was determined on, to meet the necessity of the case. Moses was the commissioned agent, through whose administration this was accomplished, with a strong arm, and great judgments.

The oppression of the slave is still hateful to God, and

deliverance is in store for him under some leader, or leaders. Clarkson was providentially raised up to lead in this great work. Wilberforce, and others of like spirit, were his associates. Buxton, Lushington, and others, pleaded the cause in the British Parliament. Emancipation, by law, was the result. Such men as Franklin, Jefferson, and the best leaders of American independence, were among the pleaders for freedom. The best divines of the age preached and pleaded the good cause, such as Wesley, Edwards, and a host of others. State after state proclaimed freedom. Happy was it for them that they obeyed the voice of justice and mercy.

But many states refused to let the oppressed go free. They have fortified themselves, like Pharaoh and the Egyptians, against freedom, and have resorted to the most subtile policy of plans, ways and means, to keep the people in bondage. Perhaps they will soon hear the expostulations of our Moseses and Aarons. We hope and pray that they may. But Moses had a commission, not merely to petition and expostulate—he had one to do the work itself, should expostulation be in vain. What deliverers God may raise up from among the sons of the oppressed, even fugitives from labor, like Moses, we can not tell. Such men as Frederick Douglass may not be despised. Judging from some specimens of his writing, and speeches which we heard, he is not a man to be despised, and will compare with the best of our southern statesmen in ability. We can not tell what sons of oppression may now, or will be, in reserve, under God's providence, to head insurrections, or foreign black troops, out of the fourteen millions of colored people now in the western continent and its islands. We pray that the voice of justice and mercy may be heard in due time, to avert these calamities.

12. The punishments on the Egyptians, for persevering

in their oppression, are mere specimens of what God has done in former ages, and what he hath declared he will do in the future in like cases. The ten plagues of Egypt are well known, as the judgments of God on account of oppression. Out of the very system of slavery its plagues will arise. The slaves and their masters, in the nature of the case, are converted into enemies. On the side of the oppressors are to be found the instrumentalities of war. There is the armed force, the domination, the expedients of disabilities, and the prohibitions of emancipation operating.

On the other hand, there is the *sense* of wrong, and the *judgment* of natural conscience, without any other teacher, whether preacher or book, *demonstrating* this wrong to the untutored slave. Then there is *hatred*, and *hypocrisy*, and a well-disguised spirit of resistance to all this. Then the inherent elements of slavery, which we have not space here to enumerate, furnish the seeds of future calamities growing out of the system. There is the indolence and want of economy of the slaves. There is the idleness of the masters and their families, who become consumers but not producers. There is the exhausted soil, which deteriorates its value. The very staples of production, as sugar and cotton, are liable to fluctuations. There is, too, the strong arms of the civilized world almost threatening invasion, and in due time they may come to the onset. The specimens of filibustering exhibited by southern slaveholders themselves, are pretty fair precedents for similar operations, which may be carried on in the free states, Canada, the West Indies, and other countries. There are arrows enough in God's quiver to pierce the hearts of all who make a business of oppression, and God will do this unless the oppressed are permitted to go free.

13. The deliverance of the Hebrews from bondage,

and the deliverance of slaves from slavery, are founded on the same great principles of justice and mercy.

(1.) The injustice is the same in both cases. It is as unjust for white Americans to retain black Americans in slavery as it was in the Egyptians to do the same with the Hebrews. All the *right* in either case is derived from mere power. The law of Egypt was as much law as the slave laws are. It is difficult for us to free the slaves; it was also difficult for the Egyptians to do it. Still God required them to do it, as he does also require us to do the same. The Egyptians had power to enslave the Hebrews, and they did it. We have power to enslave the Africans, and we do the same.

Besides, we have less plea on our side than the Egyptians had. The Hebrews were not mere chattels or things converted into property and marketable. Ours has this under more aggravated circumstances than any slave system that ever existed. Hence, if ten plagues were the awards of justice for Hebrew bondage, more than twenty must be our proportion. The women and children escaped the yoke among the Egyptians; but our system seizes the mother and child as soon as the infant sees the light, and puts the chains on the one, and robs the mother of her darling. This is the worst of all, and is fundamental with us. The following from the Brunswick (Ga.) Advocate, is but a *specimen:*

"WANTED TO HIRE.

"The undersigned wish to hire one thousand negroes to work on the Brunswick Canal, of whom one-third may be women. Sixteen dollars will be paid per month for steady, prime men, and thirteen dollars for women.

"F. & A. PRATT,
"P. M. NIGHTINGALE.

"*Brunswick, Jan.* 25, 1839."

(2.) The threatenings are applicable in both cases. All the parts of Egyptian bondage are condemned by almighty God. We have the same end in view to keep between three and four millions in slavery. Our means are a little different. The Egyptians killed the surplus, and made the bondage heavier in work, superintendence, and the withdrawal of material. This was simple and summary, and pronounced *wise* by the projector Pharaoh. Ours is a complicated system of arrangements. We make constitutions to do the work; in their structure all but unchangeable. We make laws to carry it out. We have federal combinations of our great Union sworn to accomplish this by supreme judges, irresponsible as to the decision, by armies and navies. Our other arrangements are subordinately administrative. We keep the slaves in ignorance, forbid them to assemble for any purpose, except under the strictest surveillance; prevent them from going from plantation to plantation; pursue them when they run away; and a thousand other means of subjugation and degradation, at variance with justice and mercy. Unless the Almighty be subject to change, our slavery is as abhorrent to him as that of Egypt was.

(3.) The judgments of God must be the same in substance in both cases. The judgments may not proceed from direct miracles. They may be of a very different class, but the same end must be accomplished—the liberty of the oppressed. A comparison of the moral, social, civil, and religious effects of freedom and slavery will furnish the answer to the inquiry here. (See American Slavery, by the author, Vol. I.)

(4.) The deliverance must be the same in both cases. The object is to deliver the oppressed from their oppressors. This is the work to be done. The jubilee among the Jews finished all *contracts* of service of every sort. Christ's jubilee proclaimed by himself—Luke iv,

18,19—will accomplish this. The second Psalm points out the way. If the voice of warning and of mercy will not be heard, the great Father will, by the stroke of justice, dash in pieces the nation who is deaf to right, truth, and mercy.

14. It remains for us to present the Scriptural arguments drawn from Egyptian bondage against slavery, and in favor of freedom.

(1.) The deliverance from the house of bondage, or the house of servants, as the margin has it, is employed as a general argument toward obedience to all God's commandments. "And God spake all these words, saying, I am the Lord thy God, which have brought thee out of the land of Egypt, out of the house of bondage or servants." Exodus xx, 1, 2. This is the preface to the ten commandments; and the deliverance from Egypt was a reason for observing them. And the observance of these commandments would prevent forever any recurrence to bondage among the Hebrews, or in the world. The fifth, sixth, seventh, eighth, and tenth commandments, are directly against slavery, and all the others are indirectly against it, and for liberty. The argument is, that as you have been delivered from bondage, observe God's commandments, as the observance of them will prevent the existence of slavery, or destroy it where it does exist. Religion and cruelty can not walk together. Justice and mercy can not endure slavery. Honesty and stealing men are at war. Marriage destroys it. Obedience to parents destroys it. Covetousness and other vices will breed slavery. Truth, righteousness, and justice, are at war with it. The very name, "the Lord thy God," as comprehending the attributes of Jehovah, is at war with the system. "The Lord, the Lord God, merciful and gracious, long-suffering, and abundant in goodness and truth, keeping mercy unto thousands, forgiving iniquity, transgression, and sin, and that will by no means clear the guilty; visiting the iniquity of the fathers upon the children, and upon the children's children, unto the third and fourth generations." Exodus xxxiv, 6, 7. God's commandments, like himself, are at variance with wrong of all sorts.

(2.) Because the Hebrews were *bondmen* and *strangers* in Egypt, they were required to remember the poor and the stranger, and not enslave them. "Ye shall not vex a stranger nor oppress him, for ye were strangers in the land of Egypt." Exodus xxii, 21. "Also, thou shalt not oppress a stranger: for ye know the heart of a stranger, seeing ye were strangers in the land of Egypt." Exodus xxiii, 9. "And if a stranger sojourn with thee in your land, ye shall not vex him. But the stranger that dwelleth with you, shall be unto you as one born among you, and thou shalt love him as thyself; for ye were strangers in the land of Egypt. I am the Lord." Leviticus xix, 33, 34. "He doth execute the judgment of the fatherless and widow, and loveth the stranger, in giving him food and raiment. Love ye, therefore, the stranger, for ye were strangers in the land of Egypt." Deuteronomy x, 18, 19.

The Israelites were required not to vex strangers, because they were once strangers in Egypt, and they ought to know both the heart and feelings of strangers. They were required not to oppress strangers, because they were once oppressed in Egypt. This applies to strangers in general, and not merely proselytes to the Jewish religion. It implies all other persons of any other country that sojourn in their land, as the Hebrews in Egypt, where the inhospitalities and the evils they met were to be remembered as motives to a different behavior. Strangers have a double title to humanity and protection, because they are especially liable to imposition and oppression. It was also wise to treat them kindly, because they would soon become proselytes to the gate, if not proselytes to the covenant. Hence, "Vex not a stranger;" "Love him as yourself;" for "ye were strangers in the land of Egypt."

The wisest and best men among the heathens considered love to strangers as one of the characteristics of the divinity. The Ζευς Ξενιος, *the god of strangers*, was the peculiar attribute of Jupiter, their supreme deity, benign to mankind, and the pattern of universal benevolence. Stabius mentions a law of Charondas requiring "to receive every stranger with kindness and humanity, and send them away in peace, in reverence to Jupiter, *the god of strangers*, who is as a god to all in common, and a narrow inspector of those who obey or violate the laws of hospitality." See Homer, Odyss., xiv, 65–69—Pope's translation—

> "It never was our guise,
> To slight the poor, or aught humane despise;
> For Jove unfolds the hospitable door,
> 'Tis Jove that sends the stranger and the poor."

The hospitality of Christians, as Sozomen in his Ecclesiastical History states, is eulogized in a letter by the Emperor Julian, apostate as he was.

Surely these lessons, taught in the texts we have quoted above, show that no Hebrew should ever treat any stranger, not born in the land, as a slave, as is fully declared in the Mosaic code, as we shall show the same is the Christian law. No stranger, or any other, is to be treated as slaves. The Anglo-Saxons themselves are strangers in America, or the sons of strangers; and because they were even politically oppressed, though never enslaved, they threw off the dominion which oppressed them. The remembrance of mere political wrongs, and that they are the descendants of strangers, should teach them to abhor slavery, and set the oppressed free. And the Africans here are just as much Americans by birth as the Anglo-Saxon race is. And for oppressed strangers to oppress another class of strangers, is doubly wrong.

(3.) The redemption of the Hebrews from Egyptian bondage was a reason why no Hebrews should be enslaved. "For they are my servants, which I brought forth out of the land of Egypt: they shall not be sold as bondmen. Thou shalt not rule over him with rigor, but shalt fear thy God. For unto me the children of Israel are servants; they are my servants whom I brought forth out of the land of Egypt: I am the Lord your God." Leviticus xxv, 42, 43, 55. As God redeemed every Israelite out of Egyptian bondage, they were, therefore, to consider themselves as his servants, and to devote themselves to him. Having thus acquired their liberty, by the interposition of God, they were bound not to enslave one another, or allow it to be done among them.

(4.) Hence, the Jewish code absolutely prohibited the enslavement of Hebrews. And as the same code forbade also the enslavement of strangers, all enslaving is forbidden expressly by the instructions given respecting Egyptian bondage. Of course the same is forbidden to all Christians. The liberty enjoyed by Christian people, whose ancestors were mostly enslaved, as is the case with the white Americans, ought to be a reason against keeping in blast the furnace of Egypt, and its severe bondage.

CHAPTER V.

THE MOSAIC CODE ON SERVICE.

THOSE who appeal to the Bible in defense of slavery, make the argument from the Mosaic laws prominent, and consider this decisive. They state that slavery existed among the Hebrews, and was tolerated by law; that it was the subject of legal enactments; that the Hebrew people might own slaves. These expositors never attempt to show what sort of service was approved by the Mosaic law. Nor have they, as far as we can learn, ever tried what effect the spirit and principles of the Mosaic code would have on our slavery. They have never allowed themselves to see how a jubilee would affect our system. Had every slave been set free at the end of the first fifty years from 1776, or in 1826, and with a prospect of another such process in 1876, there would soon be an end to the system. Or had every seventh year come in with its release, the doom of slavery would soon be fixed. If all those called slaves were to make their own contracts in the matter, and the masters could never sell slaves, how many slaves would be now in the United States?

In prosecuting our inquiries on this subject, we will pursue the following order of discussion:

I. The various classes of servants, and the different modes of becoming such.

II. The constitutional laws, principles, and usages of service among the Hebrews.

III. The rights and privileges of servants.

IV. Comparison between service and slavery.

I. The various classes of servants among the Hebrews, and the modes of their becoming servants.

The various classes of servants found among the Hebrews may be arranged in the following order. There was the hired servant, whose contract lasted for three years, or a day at a time. There was the Hebrew servant to Hebrews, for six years, or to the jubilee, whose services were bought for a price, by contract between the servant and master. There was the foreign servant, by purchase from himself, by contract to the year of jubilee. The second class has several varieties, so that the following will make as accurate a class as we can gather from the Mosaic code, concerning whom there are special regulations given, so as to prevent any of them from running into slavery, as well as to prohibit any thing cruel or unjust, either in regard to servant or master.

1. The hired servant.
2. The poor Hebrew non-slaveholder, or sexennial servant, who sold himself six years to a Hebrew.
3. The ear-bored servant, or poor non-freeholder, who sold himself for life, or to the jubilee, or to the death of his master.
4. The wife and children of the ear-bored servant.
5. The daughter sold by her father for a wife.
6. The poor Hebrew freeholder, who sold himself to a Hebrew.
7. The poor Hebrew freeholder, who sold himself to the rich stranger, or heathen.
8. The thief sold for theft.
9. The heathen servants.

1. The hired servant was one who worked for wages, by the day, or for a longer period, as was agreed on between him and his master or employer. It would seem as if some, at least, of the hired servants contracted for three years at a time. (Deuteronomy xv, 18.) A sex-

ennial servant, who served six years, was worth a double hired servant, who served only three years. This seems indicated by Isaiah xvi, 14: "Within three years, as the years of a hireling." The value, however, of the sexennial servant seems to be, that his services were procured for a small original cost; that he served for mere support for himself and family, during his term of service, and more labor was commonly exacted from him than from a hired servant. (Leviticus xxv.) No rigor was exercised over a hired servant; whereas, over the sexennial servant a moderate degree was expected, if not allowable.

2. *The sexennial servants.*

The Mosaic code on this class of servants is as follows: "If thou buy an Hebrew servant, six years he shall serve; and in the seventh he shall go out free for nothing. If he came in by himself, he shall go out by himself: if he were married, then his wife shall go out with him." Exodus xxi, 2, 3. The law reads more full in Deuteronomy, and is as follows: "And if thy brother, an Hebrew man, or an Hebrew woman, be sold [or *sell himself*] unto thee, and serve thee six years; then on the seventh year thou shalt let him go free from thee. And when thou sendest him out free from thee, thou shalt not let him go away empty; thou shalt furnish him liberally out of thy flock, and out of thy fleece, and out of thy winepress; of that wherewith the Lord thy God hath blessed thee, thou shalt give unto him. And thou shalt remember that thou wast a bondman in the land of Egypt, and the Lord thy God redeemed thee: therefore I command thee this thing to-day." Deuteronomy xv, 12–15.

The laws respecting male and female Hebrew servants are here delivered first; no doubt to exhibit just feelings of humanity, both to male and female; especially to females, who always have been treated worse than males by the codes of slavery. Tertullian justly calls these laws the *precepts of humanity*. Perpetual service, or slavery, is here forbidden. It was an excellent provision in these laws, that no man could finally injure himself, by any rash, foolish, or precipitate act. No man could make himself a servant for more than six years by one contract.

The utmost term of service for Hebrew men and women, was six years. The servants in this case sold themselves, or, rather, their services. Sometimes malefactors were sold by the judges. (Exodus xxii, 3.) Sometimes insolvent debtors were sold by their creditors. (2 Kings iv, 1; Matthew xviii, 25.) Sometimes very poor persons sold themselves. (Leviticus xxv, 39.) No such person was to serve more than six years; on the seventh, or on the year of jubilee, he was to go out free. It is supposed, however, that the term, six years, refers to the *sabbatic* years; for in whatever period between two sabbatical years the service began, it could not reach beyond the next sabbatical year. If the servant commenced on the *third* year after sabbatical year, he had only *three* years to serve; if the *fifth*, but *one*. This law is one of the most striking of the Mosaic code. It was an abridgment of civil liberty in favor of liberty, and to prevent injustice and oppression, and was worthy of a divine Lawgiver.

As to the *buying*, or purchase of a servant, we may here stop to examine the proper import of this transaction. The statutes quoted above—Exodus xxi, 2, 3, and Deuteronomy xv, 12–15—limit the voluntary sales of native Hebrew servants to the period of six years; while adopted foreign servants, as appears from Leviticus xxv, 44–46, and other passages, might sell themselves for still longer periods, even to the jubilee. The political reason, or policy of this course seemed to be that foreigners could not hold real estate in the nation any longer than the jubilee, when all the land in the country reverted back to its original owners, or their heirs—see Leviticus xxv, 10, 13, etc.—so that poor foreigners could contract for more than six years, though none were permitted to extend beyond the jubilee.

In the law above quoted the description is, "If thou buy [procure] an Hebrew servant," etc. The inquiry is, did the servants sell themselves as free and voluntary servants, or were they sold as free and voluntary servants, or were they sold by third persons to others, as slaves, as Joseph was sold to the Ishmaelites? The words buy and sell prove nothing either way. So far as we know any thing about the modes of sales of service, the servants sold themselves, by free and voluntary contract, just as poor foreign emigrants have done. The Egyptians sold themselves and their land to Pharaoh; and Joseph *bought* them and their land for Pharaoh. (Genesis xlvii, 19, 23.) The poor Hebrew, who sold himself to the stranger, is a specimen of the same sort of a voluntary sale of one's self. (Leviticus xxv, 47.) The use of the words and phrases here alluded to proves nothing against this view of the matter, because a person who *sells himself* is still *bought* and *sold*, just as the Egyptians were, or the poor Hebrew was. Besides, were this statute intended to regulate slave sales, they certainly would not be limited to *six years*, but the sale would be in perpetuity, like the sales of other property. The statute was, therefore, intended to regulate free and voluntary service, and to prevent its running into slavery, or perpetual service. This is further proved by the case of the ear-bored servant, who could not be continued in service over six years without a new contract.

The service among the Hebrews was for the most part voluntary. The buying a Hebrew servant legitimately implies the *buying him from himself;* that is, *buying his services.* These servants were never made to serve by force, against their will, except as a punishment for crime. We have no evidence that the law allowed any master to sell his servant. A man could *sell himself*—Leviticus xxv, 47—or an officer of the law may have sold a thief to serve long enough to make legal restitution, if he were not able to make restitution otherwise. A man's selling himself or his services, was a voluntary act, and yet the terms employed are sometimes such as though he were sold by a master.

At the end of the six years' service, or in the seventh year, the Hebrew servant, his Hebrew wife and children, were to be free from any obligation of future service. "In the seventh he shall go out free for nothing. If he came in by himself, he shall go out by himself; if he were married, then his wife shall go out with him." Exodus xxi, 2, 3. "In the seventh year thou shalt let him go free from thee." Deuteronomy xv, 12. If he and his wife came in together, they went out together. Jerome says that "he shall have the same coat in going out, as when he came in." That is, he shall have as good clothing when he went out, as a matter of *right,* as when he came in. We must infer, too, that the children will also go with the mother, were there any. For in the next class of servants, namely, the ear-bored servant, the children remained servants with the strange wife, given to him by his master, till the jubilee. And where the children of Hebrew parents are mentioned in connection with service, they go with the parents, as in the case of him who became servant to a stranger, it is said, "He shall go out in the year of jubilee, both he, and his children with him." Leviticus xxv, 54.

But though the sexennial servant, when he went out free, at the sabbatic year, could claim no more by his *right of contract,* but just as much as he brought with him, yet the master was *bound* to supply him bountifully from his own stores. The law in the code reads thus: "And when thou sendest him out free from thee, thou shalt not let him go away empty: thou shalt furnish him liberally out of thy flock, and out of thy fleece, and out of thy winepress: of that wherewith the Lord thy God hath blessed thee thou shalt give unto him. And thou shalt remember that thou wast a bondman in the land of Egypt, and the Lord thy God redeemed thee: therefore I command thee this thing to-day. It shall not seem hard unto thee, when thou sendest him away free from thee; for he hath been worth a double hired servant to thee, in serving thee six years: and the Lord thy God shall bless thee in all that thou doest." Deuteronomy xv. 13, 14, 15, 18. What a merciful law this was! Because the servant, during his service, could not make any property, he must not go away *empty,* for he must be furnished *liberally.* He was to be supplied from the *flock,* so as to have some to breed and to work; out of the thrashing floor, so as to have grain for *seed,* and for *bread;* out of the *winepress,* so as to have even the comforts of life when he retired. This was God's *command.* "I command thee this thing to-day." And it was urged from the consideration of Egyptian bondage or slavery, which no Hebrew was ever allowed to sanction in any shape. Another reason was the valuable services of the servant, on account of his six years' service, and that he was worth a double hired servant. And the third reason for God's command was, that God would bless the master in all he did, on this very account.

Not only so, but even during the sexennial term of service, any poor man, whether servant or otherwise, was to be supplied with the comforts of life. The Hebrew was not to harden his heart against him, or shut his hand, or calculate on the year of release, but to aid him liberally. (Deuteronomy xv, 7–11.)

There is clearly, in the case of the sexennial servant, no countenance to slavery. The term of service was for six years at farthest. The service was by contract, and there was no entailment of service on the posterity, as the husband, wife, and children were all free. The divine Lawgiver, considering that the purchases of human beings were entailing involuntary service, or slavery, on the nations out of Israel, ordained, by the case of this servant, to prevent the very existence of slavery among his chosen people. The servant alone, in this case, was the seller, the master was the purchaser; the transaction was a *mutual contract* between both; the time of its duration must never exceed six years, then entire freedom was to follow; and the servant must have a fair beginning of means in the world, to enable him to live in future as a freeman. No more direct antislavery arrangement could be made.

3. *The case of the ear-bored servant.*

The law in this case reads as follows: "If his master have given him a wife, and she have borne him sons or daughters, the wife and her children shall be her master's, and he shall go out by himself. And if the servant shall plainly say, I love my master, my wife, and my children; I will not go out free: then his master shall bring him to the door, or unto the door-post; and his master shall bore his ear through with an awl, and he shall serve him forever." Exodus xxi, 4–6. In Deuteronomy we have the following: "And it shall be, if he say unto thee, I will not go away from thee, because he loveth thee and thine house, because he is well with thee; then thou shalt take an awl, and thrust it through his ear unto the door, and he shall be thy servant forever; and also unto thy maid-servant thou shalt do likewise." Deuteronomy xv, 16, 17. On this law we submit the following remarks:

The servant who was now free, after six years' service, was *contractor* in the transaction, acted voluntarily, and had the right to accept or refuse the future relation of servant to his former master. This can never apply to our slaves, who do not enter on their condition by choice, but by force and necessity of law.

The master was *bound* to retain the servant in his service, if the servant desired it. And as the servant was a Hebrew, it was contrary to law for him to be a bondman, or menial servant, but to be as a hired servant. (Leviticus xxv, 50, 53.) The master was bound to retain the servant, from whose wife and children he had any claim of service, when the servant himself so desired it. The master could not be released while he retained the wife and children; and it was for the benefit of the servant, the wife, and children, that the law was made. So far from its being oppressive to the servant, it was the security of his natural right to his wife and his children, and made a separation a voluntary act on his own part.

The ceremony by which the new relation was inaugurated was a singular one. It seems to imply that he was now *attached* to his master's house and family, of which his wife and children formed a part; and that he was bound to *hear* all his master's orders, and *obey* them. The case, however, was to come under the cognizance of judges, so as to secure the legal rights of all concerned.

As to the duration of the service, it is said to be *forever*. The word *forever* here can not refer to eternity, or unending time, but to a limited period, whether the end of the servant's life, the lifetime of the master, or to the next jubilee. That it could not extend beyond the year of jubilee, is plain from the laws of this institution, which ended all servitudes, whether of the Hebrew or the stranger.

The Rabbins contend that such servants were set free at the death of their master, and did not descend to heirs. And this is the more probable, because the law was for the benefit of the servant, and it would seem to be unreasonable to extend it to heirs. At any rate, this case gives no countenance to our slavery, because our system is against the will of the slave, and knows no jubilee, or sabbatic release, and does not end at the death of the master.

4. *The wife and children of the ear-bored servant.*

The law in this case reads thus: "If his master hath given him a wife, and she hath borne him sons or daughters, the wife and her children shall be her master's, and he shall go out by himself," or with his body. (Exodus xxi, 4.) On this case we observe:

The master, who gave his man-servant a female-servant to wife, still retained authority over her as his servant, till her time of service expired. Her children were also his. But this was only for a limited period, *as* children, or minors.

As the wife must have been a heathen woman, she could not enjoy the privilege of the sabbatical year; but her husband might quit her, and enter on his liberty this year. It would not follow, however, that the marriage was dissolved, because he might serve another, and still live with his wife and children. The wife must have been a stranger, because a Hebrew had no power to *give* a Hebrew woman to another for wife, unless it were his own daughter. At any rate, the jubilee terminated the service of all persons capable of enjoying their freedom. As to the case of minors, we have no reason to suppose their service continued longer than their minority.

It has been objected by some, "that the master's property in a female-servant is here distinctly recognized, and he is allowed to dissolve her marriage, separate her from her husband, and retain her and her children in perpetual bondage." This is supposed to be analogous to American slavery, and to justify the master in disannulling the marriage relation of the slaves.

The ground assumed in the objection is false. The bondman in this case is a Hebrew. He could be bound to service only six years. His wife could not be a Hebrew, because she as well as he would be free at the end of six years, or at the same time with her husband. His wife, furnished him by his master, must therefore have been a stranger, or heathen woman. The master could have permanent control over no other. They could contract for any length of time, even to the jubilee. When the six years' service of the Hebrew had expired, the time of his wife's service had not expired, according to her contract with her master, made before her marriage, and which her marriage left unimpaired. She must therefore fulfill her bargain. But this did not annul the marriage, nor had the master any power to dissolve it.

The *children* were *born in his house.* They were part of his domestics. They belonged to his family. He was bound by the law to have the males circumcised, and all of them properly instructed and educated, till they would be of age. Nor was the husband necessarily separated from his wife and family. If he pleased, he could compel his master to retain him in his service till the year of jubilee, and his wife and children could be kept no longer. There was no clause in the law touching the case of the ear-bored servant, authorizing, or even permitting the master to sell either him, her, or the children. Even if the husband did not choose to avail himself of this law, what would hinder him from getting employ in the neighborhood, and still, at least occasionally, enjoy the society of his wife and children? There is no just likeness between this case and American slavery.

5. *The daughter sold by her father for a wife.*

The law on this case is as follows: "If a man sell his daughter to be a maid-servant, she shall not go out as the men-servants do. If she please not her master, who hath betrothed her to himself, then shall he let her be redeemed; to sell her unto a strange nation, he shall have no power, seeing he hath dealt deceitfully with her. And if he hath betrothed her unto his son, he shall deal with her after the manner of daughters. If he take him another wife, her food, her raiment, and her duty of marriage, shall he not diminish. And if he do not these things unto her, then shall she go out free without money." Exodus xxi, 7–11.

It appears very plainly from the account given in Leviticus, that the law laid down in the preceding verses, respecting the sexennial servant, held good with regard to female, as well as to male-servants. The law that governed parents selling daughters, was different from that regulating sales on other accounts; for she should not go out as the men-servants, or female-servants do, by gaining her liberty, after a servitude of six years; other and easier terms are assigned her, as the law in the case expressly provides.

No man could sell his daughter, as the Jews say, unless in cases of extreme poverty; and he had this permission only while she was unmarriageable, and it was also on the condition, that when mature, she would be the wife of her master or his son. It was something like apprenticeship, in which the parents bind the child for a term of years, and have from the master so much per week, during that period.

The daughter, sold by her father, was not sold for a

slave, but for a wife, as the law expressly declares; because,

(1.) She was purchased in her maidenhood, to become her master's wife at womanhood. After that period the master must marry her; or she might claim redemption, or, in other words, freedom. If he betrothed her to his son, it was on the condition that the marriage should be consummated when she was come to maturity.

(2.) The fact that she was purchased from her father, does not prove that she was a slave, or the property of the purchaser. She was bought for a *wife*. Wives were often bought by their husbands, though they were never to serve as servants. So Boaz bought Ruth. (Ruth iv, 10.) Merea bought his wife. Jacob bought two wives for fourteen years' service. Shechem offered to buy Dinah, Jacob's daughter. Leah and Rachel say of their father, "He hath *sold* us." The custom, indeed, was as common in ancient times, as receiving a dowry now with wives.

(3.) The master had no power to sell her to a strange nation, or, rather, to any other person. (Leviticus xxii, 10.) The Hebrews had no power to sell, in any case, any of their own people, whether male or female, to those of another nation. He must allow her to be redeemed, if he did not marry her; and all he could require was to have the money refunded that was paid for her, or a just proportion of it, according to the laws of redemption.

(4.) If she is betrothed to his son, she must be treated as a daughter. He shall give her the same dowry he would give to one of his own daughters. If the son married another woman, she must stand in the relation of a second wife; and he was bound to make no abatement to her in the privileges of the *first* wife, either in her food, raiment, or duty of marriage. If the father or the son should marry her, and afterward take another wife, her food, raiment, and marriage duty must not diminish.

(5.) Should she not be recognized any longer as a wife she could not be retained as a servant, but she was to go out free without money, that is, without being redeemed.

The case is a very plain one, that a daughter sold by her father was sold only to become a wife; and when this stipulation failed she was free. Hence, she never was, and never could be, according to the law of Moses, a slave.

In this case we see the strong, unbending antislavery nature of the Mosaic code. In the heathen nations daughters could be sold for slaves, and their children would also be slaves. The Mosaic code, in the case of the daughter sold by her father, prevented this, and required that the result should be freedom and not slavery.

6. *The poor Hebrew freeholder who sold himself to a Hebrew.*

A Hebrew reduced to poverty might sell himself to a Hebrew, not as a bond-servant, but as a hired servant, till the jubilee. The law of Moses, in this case, reads as follows: "And if thy brother that dwelleth by thee be waxen poor, and be sold unto thee; [or sell himself;] thou shalt not compel him to serve as a bond-servant, but as an hired servant, and as a sojourner, he shall be with thee, and shall serve thee unto the year of jubilee: and then shall he depart from thee, both he and his children with him, and shall return unto his own family, and unto the possession of his fathers shall he return. For they are my servants, which I brought forth out of the land of Egypt: they shall not be sold as bondmen. Thou shalt not rule over him with rigor; but shalt fear thy God." Leviticus xxv, 39–43.

(1.) This statute is very different from that in Exodus

respecting the sexennial servant. (Exodus xxi, 2, etc.; Deuteronomy xv, 12, etc.) It relates to another class of persons. The sexennial servant is bought for six years, but he may, at pleasure, extend the time of service to the jubilee. In the case of the poor servant in Leviticus no mention is made of a six years' engagement, nor of his having the ear bored as a test of additional service. The sexennial servant shall not be sent away empty, but shall be furnished liberally. Nothing is said of his returning to his possession. That in Leviticus makes no provision for furnishing liberally when he departs; but declares that he "shall return to the possession of his fathers." A servant of the one class was called an *abed.* A servant of the other could not be sold with the sale, nor be compelled to serve with the service of an *abed.* The poverty of the sexennial servant shows that he needed supplies when his service was ended. He, likely, was a younger brother who was not a landholder, while the statute in Leviticus xxv, 39, provided for the *first-born,* the possessor of the inheritance of his father, who, from poverty, had been compelled to part with his real estate till the jubilee. The difference then is between two Hebrew servants of one class, and Hebrew and heathen servants of another class.

(2.) There is a marked distinction made here between the hired or temporary servant, and the permanent or sexennial servant. Both classes were paid; but in several respects they were distinguished. Hired servants were paid daily at the close of their work. (Leviticus xix, 13; Deuteronomy xxiv, 14, 15; Job vii, 2; Matthew xx, 8.) Bought servants were paid in part in advance, and a constant maintenance, and those that went out on the seventh year received a gratuity. (Deuteronomy xv, 12, 13.) The *hired* were paid in *money;* the bought servant received the *gratuity,* at least, in cattle, grain, and the product of the vintage. (Deuteronomy xiv, 17.) The hired servants supported their families out of their wages; the bought servants and their families were supported by the masters *besides* their wages.

The bought servants were, as a class, superior to the hired servants, possessing greater privileges, and occupying a higher station in society. They were incorporated into the families of their masters; were guests at family festivals and social solemnities, from which hired servants were excluded. Marriages took place between servants and their master's daughters. (1 Chronicles ii, 34, 35.*) Hired servants did not form such alliances. Bought servants and their descendants were treated with the same respect with other members of the family. This is exemplified in the cases of Abraham, Gideon, Saul, Jonathan, Elisha, and their servants. (Genesis xxv; Judges vii, 11; 1 Samuel ix, 5, 22, and xv, 1–14.) No such ties seem to have existed between hired servants and their masters. Hired servants were mostly of the lower class. (Judges ix, 4; 1 Samuel ii, 5.) Traces of this are found in the parables of the talents, of the prodigal son, etc., in the New Testament. Hebrews and strangers belonged to each class indiscriminately.

(3.) In the enjoyment of mere *political privileges* the hired servants among the Hebrews were more favored than the bought servants among strangers. No stranger could exercise any honorable political office, nor could he own the soil. The want of ownership in the soil,

---

* "For the *purchased servant*, who is an Israelite or proselyte, shall fare as his master. The master shall not eat fine bread and his servant bread of bran; nor yet drink old wine, and give his servant new; nor sleep on soft pillows and bedding, and his servant on straw. I say unto you that he that gets a *purchased* servant does well to make him as his friend, or he will prove to his employe as if he had got himself a master." (Maimonides, in Mishna Kiddushen, Chap. I, Sec. 2.)

perhaps, forms the reason why the one served six years, and the other to the jubilee.

(4.) The servants purchased from the heathens are called, by way of distinction, *the servants*, not *bondmen.* They were *tributaries*, and were required to pay an annual tax to the government. The strangers were properly the house servants employed in the families. The Jewish servants were almost exclusively agriculturists. (1 Samuel xi, 7; 1 Kings xix, 19; 2 Chronicles xxvi, 10; Judges vi, 11.) Hence the regulation in the law under consideration, "Thou shalt not compel him to serve as a bond-servant." "As an hired servant, and as a sojourner, shall he be with thee." His family organization was to be preserved. Jarchi's comment on "thou shalt not compel him to serve as a bond-servant," is, "The Hebrew servant is not to be required to do any thing that is accounted degrading—such as all offices of personal attendance, as loosing his master's shoe latchet, bringing him water to wash his feet and hands, waiting on him at table, dressing him, carrying things to and from his bath. The Hebrew servant is to work with his master as his son or brother in the business of his farm or other labor, till his legal release." His family organization was preserved, so that he lived with his wife and children, controlled them, and did not make a part of the household of his master, as the stranger or permanent servant did for the most part.

(5.) "Thou shalt not rule over him with rigor." What is rigorous service? Service which is not determined, and whereof there is no need. To overlook the privileges of a Hebrew, and requiring services which a stranger or domestic servant might render, was rigorous. To overlook the distinction between servants of Jewish and Gentile peculiarities would be rigorous in reference to the Jew. The Egyptians made the Israelites serve with rigor. (Exodus i, 13.) This rigor is affirmed of the *amount of labor*, and the *mode* of the exaction. The expression, "to serve with rigor," is never applied to the service of servants under the Mosaic system. The phrase, "thou shalt not rule over him with rigor," does not prohibit unreasonable exactions of labor, nor inflictions of cruelty. Such were provided against otherwise. But it forbids confounding the distinctions between a Jew and a stranger, by assigning the former to the same grade of service as to the other.

7. *The poor Hebrew who is servant to a stranger.*

The law of this case reads as follows, and contains very clear expositions of the case: "And if a sojourner or stranger wax rich by thee, and thy brother that dwelleth by him wax poor, and sell himself unto the stranger or sojourner by thee, or to the stock of the stranger's family: after that he is sold he may be redeemed again; one of his brethren may redeem him: either his uncle or his uncle's son may redeem him, or any that is nigh of kin unto him of his family may redeem him; or if he be able he may redeem himself. And he shall reckon with him that bought him from the year that he was sold to him unto the year of jubilee; and the price of his sale shall be according to the number of years, according to the time of an hired servant shall it be with him. If there be yet many years behind, according unto them he shall give again the price of his redemption out of the money that he was bought for. And if there remain but few years unto the year of jubilee, then he shall count with him, and according unto his years shall he give him again the price of his redemption. And as a yearly hired servant shall he be with him, and the other shall not rule with rigor over him in thy sight. And if he be not redeemed in these years, then he shall go out in the year of jubilee, both he and his children with him. For unto me the children of Israel are servants; they are my servants whom I brought forth out of the land of Egypt: I am the Lord your God." Leviticus xxv, 47–55.

(1.) The purchaser, in this case, was a sojourner, stranger, or the son of a stranger, who became rich. As a stranger he could not be a freeholder, so as to possess real estate, especially fields or vineyards. The strangers were generally poor, but some became rich. God here provides that the sojourners should have the same legal advantages with the native Hebrew. But the Hebrew who sold himself to him had the peculiar privilege of redemption before the jubilee, or of the jubilee when it arrived. Yet the law wisely provides that the sojourner shall have full compensation, and that the price shall be exactly paid him. The stranger was required, too, to treat the Hebrew servant with the indulgence of a hired servant, in leaving him with his family, and that his service should not be rigorous or severe.

(2.) As to the Hebrew servant, he was a freeholder; but he became *poor*, so that he could not support his family, seeing his property was sold or mortgaged unto the jubilee; and to meet present wants he was compelled to sell himself, or, rather, his services, and to become a *day-laborer*, or *as a* hired servant. He, therefore, *sold himself* for money. He was not sold by another person; for no such sale occurred among the Hebrews, except the thief for restitution, or the female maid or minor for a wife, but never for a servant, much less a slave. The sale of the poor freeholder was to the year of jubilee, with the privilege of redemption at any time by himself or any other person.

(3.) The servant had the right of redemption, either by himself or any one of his kindred, at any time before the jubilee. The price was to be reckoned according to the years from the time of redemption to the jubilee, at the rate of a hired servant's wages. The *fixed* price was the wages of a hired servant for the same length of time. There were no exactions in this case, or even bargains for high or low, but a determined rate. The Jews considered themselves bound to redeem their poor brethren, lest they should be swallowed up by the heathen. On their return from the Babylonish captivity we find the following: "We, after our ability, have redeemed our brethren the Jews, which were sold unto the heathen." Nehemiah v, 8.

(4.) He was to be treated "as a yearly hired servant." Hired servants were not incorporated into the families of their masters; they retained their own family organization, without the surrender of any domestic privilege, or honor, or authority; and this, even though they resided under the same roof with their master. While bought servants were associated with their master's families at meals, at the passover, and at other family festivals, hired servants and sojourners were not. (Exodus xii, 44, 45; Leviticus xxii, 10, 11.) Hired servants were not subject to the master in any such sense as the master's wife, children, and bought servants. Hence, the only form of oppressing hired servants is that of *keeping back wages.* To take away *such* privileges from the poor freeholder would be *hard,* or *rigorous.* It would be ruling over him with rigor. He was the *head of a family,* who had seen better days, now reduced to poverty. He was an Israelite. Abraham was his father. He was not a servant born in the house, nor a minor, whose minority had been sold by his father. He was the head of a family.

(5.) He was at the utmost to be free at the jubilee. "If he be not redeemed in these years, then he shall go out in the year of jubilee, both he and his children with him," or his entire family.

(6.) The reason for this law was, 1. The Hebrews

were the servants of the most high God; and it was inconsistent that they should be under the control of men as slaves. Hence, no slave was to be found in God's heritage, which he gave to Abraham and his descendants. 2. Their ancestors had been in bondage in Egypt; and as God brought them out of the house of bondage, he would never allow that Palestine could become another Egypt for those in behalf of whom he achieved so great a deliverance. 3. "I am the Lord thy God." The supreme authority of Jehovah hath established this law, and no man should infringe on it in the least.

This was a very equitable law, both to the sojourner who had made the purchase, and to the Israelite who had sold himself. The Israelite might redeem himself, or one of his kindred might redeem him; but this must not be done to the prejudice of the master. They were, therefore, to reckon the years he must have served from that time to the jubilee, and settle on the amount to correspond with the years. The Jews held that the kindred of such a person was bound, if in their power, to redeem him lest he should be swallowed up among the heathen. And we find—Nehemiah v, 8—that this was done by the Jews on their return from the Babylonish captivity.

The Israelites were a *typical people.* They represented Christians. And Christians are not merely *servants* of God, like the Jews, but they also are his *sons*, and should never become the slaves of men. (1 Corinthians vii, 2, 3.) In the case before us, this servant was no slave. He sold himself, as a servant, for a term of years; he had, by law, the right of redemption, and, at farthest, he and his family were free at the jubilee. It is a sad sight, indeed, to see Christians buying and selling their own Christian brethren and sisters to the highest bidder; or which is, in fact, the same in reference to the sufferers, to see the great American nation engaged in this work, which God would not permit to enter Judea, but was excluded by express enactments.

(8.) *The thief sold for his theft.*

The law is, "If he [the thief] have nothing, then he shall be sold for his theft." Exodus xxii, 3.

The laws of the twelve tables ordained, "He that is attacked by a robber in the night, let him not be punished if he kills him. If the robbery be committed by day, and if the robber be taken in the fact, let him be beaten with rods, and become the slave of him whom he robbed." (Twelve Tables. Laws I, II.) The Hebrew code would not allow the thief to be made a slave; but it required that he should be sold so long as his services were required to pay the proper assessment for theft. The restitution required was fivefold, fourfold, double, etc., according to the articles stolen and the amount of injury done. (Exodus xxii, 1.) He was to be sold *for his theft*, or for services to the amount of the assessment made for such theft. The sale, too, was by the public officers. This case furnishes no analogy between it and our slavery.

(9.) *The heathen servants among the Hebrews.*

The law in this case is as follows: "Both thy bondmen, [servants,] and thy bondmaids, [maid-servants,] which thou shalt have, shall be of the heathen that are round about you; of them shall ye buy bondmen and bondmaids. Moreover, of the children of the strangers that do sojourn among you, of them shall ye buy, and of their families that are with you, which they begat in your land: and they shall be your possession. And ye shall take them as an inheritance for your children after you, to inherit them for a possession; they shall be your bondmen forever: but over your brethren the children of Israel, ye shall not rule over one another with rigor." Leviticus xxv, 44–46.

If there were any slaves among the Hebrews, they must have become such under the provisions of this law; for it is the most plausible support of slavery to be found in the Mosaic code. It, therefore, demands our most careful consideration. There can be no doubt but the Hebrews were authorized to purchase those of the surrounding nations for servants. But the question arises, of *whom*, and *how*, and under *what conditions* did they purchase them? Was this service to be during life as to the servants, and hereditary as to their children; or did they come under the operation of the jubilee, which proclaimed liberty to all the inhabitants of the land? If slavery was here authorized as to strangers and their descendants, there must have existed, in after times, a very large body of them in Judea, similar to the Helots in Greece, the slaves of Rome, and the slaves in America. We are prepared to show that no such class of Helots existed in Judea, and that this law does not authorize or establish such a system. When a southerner buys a slave, he buys of a third person, who claims the slave as his property; and he is his property according to the slave laws. But in this case the stranger *sold himself* to the Hebrew, or *consented* to the sale; and hence the purchase was a *contract* between two parties, and, therefore, the system could not be slavery. But had the purchase been from third persons, the Mosaic code interfered so as to preclude slavery.

Some very respectable names may be mentioned who have believed that this law tolerated, sanctioned, or established the slavery of aliens or strangers among the Hebrews. This was Mr. Thomas Goodwin's opinion. (See his Moses and Aaron, c. x.) The conductors of the Princeton Repertory, in an article in 1836, are very positive on this point. They say, "We do not know how this passage can be rendered plainer than it is, nor can we hope that any man, who is in such a state of mind as to prevent his seeing and admitting that it authorized the Hebrews to hold slaves, could be convinced, even if one rose from the dead." The conclusion to which we have come, on reading the above, is, that the writer of the article had never thoroughly studied the subject on which he decided *ex cathedra*, and was under the influence of those vague and pro-slavery teachings found in Cornelius a Lapide, and other Popish writers, and the general current of Protestant commentators, who follow the footsteps of their Roman predecessors on this point, without ever carefully examining the Mosaic code on the subject. Among these we place Coke, Clarke, Benson, Professor Robinson, and many others, who, with Lapide, adopted the creed on this subject as taught in the *Corpus Juris Canonici* of the Church of Rome.

First. The first part of our inquiry is, *who were the persons that might be bought?* The answer is, that they were *heathens, strangers*, that dwelt round about Palestine, or the children of strangers that were born in the country. The Hebrew word גר, *ger*, and נכר, *necher*, signifies a *traveler* or *stranger*—one who comes from abroad, or from another place. They were those who came to dwell in Judea, or who embrace the religion of the Hebrews, not being Hebrews by birth. They are called in Greek Προσηλυτος, a *proselyte*, a *stranger*, a *foreigner*. The Vulgate calls them *advenæ*, *immigrants*, and *peregrini*, *strangers, travelers*. The French, from the Vulgate, calls them *les etrangers*, *strangers*.

These may be divided into two classes—the heathens and the proselytes. The heathens comprise those who had not yet embraced the Christian religion, but had come to Judea to better their condition, and enjoy liberty.

The Hebrews distinguish two kinds of proselytes—the

first, the *proselyte of the gate;* the second, the *proselyte of justice.* The first class, without obliging themselves to be circumcised, or to receive any other ceremony of the law, feared and worshiped the true God, observing the seven precepts of Noah, such as avoiding idolatry, blasphemy, incest, adultery, and murder. These might dwell in Judea, share in its outward prosperity, be protected by its laws, and receive instruction respecting the true religion. These dwelt mostly at the *gates* or suburbs of cities, and sometimes within their walls. In the days of Solomon there were one hundred and fifty-three thousand, six hundred of these proselytes who were employed in building the temple. (2 Chronicles ii, 17, 18.) Many of these were Canaanites, who had continued in the country since the days of Joshua.

Proselytes of justice or *righteousness*, were those converted to Judaism, who had engaged themselves to receive circumcision, and to observe the whole law of Moses. They were then admitted to all the prerogatives of the people of Israel, with the exception that they could not be kings or rulers—could not own landed property, unless houses, in certain cities or their suburbs. Boys under twelve years of age, and girls under thirteen, could not become proselytes, till they had obtained the consent of their parents; or, in case of refusal, the concurrence of the officers of justice. Moses—Deuteronomy xxiii, 1, 2, 3, etc.—excludes certain persons from the privileges of the people of Israel, or from the congregation of the Lord; some forever, others only for a certain time. Eunuchs were excluded forever. Illegitimate children were not to be admitted till after the tenth generation. The same was the case with the Moabites and Ammonites. The Egyptians and Idumeans were admissible after the second generation. It was believed by the Jews, that the mixed multitude—Exodus xii, 38; Numbers xi, 4—that came up from Egypt, were at least semi-heathens. Dr. Clarke computes them at twenty thousand, and says of them, "This *mongrel* people, who had comparatively little knowledge of God, feeling the difficulties and fatigues of the journey, were the first to complain." Jethro, the father-in-law of Moses, had embraced the Jewish religion. (Exodus xviii, 10.)

From these *strangers, foreigners,* or their children born in Palestine, the Hebrews were permitted to procure, buy, or contract for servants, in the menial offices of their houses. As among the Hebrews so among the strangers, none but poor persons would become servants of any grade. For, a rich stranger would certainly not become a servant; on the contrary, he could have servants himself, even a Hebrew servant, as we have already seen. (Leviticus xxv, 45.) There is no doubt, too, that, among the strangers, those only sold themselves or became servants who were poor, and were, in consequence, compelled to bind themselves to serve for a number of years, which, by law, was limited by the jubilee. These, too, were employed in the lowest grades of service, such as household service; while the Hebrew servants were employed in the business of the field, and the more reputable pursuits of life.

Second. The strangers, as a class, especially before they became proselytes of justice, were laid under certain legal restraints and disabilities, to which Hebrews were not subject. The following are mentioned as prominent, though others might be mentioned:

(1.) The law of Moses enjoined that, whenever the Jews should determine to have a king, they should not select a foreigner or stranger. "One from among thy brethren shalt thou set king over thee: thou mayest not set a stranger over thee, which is not thy brother." Deuteronomy xvii, 15. The Talmud relates that, when

King Agrippa, at the Sabbatic service, came to this passage, his eyes filled with tears, because he remembered that he was not of the seed of the Jews. The people present being disposed to relieve him, cried out, three times, "Fear not, Agrippa, thou art our brother." On this ground the Jews proposed that insidious question to our Lord, "Is it lawful to give tribute to Cesar, OR NOT?"—Matthew xxii, 17—for they were then under *foreign* power. We may also infer, that, as strangers could not be kings, they could not hold high, if any, political office in the Hebrew commonwealth.

(2.) A Hebrew might receive usury from a stranger, but not from a Hebrew. "Unto a stranger thou mayest lend on usury, but unto thy brother thou shalt not lend upon usury." Deuteronomy xxiii, 20. As their neighbors, as the Sidonians, Syrians, Egyptians, and others, made great gain by merchandise, it would be unreasonable that they should borrow money from the Israelites for nothing. It was also reasonable that the Israelites, whose business was husbandry, should lend money freely to one another, without interest, or not beyond common interest, their land not being a country of traffic, wherein money could be profitable, as in other countries. At any rate, the stranger labored under this disability compared with the Hebrews.

(3.) A stranger could not oppress a Hebrew. Even when the Hebrew sold himself to the rich stranger, he could not exact from him the services of a menial, such as from a hired servant. "As a yearly hired servant shall he be with him: and the other [the stranger] shall not rule over him in thy sight." Leviticus xxv, 53. That is, he must allow the Hebrew the most reputable service in his power, and not treat him as a menial, or a mere hired day-laborer, as among us.

(4.) The heathen, or stranger, was as liable to be punished for wicked conduct as any other. He was subject to law. If he blasphemed God he was to be put to death, as any other transgressor. (Leviticus xxiv, 16.)

(5.) The stranger was as much bound to abstain from leaven during the paschal feast as the Hebrew was. (Exodus xii, 19.)

(6.) The uncircumcised stranger, foreigner, or hired servant, was prohibited from eating the passover. (Exodus xii, 43, 45.) The proselytes of the gate, or the heathen, could not eat the passover, or partake of the sacred festivals. But the proselytes of the covenant had the same rights as the Jews themselves, whether spiritual or temporal.

(7.) The strangers were inferior to the Hebrews, as to the time of their service. The strangers were never purchased for six years, but always till the jubilee. The Hebrew servants, even when their ears were bored, never became an inheritance to the children of their master; whereas, if the master of a Gentile died before the jubilee, the Gentile servant was inherited by the children, and retained till his whole time of service expired, reaching down to the jubilee. (Leviticus xxv, 46.)

From the foregoing we conclude, that, as the strangers were not, as was right, entitled to the full privileges of Hebrews, till after a full and long probation, their service as servants had disabilities and disadvantages attached to it that would not apply to Hebrews. As heathens, being poor and degraded, they were suited to the lowest menial service of the country; and, in this respect, the Hebrews were honored and privileged with the more reputable grades of service, even when they were compelled, through poverty, to sell their services to such as were able to purchase them.

Third. God encouraged the settlement of strangers among the Hebrews, by the protective statutes and grants of advantageous privileges. Among others we name the following:

The stranger was privileged to be a partaker of the covenant blessings of the Hebrews; and these blessings were incompatible with a state of degradation such as slavery induces. "Ye stand this day all of you before the Lord your God—your little ones, your wives, and thy stranger that is within thy camp, from the hewer of thy wood to the drawer of thy water: that thou shouldest enter into covenant with the Lord thy God, and into his oath, which the Lord thy God maketh with thee this day." (Deuteronomy xxix, 10–13.)

It was the privilege of the stranger to be incorporated into the Jewish nation, when circumcised, and be as one born in the land. "But every man's servant that is bought with money, when thou hast circumcised him, then shall he eat thereof. And when a stranger shall sojourn with thee, and will keep the passover to the Lord, let all his males be circumcised, and then let him come near and keep it; and he shall be as one that is born in the land: for no uncircumcised person shall eat thereof. One law shall be to him that is home-born, and unto the stranger that sojourneth among you." (Exodus xii, 44, 48, 49.)

The circumcised stranger, equally with the Hebrew, partook of the passover, and one law governed both, so as to place them on an equal footing as to covenant relations. (Exodus xii, 49; Numbers ix, 14.)

The strangers were protected equally with others by the laws, while there were some laws enacted for their peculiar benefit. "Ye shall have one manner of laws, as well for the stranger as for one of your own country: for I am the Lord your God." Leviticus xxiv, 22. No distinctions are made to favor the master at the expense of the servant; for the law allowed no respect of persons.

His testimony was as good as his master's. The Mosaic laws regarded the brotherhood of man.

The stranger in judgment was protected equally with others. "Thou shalt not pervert the judgment of the stranger, nor of the fatherless; nor take a widow's raiment to pledge." Deuteronomy xxiv, 17. "Cursed be he that perverteth the judgment of the stranger, fatherless, and widow." Deuteronomy xxvii, 20.

The same law applied to the stranger and Hebrew in regard to sins of ignorance. (Numbers xv, 29.)

The privileges of the sabbatic year belonged to the stranger as well as others. "And the Sabbath of the land shall be meat for you; for thee, and for thy servant, and for thy maid, and for thy hired servant, and for thy stranger that sojourneth with thee." Leviticus xxv, 6.

The stranger, equally with the Levite, the fatherless, and the widow, partook of the jubilee provisions, arising from tithes. (Deuteronomy xiv, 29; xxvi, 12.)

To secure the stranger from slavery there was an express law against oppressing him. "Thou shalt neither vex a stranger nor oppress him; for ye were strangers in the land of Egypt." Exodus xxii, 21. "But the stranger that dwelleth with you shall be unto you as one born among you, and thou shalt love him as thyself; for ye were strangers in the land of Egypt: I am the Lord thy God." Leviticus xix, 34. "Love ye therefore the stranger: for ye were strangers in the land of Egypt." Deuteronomy x, 19. The stranger was neither to be vexed nor oppressed, but loved as one born among them. And though some of them were servants till the year of jubilee, this treatment shows that they were not considered as slaves, though they were servants; and servants, too, in the menial rank of servants.

The poor man, whether stranger or Hebrew, was to be relieved with equal regard. "And if thy brother be waxen poor, and fallen in decay with thee; then thou shalt relieve him; yea, though he be a stranger, or a sojourner: that he may live with thee." Leviticus xxv, 35.

The stranger had the benefit of the fugitive law. (Deuteronomy xxii, 15, 16.)

The hired servant, whether a Hebrew or a stranger, was to be paid his wages. "Thou shalt not oppress an hired servant that is poor and needy, whether he be of thy brethren, or of thy strangers that are in thy land within thy gates: at his day thou shalt give him his hire, neither shall the sun go down upon it; for he is poor, and setteth his heart upon it: lest he cry against thee unto the Lord, and it be sin unto thee." Deuteronomy xxiv, 14, 15.

The stranger, or sojourner, could flee to the city of refuge. (Numbers xxxv, 15.)

The stranger shared, with the fatherless and widow, the gleanings of the harvest-fields. (Deuteronomy xxiv, 19, 21.)

Those were cursed who perverted the judgment of the stranger, the fatherless, or widow. (Deuteronomy xxvii, 19.)

The stranger was present at reading the law, in the year of release, and was considered as having a right and interest in the privileges of the country. (Deuteronomy xxi, 12.)

According to the foregoing collection of statutes, from the Mosaic code, respecting the reception, treatment, and privileges of strangers, it is manifest that they give no encouragement to the institution of slavery, but they are at variance with it. The stranger was a welcome candidate for covenant relations with the Hebrews. He might be naturalized by circumcision, and then partake of the passover, in common with the Hebrews, so as to become one of their nation. He was protected equally with others, in civil rights, under one and the same principles and forms of law. When poor, he was to share with the widow and the fatherless. He must not be vexed nor oppressed, but loved and dealt with as one born in the land. He enjoyed the benefit of the fugitive law. He could flee to the city of refuge. And the Hebrews were instructed constantly to treat the stranger with kindness, under the consideration that they themselves were strangers in Egypt. And, though some of these precepts are honored by many benevolent slaveholders, yet the slave system and the slave laws are in opposition to these statutes, and can never be reconciled with them.

Fourth. The religious duties enjoined upon the Gentile servants, show they were bought with their own consent, and were not reduced to a state of slavery. Willing services could not be expected of persons bought against their will, and held in perpetual slavery. The stranger was called upon to receive circumcision, the token of the covenant, in which he avowed the Lord to be his God forever—Exodus xii, 48, 49—and this covenant was occasionally renewed—Deuteronomy xix, 10–15—to eat the passover and unleavened bread seven days. (Exodus xii, 44.) The stranger was bound to attend the jubilee feasts with rejoicing. (Deuteronomy xii, 10–12.) He was bound to receive religious instruction. (Deuteronomy xxxi, 10–13; Joshua viii, 33–35.) He was required to offer sacrifices; to appear three times in the year before the Lord, and none were to appear empty. (Exodus xxiii, 14–17; Deuteronomy xvi, 11, 14, 16, 17; Numbers ix, 13.) Such duties could not be performed in consistency with slave laws. On this point the testimony of Maimonides is of value, and is a just interpretation of the Mosaic code on the subject:

"Whether a servant be born in the house of an Israelite, or whether he be purchased from the heathen, the master is to bring them both into the covenant. But he that is born in the house is to be entered upon the eighth day; and he that is bought with money on the day in which the master receives him, unless the slave be unwilling. For if the master receives a grown slave, and he being unwilling, his master is to bear with him—to seek to win him over by instruction, and by love and kindness, for one year; after which, should he refuse so long, it is forbidden to keep him longer than the twelve months, and the master must send him back to the strangers, whence he came; for the God of Jacob will not accept any other than the worship of a willing heart."

Fifth. The fact that some strangers were called bondmen, and others servants, is quoted to prove that the former were slaves. The Hebrew word *abed* affords ground for no such distinction, as it means a *laborer*, or one who does work for, or renders any sort of service to another. Indeed, there is no word in the Hebrew language that corresponds to our word slave—to the Latin *mancipium*, or the Greek *andrapodon*, a slave. A periphrasis is required in this venerable language to denote a slave, such as Egyptian bondage, oppression, theft, robbery, or hard usage. In the Hebrew, in reference to the foreign servants, there is no word nor expression which points out slavery to be the condition of these hired servants. In the statute, then, in Leviticus xxv, 44–46, in the place of bondmen, it should be servants; and in the place of bondmaids, maid-servants; or the terms bondmen and bondmaids may be used in a good, and even its proper sense, to mean those servants who were *bound by contract* to serve a term of years, just as apprentices are *bound*, or the Hebrew servant was *bound*, by contract, to serve out his term of years. The name, bondman, or bondmaid, properly, no more means a slave, than apprentice, the word minor, or hired servant does.

Sixth. The Israelites, in procuring servants of the heathen, were required to *buy* them; from which it is argued that the servants were property, and, therefore, slaves. This inference is based on the assumed principle, that whatever costs money is money or property. The children of Israel were required to *buy* their first-born from the obligation of the priesthood. (Numbers xviii, 15, 16; Exodus xiii, 13; xxxiv, 20.) The word to *buy* is still used to describe this transaction. They were bought as really as were the servants. The Israelites were required to pay money for their own souls. Bible saints, as Jacob, Boaz, David, etc., bought their wives; yet these wives were not the less wives, and surely they were not slaves.

The word buy, like other words, is governed by the *usus loquendi.* Eve said, "I have gotten [bought] a man of the Lord." She named him *Cain;* that is, acquisition, purchase. "He that heareth reproof getteth [buyeth] understanding." Proverbs xv, 32. "We, after our ability, have redeemed [bought] our brethren that were sold to the heathen." Nehemiah v, 8. Here *bought* means, not to bring into servitude, but to take out of it.

It is not long since European servants, or laborers, were bought in America; but these were not slaves. But we have said enough on this here, especially as we have noticed it in our chapter on patriarchal service.

In Leviticus xxv, 47, the Israelite who became the servant of the stranger, "SOLD HIMSELF unto the stranger." The same word, and the same form of the word, which, in verse 47, is rendered *sell himself,* is, in verse 39, rendered *be sold.*

Who sold the foreign servants? If there were a theft committed, the civil magistrate might sell the thief for so long a time as his services would satisfy for the law on theft. This, however, would be a temporary arrangement, and the penalty of a crime. It does not, therefore, apply to the case. A father might sell his daughter for a wife, but not to be a slave. The law of Moses—Exodus xxi, 16—did not allow that one man should sell another man. But a man might sell himself, as we have seen. (Leviticus xxv, 47.) In this way the Jews could obtain bondmen of the heathen. They bought them when the poor heathen men or women sold themselves. Hence, this must have been a contract between the seller and buyer.

The heathen and the stranger might be bought, and who but themselves had a right to sell? None could buy those who dwelt in the land of Israel without incurring the penalty of death. Hence, the Hebrews could purchase none but those who sold themselves; and could hold them to service no longer than the term specified. If they could buy lawfully those that were slaves, they might save their money by their own thefts. The fact of their buying slaves shows they could not lawfully make slaves of them, when they had power to reduce them to slavery without purchase; so that the servants bought were bought from themselves and paid for their services. Perhaps parents, who were unable to maintain their children, might sell them for the term they had a right to their services; but no man could justly sell his children for life. And as God did not allow a father to commit such a crime against natural affection, surely he would not allow his people to commit such wickedness. If the parent had no right to sell, the Hebrews had no right to purchase. The fact that purchase was required shows that the principle of justice was dominant, and that an equivalent was paid for the services.

Seventh. The word FOREVER, in the statute, is quoted to prove that the servants were to serve during life, and their posterity from generation to generation. No such idea is contained in the passage. It is certain that the word *for-*

ever here conveys the idea of limited time, and not of endless duration; because slavery must end, at least, at the end of the world. It must mean, therefore, here a limited period. The word here means *always*. As if it were said, you shall always get your permanent laborers successively from the strangers, or, as the original literally runs, "forever, or always, shall ye serve yourselves from the strangers." Or the sense is, that from generation to generation the Hebrews might obtain a constant succession of servants from the strangers, according to the law regulating this class of servants. For whenever *forever* refers to individual cases, it is limited by the jubilee. The word is applied to the ear-bored servant who was free at the jubilee. (Exodus xxi, 2–6; Deuteronomy xv, 12–17.) But as these servants were free at the jubilee, they could not be slaves.

Eighth. That the foreign servant was free at the jubilee we have ample proof. "And ye shall hallow the fiftieth year, and proclaim liberty throughout all the land to all the inhabitants thereof." Leviticus xxv, 10. This law must apply to the stranger. The release of the Hebrew servant was secured by other enactments, as we have seen, at the end of six years, except those who chose to continue to the jubilee. The year of jubilee, therefore, could bestow no privilege to any Hebrew, but to the few who voluntarily remained in service at the close of the usual period of six years, or to freeholders who became servants. *All the inhabitants* of the land included these servants as well as others; for the strangers are mentioned expressly verse 6.

Ninth. From the use of the terms *inheritance* and *possession*, it is argued that the service was transmitted by inheritance from generation to generation. The law says, "Ye shall take them as an inheritance for your children after you to inherit them for a possession." We contend this refers to the individuals only for the term of service; that is, to the jubilee. That the servants were not property is certain, because they could not be sold; yet their term of service, in consequence of the price paid for it, was property, to be possessed and inherited by children as other property. But that the descendants of these servants could not be in successive generations slaves, we have proved from the historical fact, as well as from the law of the jubilee, that no such class of servants existed among the Jews in subsequent ages. If the jubilee had not terminated this service of strangers, and if children followed the condition of the mother under almost all slave codes, the land of Judea would abound with these Helots, like Greece, Rome, America, and all slave countries. In consequence of the law of the jubilee the foreign servants becoming free and incorporated into the Jewish population, very few servants from strangers were to be found. The only servants mentioned in the narratives of the evangelists, except where the words occur in Christ's parables, are the centurion's servant miraculously healed, and the servants of the high-priests' palace. (Matthew viii, 5–13; Mark xiv, 65; Luke xxii, 50.)

Tenth. On a careful survey of this law—Leviticus xxv, 44–46—we must conclude that it gave no toleration, sanction, or authority to slavery. The Hebrews were forbidden to buy human beings from third persons in view of enslaving them. The strangers were to be treated with such regard to their well-being as to preclude slavery. Their attendance to religious duties, by divine command, was at variance with a slave system. These foreign servants, however, were not equally privileged with Jewish servants, as they might be inherited by children at the death of their fathers; were employed in domestic or menial services; had not the right of redemption, and served to the jubilee. But whenever its first trumpet sounded they were released. And all this is established by the historical fact, that no hereditary class of servants existed among the Jews down to the time of Christ. On this point, however, we shall take pains to show, from historical data, that we give the proper view of it.

CHAPTER VI.

MOSAIC CODE—CONSTITUTIONAL LAWS.

II. On examining the various classes of servants, respecting which the Mosaic code legislated, we find that not one of them could be classed under the head of slaves. Still, in some of them, if not in all, we perceive several characteristics which go to say that some usages existed even among the Hebrews, and others among the surrounding nations, which, if not restrained or forbidden, would ultimately embody slavery in the Jewish polity. But the Mosaic restrictions respecting these, and the principles established, prevented slavery proper. For instance, the case of the ear-bored servant, who was to serve forever, might be a sort of specimen on which to graft slavery, did not the jubilee interfere. The case of the daughters sold for wives would readily run into the common surrounding heathen usage, that the child follows the condition of the mother, did not the Mosaic statute expressly provide otherwise. The man sold for debt would be a capital case on which to adjust a slavery department, and then the strangers would be readily the types of an imported African, had there been no jubilee. In the Mosaic code there are several great constitutional laws which completely prevent the tendency of human nature, the enslaving examples of strange nations, and the kindred honored usages of those among the Hebrews from running into slavery. We will now present these to our readers; and though the manner of procuring servants among the Hebrews, and even the treatment of them, might run into a modified slavery, the great constitutional guards entirely prevent this. Hence, no slave could tread the Hebrew soil except for the purpose of knocking off forever his chains. We will now in order present these great constitutional laws.

1. Because Canaan was the land to be inherited by promise to Abraham, Isaac, and Jacob, and their posterity, it was not to be a land of slavery.

In the original grant to Abraham, after reciting that his name should be great, that he would be a blessing, and that in him all the families of the earth should be blessed, the Lord said, "Unto thy seed shall I give this land." Genesis xii, 7. This was especially renewed in reference to Abraham when circumcision was enjoined as the seal of the covenant. It is stated in the promise, "And I will give unto thee, and to thy seed after thee, the land wherein thou art a stranger, all the land of Canaan, for an everlasting possession; and I will be their God." Genesis xvii, 8. The token of the covenant was circumcision. This comprehended every male child—he that was born in the house, or bought with money of any stranger which was not of the seed of Israel. Hence, every Hebrew was to be free, and every stranger who became a proselyte was to be treated as a Hebrew, being, like the Hebrew, exempt from usury, whereas other strangers were to be charged usury or interest.

In the fulfillment of this promise to strangers and Hebrews, we have the following regulation: "And if thy brother be waxen poor, and fallen in decay with thee; then thou shalt relieve him; yea, though he be a stranger, or a sojourner; that he may live with thee. Take thou no usury of him, or increase; but fear thy God; that thy brother may live with thee. Thou shalt not give him thy money upon usury, nor lend him thy victuals for increase.

I am the Lord your God, which brought you forth out of the land of Egypt, to give you the land of Canaan, and to be your God." Leviticus xxv, 35–38. The poor, and these only—except criminals—were liable to become servants, or bond-servants. All, whether strangers or others, were to be relieved so as to be saved even from bond-service, in consequence of poverty. But if this did not meet all cases, then the other regulations would prevent slavery, as the limited periods of service, the right of redemption, and the jubilee. Thus the land devoted to the descendants of Abraham should never be the seat of slavery, either to the Hebrew, or to any stranger who dwelt among them.

2. Slavery is prohibited to the Hebrews in those declarations which forbid them to allow of any such bondage in Canaan as existed in Egypt. "For they are my servants which I brought forth out of the land of Egypt; they shall not be sold as bondmen," or with the sale of bondmen. "Thou shalt not rule over him with rigor; but shalt fear thy God. For unto me the children of Israel are servants; they are my servants whom I brought forth out of the land of Egypt: I am the Lord your God." Leviticus xxv, 42, 43, 55. And as strangers could ally themselves to the Israelites by receiving their religion, then it is clear all the inhabitants were to be saved from such bondage as the Egyptian, or from any form of slavery. And this is repeated in Deuteronomy. "And thou shalt remember that thou wast a bondman in the land of Egypt, and the Lord thy God redeemed thee: therefore I command thee this thing to-day." Deuteronomy xv, 15. It would be strange, indeed, that the Almighty would send the plagues of Egypt on account of slavery, and then permit or establish the same, or something as bad, or worse, in Canaan.

3. The essential acts of enslavement of any human

being, such as stealing a man, selling the stolen man, or retaining the stolen man, is expressly prohibited in the Mosaic code on pain of death.

The fundamental law in Exodus, and the somewhat exegetical one in Deuteronomy, reads thus: "And he that stealeth a man, and selleth him, or if he be found in his hand, he shall surely be put to death." Exodus xxi, 16. "If a man be found stealing any of his brethren of the children of Israel, and maketh merchandise of him, or selleth him; then that thief shall die; and thou shalt put evil away from among you." Deuteronomy xxiv, 7. In the first passage either to *steal any man, to sell a man,* or to have in custody a stolen man, is expressly forbidden in this fundamental law of God. The punishment for the crime is capital, or death. It ranks with *smiting* or *reviling* a parent. Whether the act of theft is done secretly, as in some cases, or by violence, as in other; whether by law, or assault and battery, as the act in reference to the sufferer is to *deprive him of liberty*, the dearest gift of God to man, the criminality is the same. In the passage in Deuteronomy the explanation is remarkably significant. The stealing is that of a brother, like the stealing of Joseph. The man was converted into an article of merchandise, as if he were a horse, or any thing else, and a *mere sale* is only a part of the mercantile transaction. Death was the penalty, and unless the culprit were put to death the evil was not put away. This fundamental law in terms prohibited slavery to the Jews, whether in reference to Hebrews or to foreigners. If the stolen man was found in the hand of his captor, the man was, of course, set at liberty, and his captor was put to death. If all the retainers of stolen men in our land were put to death, or, in other words, were this law in vogue among men, as it always must be in the sight of God, our handful of slaveholders would be all exterminated, while the three and a half millions of slaves would be set at liberty. God's laws, according to which he will judge the world in the last day, would make sad work with many human laws of most countries.

4. There is not only an entire *absence* of any slave code, or body of slave regulations, in the Mosaic law, or in any part of the Old Testament, but, on the contrary, the direct reverse of all this. The omission and antagonism are unaccountable on the hypothesis of slavery among the Hebrews. Every slave nation has adopted two distinct codes—one for its free inhabitants, and another for slaves; the latter being always barbarous and cruel. According to Stroud more than seventy acts, punishable with death when committed by slaves, are not either punished at all, or else in a slight degree, when committed by freemen. The omission of this by Moses is accounted for only on the supposition that slavery was not authorized by his law. Had God authorized slavery by that law, he certainly would have enacted a slave code to support it.

5. But this great code was formed to *prevent* every sort of oppression. "Ye shall not oppress one another;" "Ye shall not therefore oppress one another; but thou shalt fear thy God: for I am the Lord your God;" "Thou shalt not rule over him with rigor; but shalt fear thy God." Leviticus xxv, 14, 17, 43. Thus mutual oppression, as well as oppression of every sort, was forbidden. And as slavery is oppressive, though all oppression is not slavery, therefore slavery is forbidden. (See Genesis vi, 11; Exodus iii, 9; xii, 29; xiv, 28. See particularly Job xxvii, 13; Isaiah lviii, 6, 7; Ezekiel xviii, 10–13; xxii, 29, 31; Amos iv, 1; viii, 4–8; Zechariah vii, 9, 14.) More ancient nations were destroyed on account of this sin than for any other. The Israelites were forbidden under heavy penalties to oppress strangers

or foreigners. (Exodus xxii, 21; Leviticus xix, 33, 34; xxv, 35; Deuteronomy i, 16; x, 18, 19; xxiv, 14, 15, 17.)

6. The fifth, seventh, eighth, and tenth commandments directly condemn the system of slavery; and the other commandments condemn it indirectly.

The fifth commandment teaches, "Honor thy father and mother." It teaches the duties of parents to children, and the duties of children to parents. It is the duty of parents to instruct their children in the principles of knowledge; protect them, provide for them, and prepare them for the duties of life. They are required to instruct them in the principles of religion—discipline them in its practice and precepts, and leave them a good example. On the other hand, children are bound to reverence and love their parents—obey them in all things in the Lord—provide for them in sickness, poverty, and old age—receive their good instructions, and imitate their good example. Slavery pays no regard to the reciprocal duties of parents and children. It transfers to the master the authority of parents over their children, and the right obedience of children to their parents. Thus the authority of the master was above the moral law, and especially above the fifth commandment. Slavery goes beyond the farthest extent of the civil power; for the proper civil power claims no authority over the private rights and duties of citizens. Hence, as slavery does thus interfere, it is condemned by the commandment, "Children, obey your parents."

The seventh commandment, "Thou shalt not commit adultery," destroys slavery. God intended marriage, and enjoined it as much on servants as on others, as we have seen in considering the various classes of servants. Slavery does not regard marriage, but entirely annuls it, as all the slave laws declare. Now, as slavery either forbids or annuls marriage, and God enjoined it on all servants in Judea as well as on others, therefore, the service concerning which Moses legislated was not slavery. Slavery places the slaves entirely in the power of the master. Hence, every female slave is entirely in the power of the master—his sons—his overseer—his driver, or of any white man. No violence to the person of a slave is to be considered a rape. Hence the process of amalgamation in the south, and the high market value of handsome white slaves. The seventh commandment forbids slavery.

The eighth commandment, "Thou shalt not steal," forbids slavery. "Theft is an unjust taking or keeping to ourselves what is justly another man's." Slaveholders are called, by St. Paul, *man-stealers*, or, in other words, the *stealers*, *venders*, or *holders* of men as slaves. (1 Timothy i, 9, 10.) And these are reckoned by him as among the most flagrant transgressors of the moral law. As slavery is theft, it is forbidden by this commandment.

Slavery is condemned by the tenth commandment, which says, "Thou shalt not covet." By the law of God every man owns himself. The slaveholder first *covets*, then steals, secretly, violently, or by law, the man, and makes him a slave. The act or acts are breaches of the tenth commandment.

As the apologists for slavery have no solid grounds, on the score of justice, or the law of God, to maintain their cause, they have recourse to the perversion of Scripture to prove their point. For this purpose the fourth and tenth commandments are chosen. In the fourth commandment it is said, respecting the Sabbath, "In it thou shalt not do any work, thou, nor thy son, nor thy daughter, thy man-servant, nor thy maid-servant, nor thy cattle, nor thy stranger that is within thy gates." The tenth commandment says, "Thou shalt not covet thy neighbor's house, thou shalt not covet thy neighbor's wife, nor his man-servant, nor his maid-servant, nor his ox, nor his ass, nor any thing that is thy neighbor's."

On the foregoing we remark:

(1.) Of the various classes of servants among the Hebrews, none of them were slaves, but either hired servants, servants for six years, or till the jubilee. And the right of property or possession in them, as expressed by THY *man-servant*, THY *maid-servant*, only referred to the right of the master to the *service* of the servant during that period.

(2.) The command, "Thou shalt not covet," does not prove that the servants were held as property, any more than that a *wife*, *son*, or *daughter* was property in common with cattle, houses, etc. Men are possessed as servants, without being possessed as property. Children and wives are possessed as children and wives, but not as chattels. They may be claimed by the title of children and wives, but not by the title of chattels.

(3.) The command says, "Thou shalt not covet any thing that is thy neighbor's;" that is, any thing that justly belongs to him. To every man belongs, by the law of nature, and the law of God, and by all just human laws, *personal liberty*, *personal security*, and *the pursuit of happiness*. These must not be coveted by any person, because these are the property of another. But the *contract* for services, by which one person voluntarily binds himself to another, becomes the just right of the other, and should not be coveted or seized by another.

(4.) These servants could not be slaves, because the fifth, seventh, and eighth commandments condemn slavery, in condemning the acts which originate or continue it. To enslave is to steal a man, or to use him as stolen. And then the commandments on obedience to parents, and on marriage, clearly condemn the system. Those, therefore, mentioned as servants, in the fourth and tenth commandments, could not be slaves; seeing the fifth, seventh, eighth, and the same tenth commandment condemn slavery. The conclusion is, that the decalogue condemns, prohibits, and makes penal the entire system of slavery.

7. The *respect of persons* forbidden in the law of Moses, and in other portions of Scripture, is at variance with a state of slavery. "Ye shall do no unrighteousness in judgment: thou shalt not respect the person of the poor, nor honor the person of the mighty; but in righteousness shalt thou judge thy neighbor." Leviticus xix, 15. "Hear the causes between your brethren, and judge righteously between every man and his brother, and the stranger that is with him. Ye shall not respect persons in judgment: but ye shall hear the small as well as the great; ye shall not be afraid of the face of man: for the judgment is God's." Deuteronomy i, 16, 17. "For the Lord your God is a God of gods, and Lord of lords, a great God, a mighty and a terrible, which regardeth not persons, nor taketh reward." Deuteronomy x, 17. In other parts of the Old Testament the same instructions are given. "It is not good to accept the person of the wicked, to overthrow the righteous in judgment." Proverbs xviii, 5. "It is not good to have respect to persons." Proverbs xxiv, 23. "To have respect of persons is not good: for for a piece of bread that man will transgress." Proverbs xxviii, 21. The justness of the cause was to be decided without regard to rich or poor. The claims of slavery are founded on respect of persons—on injustice—on gain—and are at variance with the above texts and the righteous jurisprudence of the Bible.

8. The legal rights and privileges secured to servants among the Hebrews, both in the Mosaic code and other places of the Bible, excluded the very idea of slavery

from the nation. According to slave laws, the slaves have no rights, because they are property. Among the Hebrews all classes of servants were circumcised. They had a right of covenant with God. They had a right to the passover and other feasts. They enjoyed the Sabbath and its privileges. They received remuneration and good treatment. They were instructed in religion. They had a right to hold property, and have servants of their own. They were governed by equal laws. They might be heirs to their masters. They exercised the highest offices. If their masters abused them to the extent of *mayhem*, they were set free. They might leave their master's house for ill usage. Their contract of service ended at the year of release, or at the jubilee. They married into their master's families. The children and heirs of masters seem to have no greater privileges than the servants. The legal exercise of these rights would destroy slavery. And surely God would not establish an institution in a code of laws, which he would destroy by antagonistic laws, in the same code. Something the very opposite of this, however, is done by all slave codes. The Roman law declared that all men were born free, and that liberty was the right of every man. It also declared that slavery was contrary to natural law and the divine law. But they gave the dominance to unjust human laws, so as to annul the divine law. In the United States it is declared that all men are created free and equal—copying the Roman law, as well as the divine. Yet the slave laws, though merely statutory, counteract and annul the Declaration of Independence—the declaration of rights—the Constitution of the United States—the decisions of judges, and the principles of the decalogue. But God's laws do not conflict; and, hence, there is no law of his which authorizes any person to *steal a man*—to compel him to serve him without wages and without a contract—

to part husbands and wives—to sell children from their parents—to hunt men with dogs and guns, who are fleeing for liberty. It is for our *free America* to do this.

9. There is no word in the Hebrew language corresponding in meaning with our English, and the ancient and modern word *slave, slaveholder, slavery*, etc. This certainly could not have happened, had the practice of human slavery existed among the ancient Israelites, either with or without the Mosaic law. No such word was formed during the use of the Hebrew language, down to the time of our Lord. Never did an important public institution, custom, or practice, exist in any country in the world, without a distinct and specific name given to it, in the language of the country. Accordingly, the ancient Greeks and Romans, the English, French, and Spaniards, have distinct names for slave, slavery, and slaveholders. While the Latins had *servus*, a servant, for any sort of a servant, the word *mancipium* was the proper name of a slave. The Greeks used the word *doulos* to signify a servant of any sort; but *andrapodon*, from *aner*, a *man*, and *pous*, a foot, a *downtrodden man*, is the proper name for slave; while *andrapodistes*, from the preceding, and *istemi*, to stand, means the *slaveholder*, who *stands with his feet on the prostrate man*. Such distinctions run through all languages, as far as we can learn, where slavery has existed.

The Hebrew word *abed*, a *laborer, husbandman, servant*, is derived from *abad*, to *labor, cultivate*, to *labor for another*, to be *tributary*. So it is said there was not a man *to till*, or *cultivate*, the ground. The word is used as a noun in the sense of *husbandman, laborer, servant.* It retains this meaning in composition in proper names, as *Obededom, the servant of Edom; Obadiah, the servant of Jehovah; Abednego, the servant of light; Ebedmelech, the servant of the king.* How is it possible that the Hebrew language has no word for slave as distinguished from servant, if slavery had existed from the earliest patriarchal times among the people of God, especially as this was their language from Adam to Christ?

10. Another fundamental law in regard to Hebrew service was, that the servant could never be sold. A man, in certain circumstances, *could be bought;* but when bought he could not be sold. Permission is given in the law of Moses to *buy* a servant, but none is given to *sell* him again; and because no such permission is given, it is full proof that it was not designed. The Mosaic code gives no authority to take servants in payment for debts; they were not given as pledges, nor given as presents. This is positive as to the Hebrew servant, and its principle must apply to all. "They shall not be sold as bondmen." Leviticus xxv, 42. Before a slave came into the hand of an Israelite he might have been bought and sold many times; but in the hand of the Hebrews he could not be an article of merchandise. Many good men have bought slaves; but they would not for the world sell one.

As servants were not subject to the ordinary uses of property, they were not property, and could not be sold as property. The law forbade to steal, buy, sell, or make merchandise of a man. (Exodus xxi, 16; Deuteronomy xxiv, 7.) No Israelite could buy a stolen man. In the case where damages were paid the master, as when an ox pushed the servant—Exodus xxi, 32—there is no recognition of the master's property in the servant. It only refers to his services. The master had paid a full price for his services. Hence, if the person of the servant were injured, the loss fell on the master. And if the servant were killed, the master was bound to support the family of the servant.

The servant in the family of an Israelite was one of his *own accord.* For to abjure idolatry; to enter into covenant with God; to be circumcised in token of it; to observe the Sabbath, the passover, the pentecost, and the feast of tabernacles; and to receive instruction in the moral and ceremonial law, were all voluntary acts.

As the servants of the Jews became such *voluntarily*, they also received wages, pay, or remuneration. "Woe unto him that buildeth his house by unrighteousness, and his chambers by wrong; THAT USETH HIS NEIGHBOR'S SERVICES WITHOUT WAGES, and giveth him not for his work." Jeremiah xxii, 13. God here testifies that to use the service of others without wages is *unrighteousness*, and he pronounces a woe on the *doer* of the *wrong*. To buy a person against his will of a third person; to reduce him and his posterity to perpetual slavery; to give him barely food, clothing, and lodging only; and all this at the pleasure of the master, can have no pretenses to wages or remuneration. The answer of Rev. R. J. Breckinridge to such a substitute for wages is in point. "Out upon such folly! The man who can not see that involuntary domestic slavery, *as it exists among us*, is founded on the principle of taking by force that which is another's, *has simply no moral sense.*"

11. The law of Moses, which forbade to restore runaway servants or slaves to their masters, proves that no slavery proper could exist in Judea. The law reads thus: "Thou shalt not deliver unto his master the servant which is escaped from his master unto thee: he shall dwell with thee, even among you in that place which he shall choose in one of thy gates, where it liketh him best: thou shalt not oppress him." Deuteronomy xxiii. On this law we remark as follows:

(1.) The servant, we maintain, was not a Hebrew servant, because such servants were such by contract. They could not be slaves, and were protected equally with others, as well as paid beforehand their wages, if they were servants bought with money from themselves. It would have been unjust to have harbored such runaways. It is, moreover, absurd that God would make so many laws respecting servants "born in the house or bought with money of any stranger," and who had received their wages or support in advance, or as they had need, and then introduce a law to encourage them to run away, and thus refuse to meet their contracts or agreement, honorably entered into. To prove further that Hebrew servants, or the servants of Hebrews, were not thus protected, we adduce the case of the servant that might be punished, whose services, though not the person, were "*the money* of the master." Exodus xxi, 20, 21. The servants of Shimei, who escaped to the king of Gath, were brought back by their master. (1 Kings ii, 39, 40.) A servant in Judea, who was not, and never could be a slave, had no more right to run away than any other person, as he had the same means of redress.

(2.) The fugitive, as Hanligant says, was a foreign servant or slave, not of the Jewish nation. The pagan master was often cruel. He might beat, maim, or kill his slave. The slaves were often selected as sacrifices to idols. The words, "escaped from his master," show that he was in jeopardy and saved himself by flight. The design of the law seems to be to provide an asylum for all oppressed foreign slaves who would flee to Judea for liberty, on whose territory there were no slaves, and where laws of equity governed.

(3.) It is evident this law is addressed to the magistrates, and not to individuals, or the common people. The character of the fugitive—the causes of his flight—the granting of the rights of citizens, implied in the phrase, "in one of thy gates," all came properly under the power of the civil magistrate; and no magistrate could, on any account, deliver up a runaway slave. The moment his foot touched Hebrew soil the magistrate became his protector, so that he should not be taken back to his master, or oppressed, or even restrained by the Hebrews. He was to dwell unmolested wherever he chose.

(4.) Hence, Palestine became an asylum for freedom. The foreigner who voluntarily came there was a freeman, and no longer a slave. No power could oppress him, nor compel him to return to slavery, nor force him to become even the servant, much less the slave, of any man in his new residence, unless he made a voluntary contract himself to become the servant of some one, and that contract could be made only to the jubilee. The whole civil power of Judea was engaged to protect the stranger, who was now free and no longer a slave.

(5.) Heathen service or slavery was compulsory, having no regard for the rights of man, and the Jewish law forbade the system which compelled the poor and defenseless to toil for the rich and powerful. Hence, the Hebrews had none but voluntary servants, who sold themselves for a term of years; and, therefore, justice and humanity forbade all Jews to countenance the claim of foreign slaveholders by restoring their runaways; and they would not allow their soil to be polluted as a race-ground for seizing forcibly those who were escaping from oppression.

(6.) Therefore, as there was no law to seize runaway slaves, so the law in Deuteronomy xxiii declared that no law could ever be made to restore a slave to his master. No future law could ever change this principle of the Jewish constitution.

(7.) This law of Moses deeply impresses the mind with the evil of slavery. This law impressed this great truth on the public mind, that every man ought to be a freeman. It taught every Hebrew that it was wrong to subject any man as a slave. It taught the heathen world that there was one nation, at least, that regarded the voice of natural law, as uttered by Justinian in the Roman code, "All men from the beginning were born free"—"*Omnes liberi ab initio nascebantur.*" We quote from memory.

(8.) And the Jewish nation themselves were an example of this. The whole nation of the Hebrews were a fugitive race, who fled as precipitately from Egypt as a slave does from his master. The example of the whole people, in the glorious exode from Egypt, was one great rush for freedom, under the direction of God. And as God is as watchful over *one* of his creatures as over *all*, so every individual, who is escaping from slavery, is as much under God's protection as the Israelites were in their escape, their flight, and their settlement in Canaan. Hence, the law of the fugitive is, that he should not be delivered to his master; that he may dwell where he pleases; that he should not be oppressed or enslaved, but protected by the civil magistrate.

(9.) Hence, the American Fugitive-Slave law is in direct opposition to the divine law, and can not bind the conscience of a Christian. It is also unconstitutional in reference to the Declaration of Independence, the bill of rights, and the Constitution of the United States. It is at variance with natural law. It has, therefore, no force to bind the conscience of any man, except so far as it forms a part, though an anomalous one, of a great system of the best laws in the world; and even this is to have such respect shown to it as not to impair a good system in doing away the unsound portion of it. This is a nice point.

(10.) How different the Mosaic code from our slave codes! In the year 1705 a law was enacted in Virginia authorizing any two justices of the peace, "by proclamation, to *outlaw* runaways, who might thereafter be killed and destroyed by any person whatsoever, by such ways and means as he might think fit, without accusation or impeachment of any crime for so doing." And then the law authorizing the hunting of men with dogs, guns, advertisements, in any county, is among the most scandalous, unjust, and wicked laws ever enacted by a barbarous or civilized nation.

12. The sabbatical year, as established in the Mosaic code, is at utter variance with a system of slavery. The following texts contain the principal regulations of the sabbatical year: "And six years thou shalt sow thy land, and shalt gather in the fruits thereof: but the seventh year thou shalt let it rest and lie still; that the poor of thy people may eat: and what they leave the beasts of the field shall eat. In like manner thou shalt deal with thy vineyard, and with thy olive-yard." Exodus xxiii, 10, 11. "Six years thou shalt sow thy field, and six years thou shalt prune thy vineyard, and gather in the fruit thereof; but in the seventh year shall be a sabbath of rest unto the land, a sabbath for the Lord; thou shalt neither sow thy field, nor prune thy vineyard. That which groweth of its own accord of thy harvest, thou shalt not reap, neither gather the grapes of thy vine undressed: for it is a year of rest unto the land. And the sabbath of the land shall be meat for you; for thee, and for thy servant, and for thy maid, and for thy hired servant, and for thy stranger that sojourneth with thee, and for thy cattle, and for the beast that are in thy land, shall all the increase thereof be meat." Leviticus xxv, 3–7. The following are the regulations of the law:

The Hebrews were neither to sow their fields nor prune their vines on the seventh year, that the land might enjoy its *rest* or *sabbath* every seventh year, as the Israelites had enjoyed their rest every seventh day. (Exodus xxiii, 11; Leviticus xxv, 4.)

The produce of that year, which, of course, was spontaneous, was common to all, without exception, as the poor, the servants, the stranger, and cattle. This reminded the owners of the land that they depended on God for their lands, and that their duty was to feel charity for the poor, for servants, and for strangers, and humanity to brutes. (Leviticus xxv, 6, 7; Exodus xxiii, 11.)

This institution was intended to demonstrate a particular providence; for the produce of every sixth year was promised to be such as would support them till the harvest of the ninth year. (Leviticus xxv, 20–22.)

The sabbatic year was intended as a release from any debts in the way of borrowing and lending, which had been contracted between the Israelites. (Deuteronomy xv, 2.) And they were cautioned not to shut their bowels of compassion on that account. (Deuteronomy xv, 7–11.) But of a person of another nation, not a proselyte, it could be exacted. (Deuteronomy xv, 3.)

But the most important matter that concerned the sabbatic, or seventh year, was, that it terminated the term of service of Hebrew servants. The *land* was to *rest* on the seventh year. So the Hebrew servants who sold themselves, for wages or money, were also to enjoy this year of release. "Six years he shall serve: and in the seventh he shall go out free for nothing." Exodus xxi, 2. "And if thy brother, a Hebrew man, or a Hebrew woman, be sold [sell himself] unto thee, and serve thee six years; then in the seventh year thou shalt let him go free from thee." Deuteronomy xv, 12.

In the sabbatical year, at the feast of tabernacles, they were enjoined to read the law in the hearing of all the people, comprising the women, children, and the strangers, to the end that they might hear, learn, fear the Lord, and "observe to do all the words of this law." Deuteronomy xxxi, 12. In the sabbatic year, or year of release, we see an institution which would destroy slavery in its stronghold. And did the Almighty approve of such a system, he would not annul or counteract it by the year of release. And this was proclaimed to all Israel as the standing law of the country, on reading the law in the sabbatic year.

13. The law of the jubilee is thus described: "And thou shalt number seven sabbaths of years unto thee, seven times seven years; and the space of the seven sabbaths of years shall be unto thee forty and nine years. Then shalt thou cause the trumpet of the jubilee to sound, on the tenth day of the seventh month, in the day of atonement shall ye make the trumpet sound throughout all your land. And ye shall hallow the fiftieth year, and proclaim liberty throughout all the land unto all the inhabitants thereof: it shall be a jubilee unto you; and ye shall return every man unto his possession, and ye shall return every man unto his family. A jubilee shall that fiftieth year be unto you: ye shall not sow, neither reap that which groweth of itself in it, nor gather the grapes in it of thy vine undressed. For it is the jubilee; it shall be holy unto you: ye shall eat the increase thereof out of the field. In the year of this jubilee ye shall return every man unto his possession." Leviticus xxv, 8–13. The jubilee year began on the first day of Tizri, answering to our September, and about the autumnal equinox. On this year no one either sowed or reaped. Each took possession of his inheritance that had been sold, mortgaged, or alienated. Hebrew servants, with their wives and children, were free from all previous contracts of service, which could last only to the year of jubilee at the furthest. All foreign servants also enjoyed the right of the jubilee.

The most natural derivation of the word jubilee, is

from הֹבִיל, *hobil*, or *hovil*, the Hiphil from יבל *yaval, to recall, restore, bring back*, because this year restored all slaves or bound servants to their liberty, and brought back all alienated estates to their primitive owners. Accordingly, the Septuagint renders the word by αφεσις, a *remission*. And Josephus—Antiq., b. ii, chap. x—says it signifies ελευθεριαν, freedom. Hence he says, ‘οι δουλευοντες ελευθεροι αφιενται—"Those rendering service are sent out free;" or, as his Latin translator has it, *Servi manumittuntur, slaves are manumitted.*

The jubilee was a wonderful institution, and of great service to the religion, freedom, and independence of the Hebrews. It was calculated to prevent the rich from oppressing the poor, and reducing them to perpetual slavery, and to hinder them from getting possession of all the lands, by purchase, mortgage, or usurpation. It was further intended, that debts should not be multiplied too much, lest the poor should be entirely ruined—that servants should not always continue in servitude, and that personal liberty and equality should be preserved, as far as possible.

Some contend, that, because the law of emancipation is found in the tenth verse, and the law on service in verses 44–46, that the jubilee did not reach to the strangers or heathen. We might as well affirm that the Babylonish captivity took place after the latter-day glory, because it is written subsequently in the book of Micah iv, 1–3, 9, 10. The Hebrew who sold himself, or he who was sold by the magistrate, was free at the end of six years. The jubilee must therefore apply to all servants of every description.

The jubilee was to be a universal proclamation of freedom throughout the land. So the law says, "Proclaim *liberty* throughout *all* the land, unto *all the inhabitants thereof.*" The law is not ambiguous—*liberty* is to be the boon to be bestowed. The Septuagint renders the Hebrew דרור, *deror,* liberty; αφεσιν, *remission.* So Luke iv, 18.

All the *inhabitants* of the land, must certainly include all servants. The servants belonged to the *households;* and, therefore, to the regular inhabitants, whether strangers by birth or not. The lxx use a phrase which includes all sojourners, πασι τοις κατοικουσιν αυτην—*to all* who inhabit it. It is not worth while to dwell here respecting the meaning of inhabitants; as this word can not apply to transitory sojourners, in the case in hand, but to the *bought servants,* who were incorporated among the Hebrew families, became their *possession, as servants,* were *inherited* as such by their children, and that *forever,* or to the jubilee. Such is the plain meaning of the law of the jubilee, which applies to all servants of every grade, and proclaims liberty to all of them. If any doubts, let him just read the texts in a concordance under the word *inhabitant,* and he will be convinced of the truth of this statement.

The following passage from Isaiah will show the light in which the stranger is viewed, and, therefore, the servant who is a stranger: "The sons of the stranger, that join themselves to the Lord, to serve him, and to love the name of the Lord, to be his servants, every one that keepeth the Sabbath from polluting it, and taketh hold of my covenant; even them will I bring to my holy mountain, and make them joyful in my house of prayer: their burnt-offerings and sacrifices shall be accepted upon mine altar: for my house shall be called a house of prayer for all people." Isaiah lvi, 6, 7.

14. There is no Scriptural or other account of the existence of a slave system among the Jews. Every country in which slavery existed, has exhibited a class of persons who were hereditary slaves. Among them the common maxim, the child followed the condition of the

mother, prevailed. The Helots among the Greeks are a sample. So also the Hebrews among the Egyptians. The case of America and other modern countries presents examples. No such class of slaves existed in Judea. Besides, had the Jews practiced slavery, even in violation of the Mosaic code, they would have left some historical tradition of the matter, such as the Greeks and Romans did. Josephus relates no such custom; and, though the word *slave* occurs in the English translation, it must be considered a false rendering, because there is no word in the Hebrew language for slave.

15. The penal sanctions delivered respecting the treatment of servants, go to show that slavery was not the system of servitude which the Mosaic code regulated. We will notice the principal cases under this head.

(1.) The following law is given: "And if a man smite his servant, or his maid, with a rod, and he die under his hand; he shall be surely punished. Notwithstanding, if he continue a day or two, he shall not be punished: for he is his money." Exodus xxi, 20, 21. This law refers to servants in general, and not to Hebrew servants in particular. Cruelty is here forbidden, by appointing to that master who should beat his servant, so as to kill him, the punishment due to a murderer. If the death of the slave was not owing to the correction, the master was thought sufficiently punished by the loss of his servant's services; for, in this respect, *he was his money;* and in this view it was clear, that the master did not design to kill him. The servant being his master's money, is, therefore, not adduced as any proof that he was his master's property, but as evidence that his master had no design to kill him.

How different the spirit manifested here to servants, to the absolute power allowed over them among the heathen nations, who gave the master the power to kill his slaves! Plato, in his Republic, says, "He who kills his own slave, shall be acquitted; whoso, in anger, kills another's, shall pay double the price of him." The Emperor Adrian first softened the rigor of the laws respecting putting slaves to death. The Mosaic law here would badly suit a slave code.

(2.) The Mosaic law decided that, if an ox killed a man, the ox must be killed, and his flesh must not be eaten; and the owner of the ox would be quit. But if the ox were wont to assault persons, and the owner did not confine him, he was put to death. Yet he might, in that case, ransom his life, according to the decisions of the judges, by paying whatever sum they laid on him. (Exodus xxi, 28–31.) The fine was not determined, in this case, as to the amount. In the case of a servant, however, the fine was fixed. "If the ox shall push a man-servant or maid-servant; he shall give unto their master thirty shekels of silver, and the ox shall be stoned." Verse 32.

The law is express. There is no distinction made between a freeman and a bondman, except as to the *amount* of the fine, when that was commuted for death. "If an ox gore a *man* or a *woman*." Bondmen and bondwomen were not then excluded from the class of men and women; for the law is, a *man* or a *woman;* also, a *son* or a *daughter*. It applies equally to all human beings. Death is the punishment to be inflicted upon the owner of the ox, if, in the opinion of the judges, the same was murder, whether the person killed was bond or free; the law made no difference.

But, when the case was not pronounced murder, there was a difference between the freeman and the bondman. If there be alleviating circumstances, in both cases, a ransom is to be paid. In the case of the freeman this amount was to be decided by the judges. In the case of the bondman the sum was fixed at "thirty shekels of silver," or from fifteen to twenty dollars.

(3.) The following is another of the penal laws on service: "And if a man smite the eye of his servant, or the eye of his maid, that it perish; he shall let him go free for his eye's sake. And if he smite out his man-servant's tooth, or his maid-servant's tooth; he shall let him go free for his tooth's sake." Exodus xxi, 26, 27. The servant in this case, as in others under the Mosaic code, was not a slave, but a servant. As a servant he was to serve either till the year of release, or till the jubilee. The loss of his eye or tooth, exonerated him from the service, and he therefore kept the money by which he sold himself, or he canceled the obligation of service, whatever it was, by the loss of his eye or tooth. In this the service differed from slavery; as slavery proper knows of no such condition of emancipation. If mutilated members, scourged backs, or the like, would produce freedom with us, there would not be many slaves in the country at this time.

(4.) Here is another penal case. "And whosoever lieth carnally with a woman that is a bondmaid betrothed to a husband, and not at all redeemed, nor freedom given her; she shall be scourged: they shall not be put to death, because she was not free." Leviticus xix, 20. Had she been free, the law required that she and the man should be put to death. (See Deuteronomy xxii, 24.) As she was a servant, she had less control over herself; but as she made no resistance, she was to be scourged, and the man was required to confess his guilt and make an offering. But the girl was no slave, because she was "betrothed to a husband;" and, therefore, might soon have a husband; but a slave could not be betrothed, married, or have a husband; therefore, she could not be a slave. She was punished, however, with correction.

The man was censured, and was required publicly to atone for his sin. Such crimes as this pass entirely unnoticed by our slave laws. In all such acts among us, were the slave women to be publicly scourged, and the slaveholders publicly censured, and fined before an ecclesiastical tribunal, it would be a strange thing, indeed, in the annals of slavery. Therefore, the penal censure here administered does not agree with a slave system ; and, therefore, service among the Hebrews was not slavery.

16. We will here sum up the great antislavery constitutional principles of the Mosaic code, so as to place before our readers the mere outline of it in one general survey. There was slavery in some form in all the nations which surrounded the Hebrews. From their inevitable connection with these nations some of the usages of slavery were incorporated with the customs of the Hebrews. These customs, unrestrained and extended, would lead to slavery. To preserve liberty among God's people, and to prevent the introduction of slavery into the model republic, the antislavery principles were embodied into the Mosaic code, not only in its very constitution, but into all its civil statutes, ordinances, etc., so as entirely to prevent the establishment of slavery in Judea. Add to this, the great principles of liberty in the Jewish code were to be a standard for Christianity, so that the Christian Church should never be infested with a slave system. So Isaiah declared very clearly. (Isaiah xli, 1–4.) Our Lord proclaimed to the Jews this great jubilee. (Luke iv, 18.) Isaiah calls it proclaiming liberty to the captives, and the opening of the prison to those that are bound; to proclaim the acceptable year of our Lord and the day of vengeance of our God. Our Lord expresses it thus: "To preach or proclaim LIBERTY TO THE CAPTIVES—to set at LIBERTY THEM THAT ARE BRUISED or DOWN-TRODDEN," as the ANDRAPODA, or slaves of the heathens,

were thus trodden on by their captors and enslavers. With these remarks we introduce the summary of the antislavery constitutional laws of the Hebrew code.

By the appointment of God Canaan was to be a free country, on whose soil no slave could tread and remain without becoming a freeman, and thus resume the exercise of his natural rights, of which, like our slaves, he had been feloniously and violently deprived in spite of justice. In this free country, it was provided that no such bondage as that of Egyptian bondage should ever be introduced. So that, in denouncing the bondage of Egypt, the system of slavery was condemned in the same sentence of prohibition. Hence, the essential elements of slavery were condemned as capital offenses, and the punishment for this was death equally with murder, or beating, or reviling a parent. (Exodus xxi, 16; Deuteronomy xxiv, 7.) Thus there is the total absence of any law in the Mosaic code which tolerates, sanctions, approves, or establishes a slave system. And yet there is also the presence of many prohibitory laws excluding all the leading characteristics of slavery. Therefore, the decalogue is altogether antislavery. The fifth, seventh, eighth, ninth, and tenth commandments directly condemn it; while the other commandments are indirectly at variance with it. And the two great commandments, love to God and love to man, are subversive of the system. The constant command in the exercise of human rights, *to avoid respect of persons*, condemns the system that reduces some to the lowest degradation; while it makes despots or tyrants of others. As God made of one blood all men, this respect of persons, as that which distinguishes the slave from the master, is clearly forbidden. The numerous rights and privileges—civil, religious, and social—can not consist with slavery. And so alien is the system to the Hebrew nation, that their language never had a word exactly to correspond to slave, slavery, enslaver. The word that most nearly approaches a proper designation, is that which, in its various forms, corresponds to the terms oppression, oppressive, oppressor. And these terms are similar to the terms in Greek, which are literally expressed by *trampling under foot, he that is trampled on,* and the *trampler on men.* The Hebrew servant, or the stranger, could never be sold, though they could be bought. And they could be bought, not to enslave them, but to set them free. As there was no oppression allowed in Hebrew service, there was no need that the servant should leave his home to escape oppression. He had the civil law on his side just as much as the master had, and could sue for the fulfillment of the contract respecting his service. But the foreign slave, who fled to Judea for protection, became a freed-man, and all Israel was bound to protect him at any cost. And there was the sabbatic year, which released perhaps two-thirds, or more, of all the Hebrew servants; while the jubilee proclaimed liberty to all the inhabitants of the land without distinction. As to the effect of these two institutions on slavery, it may be gathered from applying it to our own system. Had two-thirds of all our slaves been set free septennially since 1776, the year 1853 would have been the witness of eleven seven-year releases. This would have left few slaves in our land. Then, had there been a jubilee in 1826, and did we look forward to another in 1876, our slave system would have been far from needing a Nebraska bill, or from calling for the annullment of a national compromise in favor of slavery.

The foregoing synopsis or summary of the great anti-slavery constitutional prohibitions and regulations of the Mosaic code, go unequivocally to say that the system of service which the Mosaic code regulated and sanctioned, and which God approved, was not slavery; but a system of service consistent with liberty, and which was consistent with, and was the support of liberty and equal unalienable rights.

CHAPTER VII.

MOSAIC CODE—RIGHTS AND PRIVILEGES OF SERVANTS.

III. Under a third division of our discussion of service, as regulated under the Mosaic code, we have to show that the rights and privileges of servants, as secured by this law, or that the principles of benevolence inculcated and the treatment of servants enjoined, proves that the service was not slavery. We select the following among the various rights of servants:

1. No servant or stranger could remain with an Israelite without becoming a proselyte. (Genesis xvii, 9–14, 23, 27.) Thus, according to the Mosaic law, he was entitled to covenant privileges. (Deuteronomy xxix, 10–13.) Hence, all became brethren, and entitled to all the privileges of equal and just laws, among which were personal liberty, personal security, the pursuit of happiness, and the full exercise of religious privileges.

2. If the servant desired it, he could compel the master to keep him after the six years' contract expired. This shows that the servant, as well as his master, had the full right to contract. (Deuteronomy xv, 12–17; Exodus xxi, 2–6.) Slavery knows no such law as this.

3. There were various rights and privileges conferred on servants, which will show how unlike the service regulated was to our slavery.

The servants were instructed in the principles of morality and religion. This course of instruction commenced among the servants, household, or subjects of Abraham, who taught and commanded his children and his household after him, that they should keep the way of the Lord, to do justice and judgment. (Genesis xviii, 19.) The law of the Lord was read on the sabbatic year "to all Israel, men, and women, and children, and the stranger that is within thy gates, that they may hear, and that they may learn, and fear the Lord your God, and observe to do all the words of this law." Deuteronomy xxxi, 10–13. And the copy of the law was for all the people, "as well the stranger as he that was born among them." Joshua viii, 33. Jehoshaphat sent the Levites to teach the law throughout all the cities of Judah, to all the people. (2 Chronicles xvii, 8, 9.)

The servants were invited guests at all the national and family festivals. When circumcised they partook of the passover. (Exodus xii, 12.) "And ye shall rejoice before the Lord your God, ye, and your sons, and your daughters, and your men-servants, and your maid-servants, and the Levite that is within your gates; forasmuch as he hath no part nor inheritance with you." Deuteronomy xii, 12; see also verse 18; and xvi, 10–15.

Servants were released from their labors nearly one half of the year. The law secured for them the following portions of time:

The whole of every seventh year. While the land rested the servant who tilled rested also; and the product was to be for food for the master, and "for thy servant, and for thy maid, and for thy hired servant, and for thy stranger that sojourneth with thee." (Leviticus xxv, 3–6.)

Every seventh day was also secured to the servant as well as to others. "In it thou shalt do no manner of work, thou, nor thy son, nor thy daughter, nor thy man-servant, nor thy maid-servant." Exodus xx, 10.

The servant could attend the three great national annual festivals. "Three times in a year all thy males shall appear before the Lord." Exodus xxiii, 17. These festivals were the "passover, which commenced on the fifteenth of the first month, and lasted seven days"—Deuteronomy xvi, 1–8—the Pentecost, or feast of weeks, began on the sixth day of the third month, and lasted seven days—Deuteronomy xvi, 10, 11—the feast of tabernacles lasted eight days, commencing on the fifteenth day of the seventh month. (Deuteronomy xvi, 13, 15; Leviticus xxiii, 34, 39.) If we include the time spent going to, remaining at, and returning from these festivals, each may occupy from two to three weeks.

The rest of the *new moons*, it is said, occupied two days—Numbers x, 10; xxviii, 11 14—also the feast of trumpets—Leviticus xxiii, 24, 25—and on the great day of atonement. (Leviticus xxiii, 27.)

Thus the Mosaic system secured to servants about one half their time. They were also furnished with the opportunities of instruction. The time not spent in religious services might be employed by the servant himself, and, therefore, he could obtain much property, and even redeem himself, for which the law made provision.

4. The servants were protected by law equal to the other members of the community. "Judge righteously between every man and his brother, and the stranger that is with thee." Deuteronomy i, 16. "Ye shall have one manner of law, as well for the stranger, as for one of your own country: for I am the Lord your God." Leviticus xxiv, 22. "Ye shall have one law for him that sinneth through ignorance, both for him that is born among the children of Israel, and for the stranger that sojourneth among them." Numbers xv, 29. "Cursed be he that perverteth the judgment of the stranger." Deuteronomy xxvii, 19. Thus the servants enjoyed the

full benefit of just and equal laws, and the execution of them. This can not be said of any slave system, whether the patriarchal, as in the case of Joseph, the Grecian, the Roman, or the American. The most noted distinction descriptive of slavery is that by Justinian, where he says, "In the condition of slaves there is no diversity; but among free persons there are many; thus some are *ingenui*, or freemen; others *libertini*, or freed-men." (Institutes, Lib. I, Tit. 3, Sec. 5.) Such a distinction was not recognized by the law of Moses, as this law treated all alike.

5. The Mosaic code enjoined the greatest affection and kindness toward servants, whether foreign or Hebrew. "The stranger that dwelleth with you shall be unto you as one born among you, and thou shalt love him as thyself." Leviticus xix, 34. "The Lord your God . . . regardeth not persons, nor taketh reward: he doth execute the judgment of the fatherless and widow, and loveth the stranger in giving him food and raiment. Love ye, therefore, the stranger." Deuteronomy x, 19. It is difficult to conceive how these precepts can be reconciled to slavery.

6. The Hebrews were expressly warned against vexing or oppressing servants. "And shalt neither vex a stranger nor oppress him; for ye were strangers in the land of Egypt." Exodus xxii, 21. "Thou shalt not oppress a stranger, for ye know the heart of a stranger, seeing ye were strangers in the land of Egypt." Exodus xxiii, 9. "And if a stranger sojourn with thee in your land, ye shall not vex him." Leviticus xix, 33. As they were neither to vex nor oppress strangers, they could not enslave them, as slavery is both a vexation and oppression.

7. Relief to the poor was especially enjoined to all the Hebrews. "If thy brother be waxen poor, thou shalt

relieve him: yea, though he be a stranger, or a sojourner; that he may live with thee. Take thou no usury of him, or increase; but fear thy God." Leviticus xxv, 35, 36. "For the poor shall never cease out of the land: therefore I command thee, saying, Thou shalt open thy hand wide unto thy brother, to thy poor, and to thy needy, in thy land." Deuteronomy xv, 11. The stranger, the fatherless, and the widow were to be relieved, "that they may eat within thy gates, and be filled." Deuteronomy xxvi, 12. Poverty among the Hebrews was the *principal* cause of service for a term of years; in order to take away the very cause or necessity for this service, the relief of the poor was particularly enjoined. Poverty is not the reason for slavery among us; its cause is a very different one, as all know.

8. Servants might hold property, and were sometimes the heirs of their masters. Saul's servant had money of his own. (1 Samuel ix, 8.) Ziba, the servant of Mephibosheth, made David a present of bread, fruit, and wine. (2 Samuel xvi, 1.) He also had twenty servants of his own. (2 Samuel ix, 10.) David also divided the property of Saul's house between Ziba and his master. (2 Samuel xix, 24, 30.) Eliezer was selected before the birth of Isaac to be the heir of Abraham. (Genesis xv, 2, 3.) "Now Sheshan had no sons, but daughters. And Sheshan had a servant, [*abed*,] an Egyptian, whose name was Jarha. And Sheshan gave his daughter to Jarha, his servant, to wife, and she bare him Attai." 1 Chronicles ii, 34, 35. Solomon says, "A wise servant shall have rule over a son that causeth shame, and shall have part of the inheritance among the brethren." Proverbs xvii, 2. Thus servants sometimes inherited with children. The slave law is, "Slaves have no legal rights of property in things real or personal; and whatever property they may acquire belongs, in point of law, to

their masters." The Louisiana code says, "A slave is one who is in the power of a master. . . . He can do nothing, possess nothing, nor acquire any thing, but what must belong to his master."

9. The servant among the Hebrews received *wages*. We do not say that he received daily wages as did the hired servant. But he received wages in some form, or what he himself agreed to serve for. The wages was either money, or maintenance for a certain term of years, by contract, and was as much wages as the consideration of the apprentice, the minor, or the hired servant. Slavery knows no such thing as wages as a part of its code, in any *remunerative* or just sense.

10. Servants were placed upon a level with their masters in all civil and religious rights. "As ye are, so shall the stranger be before the Lord. One law and one manner shall be for you, and for the stranger that sojourneth with you." Numbers xv, 15, 16, 29. (See also Leviticus xxiv, 22; Deuteronomy i, 16, 17.) Were the same legal and moral principles applied to our southern masters and slaves, it would require to alter the constitutions of the southern states and their laws, and then slavery would perish under this *one law* and *one manner*.

11. The treatment of servants at the end of the sexennial term of service does not comport with the usages or laws of slavery. The servant who completed his six years' service was liberally supplied by his master from the thrashing-floor, the flock, and the vintage. (Deuteronomy xv, 13, 14, 17.) Not only was the servant, his wife, and family released from service, but they were also well supplied with what was necessary to commence the world again. This alone shows how unlike our system was to theirs.

12. From the foregoing we learn that servants were

received into covenant relation to God among the Hebrews, whether they were Hebrews or strangers. Hence they possessed, on this account, various rights and privileges, religiously, socially, and civilly, which never belonged to slaves in any country. They were invited guests at all the national festivals; were instructed in morality and religion; were protected by laws equal with others; were placed on a level with others in civil and religious respects; if poor, they were relieved; they received wages for their services; they could hold property; they were dismissed from their term of service with noble gratuities. Such rights and privileges do not belong to a slave system; and the enactment of them would destroy any system of slavery, as the history of the world fully shows. As examples, we adduce the service among the patriarchs, Abraham, Isaac, and Jacob; the effect of the Mosaic code among the Hebrews; the effect of the same principles under the Christian dispensation. And to correspond with these cases, we mention the absence of such rights and privileges in our slave system, and in all the slave systems under heaven.

IV. Comparison of Hebrew service with American slavery.

We have seen that the Mosaic code respecting service was intended to root out those incipient elements among the Hebrews tending to slavery, to prevent the introduction from heathen nations of any shade of slavery, to establish universal freedom in the land of the Hebrews, and thus make it the model free country for the world, in view of establishing the great jubilee of political and religious freedom throughout the earth. Let us now turn to the slave laws of the south, and see the plain, irreconcilable contrast between the Mosaic service and American slavery, and between the slave code and the code of Moses.

1. As to the origin of the two codes; they may be traced to two very distinct and opposite sources.

The Mosaic code, regulating service, had its origin in generous compassion to the poor. Its provisions were framed for their benefit. It required a kind and benevolent disposition in the rich. It elevated the poor, and so restrained the tendency toward slavery by law as forever to prevent its establishment in the land.

The American slave laws had their origin in avarice. The system they support is derived from the African slave-trade, and is identical with it now in evil principles and practices. The laws are formed to promote the interests of the master—to degrade the servant, as well as to foster cruelty in the master, and those wrong dispositions which are at variance with the supreme law of laws.

2. American slavery is hereditary and perpetual to the last moment of the slave's earthly existence, and to all his descendants, to the latest posterity.

The service of the Hebrews was not hereditary. Perhaps about two-thirds were free at the end of six years. The greater portion of them had the right of redemption. The jubilee, or every fiftieth year, gave liberty to all without exception.

3. The law of Moses required every one to love the stranger and the poor servant, and forbade any one to oppress him; or, in other words, to make him a slave. The slave law views its victim as an enemy, and treats him as such, by bonds, imprisonment, and subjugation. Hence, it is contrary to the Mosaic code, which taught love to the servant, and the poor and needy. The service of the heathen, authorized by Moses, was founded on moral and religious principles, and did not involve injustice of any kind.

4. The Jewish service was voluntary, except where it

was the penalty for crime. Slavery is involuntary and inflicted for no crime. The labor of the slave is compulsory and uncompensated, and dictated by the master. The master, under the Jewish economy, possessed no greater authority over the servant than over his children. Servants might contend with their masters about their rights, and to despise their cause was reckoned a heinous crime. (Job xxxi, 13.) Slaves can make no contracts, and can have no legal right to any property—all they have belongs to their masters.

5. The labor of the servant, under the Mosaic servitude, was for value received. The servant submitted to this either to cancel an obligation of justice, or to procure for himself special benefits, which, in his opinion, he could not so well secure by any other means. Slavery does not recognize the principles of justice. It does not concede the right to a full compensation for servile labor.

6. According to the Mosaic code the servant was not property, and could not be sold or transferred from one master to another. The slave, being regarded as property, may be sold, left by will, alienated, or disposed of as any other property is disposed of. He may be sold irrespective of his being a husband, or father, or brother, or any other relative. In the slave-growing states the principal profit of the system is, that the slave may be sold. Some states throw in some restrictions as to sales; but these are so limited and partial, that the general merchandise in slaves continues with little restraint.

7. Among the Hebrews the testimony of the servants was as valid as that of any other person. According to our slave system, neither a slave nor a free colored person can be a witness against any white or free person, in a court of justice, however atrocious may have been the crimes they have seen him commit, if such testimony should be for the benefit of the slave. But they may

give testimony against a fellow-slave, or a free colored person.

8. The law of Moses granted a release from labor to the servant who had been cruelly or unreasonably punished. (Exodus xxi, 26, 27.) An American slave may be punished, at his master's discretion, without the means of redress. The master can transfer the same despotic power to any other person. Thus, on the side of their oppressors, there is power; but they have no comforter. There is also a great inequality of law and right, in our slave system. What is a trifling offense in the white man is considered highly criminal in the slave; as the same offenses which cost a white man a few dollars, are punished in the slave with death.

9. Servants among the Hebrews were guarded in all the privileges of marriage, whether it regards husband and wife, parents and children. In case the mother was not free from service at the same time with the wife, the children remained with her, and the master was bound to receive him to service again, if he chose to live with them. American slaves are entirely unprotected in their domestic relations; so that husbands and wives, parents and children, may be separated at the sovereign will of the master.

10. In the laws of Moses on service, the life of the servant was as much protected as the life of any other person; and the same principles applied to both. According to our slave laws, as presented by Stroud, page 35, "The master may, at his discretion, inflict any species of punishment upon the person of his slave." The murder of a slave is generally punished with a pecuniary fine. Yet, according to statute, the *deliberate* murder of a slave is punishable with death. But, considering the general character of the slave laws, the master mostly can escape, especially when no colored person can be a witness in the

case. The laws of some states acquit the master for killing a slave, if it be done *when inflicting moderate punishment.* The law of North Carolina, of 1798, after deciding that the willful murder of the slave incurs death, gives the following proviso: "Provided, always, this act shall not extend to the person killing a slave outlawed, by virtue of any act of assembly of this state, or to any slave in the act of resistance to his lawful owner or master, or to any slave dying under moderate correction."

11. The law of Moses secured to the servant a large portion of time. He had, like his owner, every seventh day, every seventh year, the whole of the national feasts, and the family festivals. This arrangement gave him about one half of his time. According to our slave laws, there is no portion of time allowed to the slave, in which he may labor for himself, read or pray. The Sabbath is not secured expressly for him by law, except in Louisiana or Mississippi. In this the Mosaic code differs from our slave code. The reason is, that Moses legislated for servants who were free; but we legislate for servants who are slaves.

12. The slave can have no property. He can not own land, a horse, or any article of husbandry. If he receives even a grant of land, for serving as a soldier to defend his country, which denies him liberty, he can not hold it, as the master may take it as his own. But, according to the law of Moses, the servant might become possessed of property. He might purchase his freedom at a fair valuation. At the end of his term of service a liberal gratuity was conferred upon him. He also might become heir to his master, did his master see fit to make him such.

13. The law of Moses secured to servants the means of religious instruction, and of religious privileges. Servants were received into covenant with God, and enjoyed

religious privileges as amply as any other portions of the Hebrew people. With us the means of religious instruction are not bestowed upon the slaves. On the contrary, the efforts of the charitable and humane to supply these wants are discountenanced by law. Indeed, in several states it is made criminal even to teach the slave to read.

14. The Mosaic code made the same provision for the education of the servant as for any other; and there was no prohibitory law to prevent him from learning any more than others, as far as he had opportunity. The benefits of education are withheld from our slaves. And this is not the effect of mere custom or neglect on the part of the master. It is an essential part of the system, and is ordained by law. In Virginia it is ordained, "that all meetings or assemblies of slaves, or free negroes, or mulattoes, mixing or associating with such slaves, at any meeting or any other place, etc., in the night, or at any school or schools for teaching them reading or writing, either in the day or night, under whatever pretext, shall be deemed and considered an unlawful assembly."

15. Slaves can not redeem themselves, or obtain a change of masters, though such a change may render this necessary for their personal safety. Under the Mosaic constitution the *law* provided a way by which this could be done, if the servant or his friends could do it. The price of redemption, too, was fixed by the statute. A just valuation was to be made of the services of the servant in proportion to the proximity to the year of jubilee, and the value of a hired servant's wages; and the master was bound to accept that as the price of his release. Our slave code has no law compelling the master to sell a slave to himself or his friend, any more than requiring him to sell his horse or ox. A husband or father can not compel a master to release his wife and children at *any* price or for any consideration. In Egypt

and Arabia, if a slave is maltreated, he may appeal to the magistrate, and *compel* his master to sell him.

In the Louisiana code there is a law which does allow of an exception, but under such restrictions as to be no real substitute for the Mosaic code in the case. It reads thus: "No master shall be compelled to sell his slave, but in one of two cases, to wit: first, where, being only coproprietor of the slave, his coproprietor demands the sale in order to make partition of the property; second, where the master shall be CONVICTED of cruel treatment of the slave, and THE JUDGE SHALL DEEM IT PROPER to pronounce, besides the penalty established for such cases, that the slave shall be sold at public auction, in order to place him out of the reach of the power which the master abused." (Louisiana Code, article 192.) In Kentucky there is, we believe, a similar law, and perhaps in some other states.

This law, however, is almost, if not altogether, a practical nullity; because no slave or free colored person can be a witness in the case; the master must be *convicted* of cruelty, a thing very difficult, indeed; and it is *optional* with the judge whether he shall make the decree in favor of the slave or not. But when, in any case, the law is carried into effect, it furnishes little or no relief to the slave, because the slave is not made free, as the servant was under the Jewish law. The degradation of slavery still remains, that the slave may be *sold* at public auction as property. And then the slave may pass into the hands of as cruel a master as his former owner.

16. If a servant escaped from his master, and fled to the land of Israel, the law commanded every one to protect him, and forbade every one to deliver him to his master. By this law, and the laws on service, the land of Judea became consecrated to freedom, so that no slave could tread its soil or breathe its free air. But the Consti-

tution of the United States has adopted an opposite law, at once at variance with the word of God and the other parts of the Constitution. The provision of the Constitution is: "No person held to service or labor in one state, under the law thereof, escaping into another, shall, in consequence of any law or regulation therein, be discharged from such service or labor, but shall be delivered up on claim of the party to whom such service or labor may be due." (Article iv, section ii, clause 3.) On this article in the Constitution the notorious enactment was passed, called the Fugitive-Slave law. The law of God provides that every man who can secure his freedom by escape, has a right to do so. The Constitution and laws of the United States decide that he has no such right. No two laws can be more at variance than the law of God and the Fugitive-Slave law.

17. There is, in our slave laws, no provision made for general emancipation; in most cases it is absolutely forbidden; and in the few cases in which it can take place, it is accompanied with unjust and degrading treatment of the person. In the Mosaic code the Hebrew servant was to be set at liberty at the close of the sixth year, in most cases; at the jubilee there was a general proclamation throughout the land. Under such laws the system could not be perpetuated. If the laws of the Pentateuch had been applied to our slavery in 1776, when the Declaration of Independence was made, there would not have been many slaves in this country now. Had the service of the greater number been terminated at the end of every six years since 1776, this would have nearly ruined slavery at this time. And had there been one jubilee in 1826, and another confidently looked for in 1876, and had the privilege of redemption been enjoyed, where could we look for slavery in 1876, after the blasts of the second American jubilee had died away?

18. Let us more especially consider here the *effect* of the Mosaic laws on service upon our slave system. Were slavery to originate with us, as service did with the Jews—the masters and the servants having to make the *contract* as to the time and conditions of service—there would be no small obstacle to completing gangs for the southern market. And then the refusal of wages, the prospective sales of near relatives, the punishments that awaited the disobedient, would not be very high motives to choose a state of slavery, because it was better than the condition of northern or British laborers. Add to this the precarious tenure of life among slaves, and the disability to hold property. And then when you apply the year of release and the jubilee to the system, it gradually, yet rapidly, vanishes away.

19. We may close our argument here with some remarks upon the laws on slavery, contrasted with those of Moses on service.

It is admitted here, that all these laws are not always enforced by individuals, whose sense of morality prevents them from practicing according to the laws. This is truly a strong protest against that system, the support of which, according to law, shocks the moral sense of a Christian. No such laws exist in the moral code of Moses, either in regard to service or any other subject.

Yet, in very many cases, the laws, in all their harshness and cruelty, *may* be executed; and in many cases they *are* and *must* be put in force. The plea, then, of relaxation can not be pleaded in favor of the law or the system of slavery, but in favor of the pious protest of enlightened minds and a good conscience.

The laws, therefore, fairly represent the system of slavery. And since our slave laws are at variance with the Mosaic laws on service, the inference is just, that the service in the one case is altogether different from the slavery in the other. For if the system of slavery is right, the laws which support it must also be right. And if the laws be just and good, they can not be the support of that which is wrong in itself.

20. In conclusion, we may here refer to the leading points in the Mosaic code; from which it will appear, that, though slavery existed in all the nations around Palestine, and shreds of it existed among the Hebrews themselves, yet the Hebrew laws prevented the establishment of slavery among their own people by necessary laws, and these laws would never allow the foreign slave, as such, a residence among them.

CHAPTER VIII.

WORKING OF THE MOSAIC CODE.

1. In our second chapter, on patriarchal service, it was shown that the service under Abraham, Isaac, and Jacob was not slavery, nor did it sanction or tolerate a slave system. On the other hand, it neutralized the elements of slavery around and laid the platform of freedom. In another chapter it was proved, we think, that the case of Joseph is the proper specimen of slavery. In Egyptian bondage we found a system which is nearly akin to slavery; which was condemned by the word of God, and destroyed by miraculous influence. It was also shown that the Mosaic code condemned the bondage of Egypt as well as the slavery in the case of Joseph, and such as existed in the heathen nations around the Israelites. Still, even among the Hebrews, there were some of the usages of the slave system, derived from their association with the Egyptians and others. The code of Moses legislated respecting the whole subject so effectually as to prevent the establishment of slavery in Canaan, as well as furnish a model free government, regulated by just and equal laws, at perfect variance with oppression and wrong.

We will now consider the *working* of the Mosaic system. What was the operation of the Mosaic laws in regard to slavery? In answer to this question, we have to reply that no system of slavery existed among the Jews from the delivery of the Mosaic code to our Lord. We find no class of persons among the Jews to correspond with our slaves, or with the Helots among the Greeks. We seek in vain, from the historical writings of the prophets, for the slave system. Indeed, the prophets, where reference is had to service, denounce every thing of the nature of slavery as fully as Moses did.

2. Had the Mosaic institutions contemplated slavery, we should certainly look that the Canaanites would be reduced to that condition. Yet none of them were to be spared. (Deuteronomy vii, 1–6.) They were an idolatrous, wicked people, who were beyond the reach of reformation, like the antediluvians and Sodomites, and they must, therefore, be cut off. The reason, too, is given; namely, that they would, like all hardened sinners, lead the Israelites astray. They were to be destroyed as nations or bodies politic. Yet, had they forsaken their idolatries and become converts to the true religion, they would be, what God required, true penitents, and proper objects of forgiveness. For this rule is laid down in Scripture and founded in reason. (Jeremiah xviii, 7, 8.) No permission was given to kidnap the Canaanites, or, when they were captured, to sell them as slaves. None of them were sold as slaves, nor were they attached as *serfs* or *villains* to the soil, nor exported to be sold in a foreign market.

Two exceptions to this have been quoted. The one was the case of the Gibeonites, the other those whom Solomon made tributary.

3. The Gibeonites were a portion of the Canaanites, who, by stratagem, obtained protection from Joshua. The history is given in Joshua, chapter ix. Through false pretenses they secured their lives. Joshua and the princes swore to spare and protect them. They were then made hewers of wood and drawers of water in the public service of the temple. The error of Joshua and the princes was, that they asked not counsel of God. Had the Lord been consulted there is no doubt but the

Gibeonites would have been spared by his approbation, because they feared the Lord and embraced the true religion. The manner of making the league appears to have been wrong. That the league itself was lawful appears, 1. Because Joshua and the princes, on reviewing it, concluded it to be so, and spared them accordingly. 2. Because God punished the violator of it long after. (2 Samuel xxi, 1.) 3. Because the other nations hardened their hearts—Joshua xi, 19, 20—which went to say that their destruction was the result of their own obstinacy and wickedness. All these circumstances laid together show that the command of God to destroy the Canaanites was not so *absolute* as some suppose, and should be understood as referring rather to the *political existence of their nations* than to the destruction of their *lives*. (See Deuteronomy xx, 10, 17.)

The Gibeonites possessed four cities: Cephirah, Beerath, Kirjath Jearim, and Gibeon their capital. All these cities were given to Benjamin, except Kirjath Jearim, which fell to Judah. The Gibeonites embraced cordially the Jewish religion, but continued subject to the burdens which Joshua imposed on them, and were faithful to the Israelites. When they were cruelly treated by Saul, their wrong was avenged by David at the command of God. (2 Samuel xxi, 1, 2, 3, 4.) From this time they ceased to form a separate people, or were classed among the *Nethinim*, as *given up* to the public service of the temple. (1 Chronicles ix, 2.) Afterward those of the Canaanites who were subdued and had their lives spared were added to the Gibeonites. We see that—Ezra ii, 58; viii, 20; 1 Kings ix, 20, 21—David, Solomon, and the princes of Judah gave many such to the Lord. These Nethinim being carried captive with Judah and the Levites, returned with Ezra, Zerubbabel, and Nehemiah, from the Babylonian captivity, and continued in the temple in the temple service under the priests and Levites.

Now let us see what ground the case of the Gibeonites gives to support slavery among the Jews. The condition of the Gibeonites under the Israelites will not comport with a state of slavery.

Their service was *voluntary*. It was their own proposition to Joshua to become servants. "We are your servants; therefore now make ye a league with us." Joshua ix, 11. They wished to make a *league* or contract, and become the servants or subjects and allies of the Hebrews; and for this *protection* they were, of course, to pay tribute as a *consideration* for the protection.

They were not slaves, nor even domestic servants in the families of the Hebrews. They still resided in their own cities, cultivated their own fields, tended their flocks and herds, and exercised the functions of a *distinct*, though not fully an independent community. When attacked by the Ammonites they were protected by Joshua. (Joshua x, 6–18.) The whole transaction was a formal recognition of the Gibeonites as a distinct people. There is no intimation that they served families or individuals of the Israelites, but only "the house of God," or the tabernacle. This service was their *national tribute* to the Israelites for the privilege of residence and protection under their government. The services seem to have been performed by rotation, and each class served a few weeks at a time. No service was required of females. The only service imposed on them was the menial service of the temple. This service was performed by a small number of their males, drafted from time to time for that purpose. Hence, only a small part of them could be employed at once on ordinary occasions. Bishop Patrick thinks that they "came up with the priests and Levites, *in their courses*, to serve at the altar."

There is clear evidence from the history, that the Gibeonites were not reduced to slavery properly so called. They were not held as property. They were not bought and sold, nor does it appear that the servitude descended indefinitely to their children; for in time they became incorporated with the Jews. No argument can be derived from this that the Hebrews designed to perpetuate the institution of slavery.

4. In the days of Solomon, or about one thousand years before Christ, he imposed a service or tribute of labor on the remnants of the Canaanites who were then in the land. "Upon those did Solomon levy a tribute of bond-service unto this day. But of the children of Israel did Solomon make no bondmen; but they were men of war, and his servants, and his princes, and his captains, and rulers of his chariots, and his horsemen." 1 Kings ix, 21, 22. The descendants of the Amorites, at this time, it is believed, became proselytes to the Jewish religion, like the Gibeonites, as they renounced idolatry. The command to destroy them, in consequence of incurable depravity, did not apply to that generation in the time of Solomon. These Solomon employed in menial services, because they seemed best fitted for such services. But the Hebrews were employed in more honorable pursuits, because they were better qualified to be soldiers, overseers, and rulers than the descendants of the Amorites. But we can see no ground for slavery here. The Hebrews and the descendants of the Canaanites were equally bound to perform their respective parts of service. The Canaanites, as being less qualified, were put to the more laborious and less honorable public duties, while the Jews were put to the most responsible and reputable services. Both were bound to *serve*, but in different sorts of service. At any rate, there are none of the elements of slavery here, such as making property of men; selling them;

breaking up the social relations. Besides, no class of slaves, answering to the enslaved descendants of the Canaanites, were to be found among the Jews. Solomon employed both Hebrews and strangers in the public service of the country; to the one he assigned the more honorable service, to the other the less honorable. The Irish and German laborers, now in this country, without any element of slavery leading to it, perform the less reputable services of the country. The native Americans generally fill the more reputable positions. The descendants of the Amorites were pressed into the public service, for the procuring of materials for building the temple, and were doubtless dismissed as soon as the temple was finished. The phrase, "unto this day," verse 21, proves only that they were held till that part of the book of Kings was composed.

Observe, also, 1. Till this time the descendants of the Amorites were not slaves; and the bond service now pressed on them was only temporary. 2. Slavery was not then in existence. It was prohibited by the law of Moses. Solomon had no slaves of his own. He was, therefore, compelled to call upon the services of freemen, as a species of taxation, to perform public service for the country.

5. An occurrence that happened in the year before Christ 893, will show the spirit of the Jewish people as taught by the prophet Elisha. The King of Syria had invaded the land of Israel with a great army. They were smitten with blindness at the prayer of Elisha, and delivered into the hand of the King of Israel in the midst of the city of Samaria, and there restored to sight. When the King inquired of the prophet whether he would smite them or not, the prophet answered: "Thou shalt not smite them: wouldest thou smite those whom thou hast taken captive with thy sword and with thy

bow? set bread and water before them, that they may eat and drink, and go to their master. And he prepared great provision for them: and when they had eaten and drunk, he sent them away, and they went to their master. So the bands of Syria came no more into the land of Israel." 2 Kings vi, 22, 23. The prophet here presented in this practical way the true spirit of the Hebrew institutions. Had slavery had a hold in the nation, either by law or custom, there certainly would have been pursued a different course toward the captives, as the general custom of heathen nations was to make slaves of those not killed in war. The Jews would not make slaves of strangers.

6. A similar event occurred about the year 761 before Christ. Because Ahaz and the people of Judea sinned against God, they were delivered into the hand of the Syrians, and many of them were made captives. They were also delivered into the hand of the King of Israel, who slew 120,000 valiant men in one day, "because they had forsaken the Lord God of their fathers." The Israelites carried away captive 200,000, and brought them to Samaria. But the prophet Oded protested against this and said: "Because the Lord God of your fathers was wroth with Judah, he hath delivered them into your hand, and ye have slain them in a rage that reacheth up unto heaven. And now ye purpose to keep under the children of Judah and Jerusalem for bondmen and bondwomen unto you: but are there not with you, even with you, sins against the Lord your God? Now hear me therefore, and deliver the captives again, which ye have taken captive of your brethren: for the fierce wrath of the Lord is upon you." 2 Chronicles xxviii, 9–11. To this the Israelites consented at the expostulation of heads of certain tribes, so that they came to the following conclusion; namely: "So the armed men left the captives and the spoil before the princes and all the congregation.

And the men which were expressed by name rose up, and took the captives, and with the spoil clothed all that were naked among them, and arrayed them, and shod them, and gave them to eat and to drink, and anointed them, and carried all the feeble of them upon asses, and brought them to Jericho, the city of palm-trees, to their brethren: then they returned to Samaria." Verses 14, 15.

We can scarcely find a parallel to this in the history of the wars which those nations carried on which were in the practice of slavery. This history settled one important point, that the Mosaic institutions did not allow that any portion of the Hebrews should make slaves of their brethren who might be taken in war. The general law of the world then was, that captives in war were to be enslaved. This settled the question that the Mosaic institutions did not sanction slavery. And when, in any instance, there were any leanings to slavery or oppression among the Jews, it was at variance with the law of Moses.

7. In the year before Christ 712, the prophet Isaiah, in the plainest terms, denounces slavery in the following language: "Is not this the fast that I have chosen? to loose the bonds of wickedness, to undo the heavy burdens, and to let the oppressed go free, and that ye break every yoke?" Isaiah lviii, 6. The meaning of this passage is that they would loose the bonds of *wickedness*, or cease to do wrong. They were to "undo the heavy burdens;" they were to release captives or slaves, as the Scripture phraseology means. "He sent a man before them, even Joseph, who was sold for a servant: whose feet they hurt with fetters: he was laid in iron: until the time that his word came: the word of the Lord tried him. The king sent and loosed him; even the ruler of the people, and let him go free." Psalm cv, 17–20. "The Lord looseth the prisoners." Psalm cxlvi, 7.

The instructions of the prophet were, that the Jews should observe the Mosaic code, so as to set free any that had been enslaved, or had been detained in service beyond the time of contract.

8. We have another historical narrative, pertinent to our subject, which took place before Christ 589, as penned by Jeremiah. "This is the word that came unto Jeremiah from the Lord, after that the king Zedekiah had made a covenant with all the people which were at Jerusalem, to proclaim liberty unto them; that every man should let his man-servant, and every man his maid-servant, being a Hebrew or a Hebrewess, go free; that none should serve himself of them, to wit, of a Jew his brother. Now when all the princes, and all the people which had entered into the covenant, heard that every one should let his man-servant, and every one his maid-servant, go free, that none should serve themselves of them any more, then they obeyed, and let them go. But afterward they turned, and caused the servants and the handmaids, whom they had let go free, to return, and brought them into subjection for servants and for handmaids. Therefore the word of the Lord came to Jeremiah from the Lord, saying, Thus saith the Lord, the God of Israel; I made a covenant with your fathers in the day that I brought them forth out of the land of Egypt, out of the house of bondmen, saying, At the end of seven years, let ye go every man his brother a Hebrew, which hath been sold unto thee; and when he hath served thee six years, thou shalt let him go free from thee; but your fathers hearkened not unto me, neither inclined their ear. And ye were now turned, and had done right in my sight, in proclaiming liberty every man to his neighbor; and ye had made a covenant before me in the house which is called by my name: but ye turned and polluted my name, and caused every man his servant, and every man his

handmaid, whom he had set at liberty at their pleasure, to return, and brought them into subjection, to be unto you for servants and for handmaids. Therefore thus saith the Lord; Ye have not hearkened unto me, in proclaiming liberty, every one to his brother, and every man to his neighbor: behold, I proclaim a liberty for you, saith the Lord, to the sword, to the pestilence, and to the famine; and I will make you to be removed into all the kingdoms of the earth. And I will give the men that have transgressed my covenant, which have not performed the words of the covenant which they had made before me, when they cut the calf in twain, and passed between the parts thereof, the princes of Judah, and the princes of Jerusalem, the eunuchs, and the priests, and all the people of the land, which passed between the parts of the calf; I will even give them into the hand of their enemies, and into the hand of them that seek their life: and their dead bodies shall be for meat unto the fowls of the heaven, and to the beasts of the earth." Jeremiah xxxiv, 8–20.

In the foregoing passage of holy Scripture there is a plain recognition of the Mosaic code respecting Hebrew service which could never legally become perpetual. The Jews are severely censured for breaking that law; yet through the persuasion of the prophet they were induced to observe its precepts and release the servants from the unjust service continued beyond the sixth year. They were threatened with the most severe judgments should they compel the servants to become slaves, by continuing them servants for life. They were to be subject "to the sword, to the pestilence, and to the famine," and to be removed "into all the kingdoms of the earth." The whole shows that the believers were not to be made slaves according to the interpretation and practice which the prophets insisted on under the Mosaic law. There was a conformity between their crime and punishment. As they promised to give liberty to their brethren, the Almighty promised to give *liberty* to the sword, pestilence, and famine to destroy them.

9. There existed among the Jews neither a domestic nor foreign slave-trade, and, therefore, there was no slavery among them, because all slave nations have a slave-trade of some sort or other.

We can find no traces of a *domestic* slave-trade among the Jews from Moses to Christ. There were, we allow, such compacts as were necessary in fixing the terms of service between the different classes of servants and their masters, in reference to the various times and conditions of service. But there were no sales of men *as property* among the Jews, so as to make merchandise of men. There is a total absence of any account of such traffic in the Jewish writings.

Nor was there any foreign slave-trade between the Jews and other nations; although this trade existed in all the nations around them. To facilitate trade Solomon built Tadmor or Palmyra, and Ezion-Geber on the Red Sea. Yet, in every allusion to the trade carried on with these and other nations, there is no allusion to the traffic in slaves. There is mention of gold, silver, ivory, apes, and peacocks; but no allusion to a commerce in slaves. (Compare 1 Kings ix, 26; x, 22; 2 Chronicles ix, 21.)

A part of the commerce of the Syrians consisted in slaves. Yet, though the Jews traded with them, there is no mention of slaves, though other articles of commerce are mentioned. (Ezekiel xxvii, 13, 17; Compare Revelation xviii, 13.)

In the whole history of the Jews, there is no mention of slaves as an article of commerce. There is no mention of them in the goods received. There is no instance of public sale of slaves. We have no mention of either a market-place for slaves, nor of slave-merchants. If slavery existed among the Jews, there must have been some account of the traffic in slaves ; but, as there is an absence of all this, the conclusion is, that the trade did not exist; for slavery could not exist without a slave-trade of some sort.

Indeed, the prophets freely denounced every step in which Hebrew service might degenerate into slavery. This is manifest from the historical passages we have already quoted and considered. The conclusion is, that the Mosaic institutions did not favor slavery, but were inconsistent with it. Hence, slavery altogether ceased out of the land of Palestine.

10. In the period elapsing from the close of the Old Testament canon, till the birth of Christ, there are no declarations to be found in the apocryphal books, or in Josephus, which declare or intimate that slavery existed among the Jews. Hence, our Savior, as his ministry was exercised among the Jews, never came in contact with slavery among them.

CHAPTER IX.

THE ROMAN LAW ON SLAVERY.

1. The origin of slavery in the world may be briefly sketched as follows:

The merchandise of men is said to commence in the days of Nimrod. It was coeval with man, and we read of wars as early as the days of Abraham. The history of Joseph shows that it existed in those days. Egypt seems to have been the first market for the sale of human beings. Homer mentions Cyprus and Egypt as the common market for slaves about the time of the Trojan war, before Christ 1184–1194. (Odyssey, Lib. XVII, 48; and Lib. XXVI.) The Odyssey shows further, that this traffic was practiced in many of the islands of the Ægean Sea. The Iliad informs us that it had taken place among the Grecians on the continent of Europe, who had embarked for the Trojan war. At the end of the seventh book of the Iliad we learn this was the case. Tyre and Sidon were noted for the prosecution of this trade. (Joel iii, 3, 4, 6.) This custom, too, appears to have existed in all countries of the world, previous to the coming of Christ—the land of Judea excepted.

In the most ancient times there are said to have been no slaves in Greece. In after times they became very numerous. At Athens, three hundred and nine years before Christ, the slaves are computed by some authors to have been at four hundred thousand, by others they were reckoned at forty thousand, while the freemen were said to be only twenty-one thousand, and the metics, or sojourners, ten thousand. The other Grecian states abounded in slaves.

Among the Romans slavery abounded. Gibbon—Fall and Decline, Chapter I—estimates the population of Rome, in the days of Claudius, at one hundred and twenty millions. One half of these, according to Gibbon, or two-thirds, according to Robertson, were slaves. They were found in every province of the empire, Judea excepted. At the coming of Christ, and when the New Testament was written, the sway of Rome extended over the civilized world; and with it its laws, and those on slavery as well as other laws.

2. On this account we will, so far as our limits will allow, present the Roman code on slavery; as this, more than any other source of information, will give us an accurate view of the subject, especially as it is connected with the Church. The Justinian law consists of four principal parts—the *Institutes*, the *Digest* or *Pandects*, the *Code*, and the *Novellæ*. The Institutes are an abridged digest of the whole. To the Justinian law is also added the *Imperial Constitutions*, and other additions of subsequent times.

The Emperor Justinian, in the year of Christ 528, ordered the compilation, which was performed and published the year following, by Tribonian, and other eminent lawyers. As the Institutes are a pretty full outline of Roman law, we make our extracts from them, and refer to the Pandects, Codex, and other parts of the civil law, when necessary. We give all we can find in the Institutes on slavery, so that our selections are full, if not complete; for it would require an unnecessary minuteness to enter into all the nice legal details of the Pandects, Code, Novellæ, etc.

It is, however, proper to state, that the Institutes give quite too favorable a view of the legal ameliorations of the slave system, as it existed in the days of Christ and his apostles. The reason is, that the Institutes construe the Christian elements diffused into the old law, as they were introduced by Constantine, Justinian, and other Christian Emperors. For instance, the law empowering the ministers of religion to emancipate, by *vindicta*, at the churches, is a Christian element, and did not exist in the days of Christ. This is a mere specimen, as will be seen in our chapter on the effect of Christianity on Roman civil law.

1. LEGAL DEFINITIONS.

"Justice is the constant and perpetual disposition to render every man his due." (Institutes, Lib. I, Tit. 1.)

"Jurisprudence is the knowledge of things divine and human; the science of what is just and unjust." (Institutes, Lib. I, Tit. 1, Sec. 1.)

"The precepts of the law are, to live honestly, to hurt no one, to give every one his due." (Institutes, Lib. I, Tit. 1, Sec. 3.)

"The law of nature is a law not only to man, but, likewise, to all other animals, whether produced on the earth, in the air, or in the waters. From hence proceeds that conjunction of male and female, which we denominate matrimony; hence the procreation and education of children." (Institutes, Lib. I, Tit. 2.)

"Civil law is distinguished from the law of nations, because every community governed by laws uses partly its own, and partly the laws which are common to all mankind. The law which a people enacts for its own government, is called the civil law of that people. But that law which natural reason appoints for mankind, is called the law of nations, because all nations make use of it." (Institutes, Lib. I, Tit. 2, Sec. 1.)

"The law of nations is common to all mankind, and

all nations have enacted some laws, as occasion and necessity required; for wars arose, and the consequences were captivity and slavery; both of which are contrary to the law of nature; for by that law all men are born free." (Institutes, Lib. I, Tit. 2, Sec. 2.)

"The laws of nature, observed by all nations, inasmuch as they are the appointment of a certain divine providence, remain fixed and immutable. But the laws which every city has enacted for itself, suffer frequent changes, either by tacit consent of the people, or by some subsequent law." (Institutes, Lib. I, Tit. 2, Sec. 11.)

2. OF THE RIGHT OF PERSONS.

"The first general division of persons, in respect to their rights, is into freemen and slaves." (Institutes, Lib. I, Tit. 3. See Digest, Lib. I, Tit. 5.)

"Freedom, or liberty, from which we are denominated free, is the natural power of acting as we please, unless prevented by force or by the law." (Institutes, I, 3, 1.)

"Slavery is when one man is subject to the dominion of another, according to the law of nations, though contrary to natural rights." (Institutes, I, 3, 2.)

"Slaves are denominated *servi*, from the practice of our generals to sell their captives, and thus *preserve*—*servare*—and not slay them. Slaves are also called *mancipia*, in that they are taken from the enemy, by hand." (*Manucapti.*) (Institutes, I, 3, 3.)

"Slaves are born such, or become so. They are born such, or of bondwomen. They become so either by the law of nations, that is, by captivity, or by the civil law, as when a free person, above the age of twenty, suffers himself to be sold, for the sake of sharing the price given for him." (Institutes, I, 3, 4.)

"There is no difference in the condition of slaves; but among free persons there are many; thus some are *ingenui*, or freemen, others, *libertini*, or freed-men." (Institutes, I, 3, 5.)

3. OF INGENUI, OR FREEMEN.

"A freeman is one who is born free, by being born in matrimony, of parents who are both free, or both freed; or of parents, one free, the other freed. But one born of a free mother, although the father be a slave, or unknown, is free, notwithstanding he was conceived discreditably. And if the mother is free at the time of the birth, although a bondwoman when she conceived, the infant will be free." (Institutes, I, 4. Cod., Lib. VII, Tit. 14. *De ingenuis manumissis.*)

4. OF LIBERTINI, OR FREED-MEN—MANUMISSION.

"Freed-men are those who have been manumitted from just slavery. Manumission—*manu-datio*—implies the giving of liberty; for whosoever is in servitude, is subject to the hand and power of another; but whosoever is manumitted is free from both."

"Manumission took its rise from the law of nations; for all men, by the law of nature, are born free; nor was manumission heard of while slavery was unknown. But when slavery, under sanction of the law of nations, invaded liberty, the benefit of manumission became then a consequence; for all men, at first, were denominated by one common appellation, till, by the law of nations, they began to be divided into three classes, namely, into *liberi*, or *freemen*, *servi*, or *slaves*, and *libertini*, or *freed-men*, who have ceased to be slaves." (Institutes, Lib. I, Tit. 5.)

5. IN WHAT MODES AND TIMES THEY ARE MANUMITTED.

"Manumission is effected by various ways; either in the face of the Church, according to the imperial constitutions, or by the *vindicta*, or in the presence of friends, or by letter, or by testament, or by any other last will. Liberty may also be conferred upon a slave by divers other methods, some of which were introduced by former laws, and others by our own." (Institutes, Lib. I, Tit. 5, Sec. 1.)

"Slaves may be manumitted by their masters at any time, even on the way, as while the prætor, the governor of a province, or the proconsul is going to the bath or the theater." (Institutes, I, 5, 2.)

On manumission, see C., Lib. VII, Tit. 15. *Communia de manumissionibus.*

6. THE DISTINCTIONS BETWEEN FREED-MEN ANNULLED.

"Freed-men were formerly distinguished by a threefold division. Those who were manumitted, sometimes obtained the greater liberty, and became *Roman* citizens; sometimes only the lesser, and became *Latins*, under the law *Junia Narbonia;* and sometimes only the inferior liberty, and became *Dedititii*, by the law *Ælia Sentia.* But the condition of the Dedititii, differing but little from slavery, has been long disused; neither has the name of *Latins* been frequent. Our piety, therefore, leading us to reduce all things into a better state, we have amended our laws by two constitutions, and re-established the ancient usage; for, anciently, liberty was simple and undivided; that is, it was conferred upon the slave as his manumittor possessed it; admitting this single difference, that the person manumitted became only a freed-man, although his manumittor was a freeman. We have abolished the Dedititii by a constitution published among our decisions, by which, at the instance of *Tribonian*, our Quæstor, we have suppressed all disputes concerning the ancient law. We have, also, at his suggestion, altered the condition of the Latins, and corrected the laws which related to them, by another constitution, conspicuous among the imperial sanctions, and we have made all the freed-men as general citizens of Rome, regarding neither the age of the manumitted, nor of the manumittor, nor the ancient forms of manumission. We have, also, introduced many new methods, by which slaves may become *Roman citizens;* the only liberty that can now be conferred." (Institutes, I, 5, 3.)

7. WHO CAN NOT MANUMIT, AND FOR WHAT CAUSES.

(Institutes, Lib. I, Tit. 6. Compare and consult D., XL, Tit. 9, *Qui et a quibus;* C., VII, Tit. 11, *Qui manumittere non possunt.*)

THE FIRST CHAPTER OF THE ÆLIAN LAW, CONCERNING MANUMITTING IN FRAUD OF CREDITORS.

"Every master may not manumit by will; for, if done with intent to defraud his creditors, it is void; the law *Ælia Sentia* restraining this liberty."

CONCERNING A SLAVE INVESTED WITH LIBERTY.

"Section 1. A master who is insolvent, may appoint a slave to be his heir with liberty, that thus the slave may obtain his freedom, and become the only and necessary heir of the testator, provided no other person is also heir by the same testament; and this may happen, either because no other person was instituted heir, or because the person so instituted is unwilling to act. This privilege of masters was, for wise reasons, established by the law *Ælia Sentia.* For it became necessary to provide, that indigent men, to whom no man would be a voluntary heir, might have a slave for a necessary heir, to satisfy creditors; or that the creditors should sell the hereditary effects in the name of the slave, lest the deceased should suffer ignominy."

OF A SLAVE MADE AN HEIR WITHOUT LIBERTY.

"Section 2. A slave also becomes free by being instituted an heir, although his freedom be not mentioned; for our constitution respects not only the insolvent master, but, by a new act of humanity, it extends generally; so that the institution of an heir implies the grant of liberty. For it is highly improbable, that a testator, although he has omitted to mention liberty in his will, could mean that the person instituted should remain a slave, and himself be destitute of an heir."

8. WHAT IS MANUMISSION IN FRAUD OF CREDITORS.

"Section 3. Manumission is in fraud of creditors, if the master is insolvent when he manumits, or become so by manumitting. It is, however, the prevailing opinion, that liberty, when granted, is not impeached unless the manumittor meant to defraud, although his goods are insufficient for the payment of his creditors; for men frequently hope better than their circumstances really are. We, therefore, understand liberty to be then only impeded, when creditors are doubly defrauded, by the intention of the manumittor, and in reality.

"Section 4. By the same law, *Ælia Sentia*, a master, under the age of twenty years, can not manumit unless for some good reason to be approved by a council, and then by the *vindicta*."

9. WHAT ARE JUST CAUSES FOR MANUMISSION.

"Section 5. Just reasons for manumission, are, that the person to be manumitted is father or mother to the manumittor, his son or daughter, his brother or sister, his preceptor, his nurse, his foster-child, or his foster-brother, or to constitute him his proctor, or his bondwoman, with an intent to marry her, provided the marriage is performed within six months. But a slave who is to be constituted proctor, can not be manumitted for that purpose, if under seventeen."

A REASON ONCE ADMITTED.

"Section 6. A reason once admitted in favor of liberty, be it true or false, can not be recalled."

10. ABROGATION OF THE LAST CHAPTER OF THE LAW ÆLIA SENTIA.

"Section 7. When certain bounds were prescribed by the law *Ælia Sentia*, to all minors under twenty, with regard to manumission, it was observed that any person who had completed fourteen years might make a testament institute an heir, and bequeath legacies, and yet that no person under twenty could confer liberty, which was not longer to be tolerated; for, can any just cause be assigned why a man permitted to dispose of all his effects by testament, should be debarred from enfranchising his slaves? But liberty being of inestimable value, and our ancient laws prohibiting any person to make a grant of it, who is under twenty years of age: we, therefore, make choice of a middle way, and permit all who have attained their eighteenth year to confer liberty by testament. For since, by former practice, persons at eighteen years of age were permitted to plead for their clients, there is no reason why the same stability of judgment which qualifies them to assist others should not enable them to be of service to themselves also, by having the liberty of enfranchising their own slaves." (Institutes, Lib. I, Tit. 6. Consult D., XL, Tit. 9; and C., VII, Tit. 11.)

11. THE POWER OF MASTERS OVER SLAVES.

"All slaves are in the power of their masters, a power derived from the law of nations; for it is observable among all nations, that masters had the power of life and death over their slaves, and that whatever the slave acquires is acquired by the master." (Institutes, Lib. I, Tit. 8, L. 1.)

"All our subjects are now forbidden to inflict any extraordinary punishment upon their slaves, without legal cause. For, by a constitution of *Antoninus*, whoever causelessly kills his own slave, is to be punished equally as if he had killed the slave of another. The too great severity of masters is also restrained by another constitution of *Antoninus*, who, being consulted by certain governors of provinces concerning slaves, who take sanctuary in temples, or at the statues of the emperors, *ordained*, that, if the severity of masters should appear excessive, they might be compelled to make sale of their slaves on equitable terms, so that the masters might receive the value, and properly, inasmuch as it is for the public good that no one should be permitted to misuse even his own property." (Institutes, I, 8, 2. See, also, on this, Dig., I, Tit. 6.)

12. THE POWER OF PARENTS OVER CHILDREN.

"Our children, begotten in lawful wedlock, are under our power.

"Section 1. Matrimony is a connection between a man and woman, implying a mutual and exclusive cohabitation during life.

"Section 2. The power which we have over our children is peculiar to the citizens of Rome; for no other people have the same power over their children which we have over ours.

"Section 3. The child of you and your wife is under your power. The issue of your son and his wife, that is, your grandsons or granddaughters, are equally so; so are your great grandchildren, etc. But children born of a daughter are not in your power, but in the power of their father or grandfather." (Institutes, Lib. I, Tit. 9. See, also, C., VIII, Tit. 47.)

"Illegitimate children, or those born out of wedlock, are looked upon as having no father: they are, therefore, called, in Latin, *spurii*, and in Greek απατορες, *apatores*; that is, without a father. They are, therefore, not under the power of the father." (Institutes, Lib. I, Tit. 10, L. 12.)

But natural children become legitimate whenever the parents become married, and they are then under the power of the father. (L. 13.)

Adopted children are also under the power of the father. (Institutes, I, 11.)

"The following answer of Cato was approved by the ancient lawyers, namely, that slaves adopted by their masters obtain freedom by the adoption. Thus instructed, we have ordained, that a slave whom any master nominates to be his son, in the presence of a magistrate, becomes free by such nomination, although it does not confer on him any filial right." (Institutes, I, 11, 12.)

"A man may, by testament, assign his own slave to be a tutor with liberty. But note, that, if a slave be appointed tutor by testament, without mentioning liberty, he seems tacitly to be enfranchised, and is thus legally constituted a tutor." (Institutes, I, 14, 1.)

"Although civil policy may extinguish civil rights, yet over natural rights it has no such power." (Institutes, I, 15, 3.)

13. OF DIMINUTION.

"Diminution is the change of a man's former condition, and this is threefold—the greater, the less, and the least." (Institutes, Lib. I, Tit. 16.)

"The greater diminution is, when a man loses both the right of a citizen and his liberty, as they do who, by rigor of their sentence, become the slaves of punishment; and freed-men, who are condemned to slavery for ingratitude to their patrons; and all such who suffer themselves to be sold, to share the price." (Institutes, I, 16, 1.)

"The manumission of a slave produces no change of state in him, because he had no state, or civil capacity." (Institutes, I, 16, 4.)

"By the greater diminution, as by slavery, the right of cognation is wholly destroyed, even so as not to be recovered by manumission." (Institutes, I, 16, Sec. 6.)

"Patrons and their children shall succeed to the inheritance of their freed-men, or freed-women, who die intestate." (Institutes, I, Tit. 17.)

CHILDREN INHERIT THE SLAVES OF THEIR PARENTS.

"The condition of a slave is not altered at the death of his master; for he then becomes a slave to the children of the deceased." (Institutes, Lib. I, Tit. 19.)

"When a tutor under the greater diminution of state loses his liberty and his citizenship, his tutelage is extinguished." (Institutes, Lib. I, Tit. 22, Sec. 4.)

"Males arrived at puberty, and females marriageable, do, nevertheless, receive curators till they have completed their twenty-fifth year; for they are not yet of an age to take proper care of their own affairs." (Institutes, I, Tit. 23.)

"What we take from our enemies in war, becomes instantly our own by the law of nations; so that freemen may be brought into a state of slavery by capture; but, if they afterward escape, and return to their own people, they obtain again their former state." (Institutes, II, Tit. 1, Sec. 17.)

14. WHAT ARE FRUITS.

"Among the produce of animals, we not only reckon milk, skins, and wool, but also their young; and, therefore, lambs, kids, calves, colts, and pigs appertain by natural right to the usufructuary; but the offspring of a female slave can not be thus considered, but belongs to the proprietor of such slave; for it seemed absurd, that man should be enumerated among the articles of produce, seeing that for his use nature hath furnished all kinds of produce." (Institutes, II, Tit. 1, Sec. 37.)

"Things corporeal are tangible; as lands, slaves, vestments, gold, silver, and others innumerable." (Institutes, II, Tit. 2.)

"The *usufruct* not only of lands and houses is grantable, but also of slaves, cattle, and other things, except those which are consumed by use." (Institutes, II, Tit. 4, Sec. 2.)

WHAT MAY NOT GIVE THE RIGHT OF POSSESSION.

"No length of time will be sufficient to found a prescription; as when a man holds a free person, a thing sacred or religious, or a fugitive slave." (Institutes, Lib. II, Tit. 6, Sec. 1.)

"No prescription lies for things that have been stolen, or seized by violence, although they have been possessed *bona fide*, during the length of time required by our constitution; for prescription to things stolen is prohibited by a law of the twelve tables, and by the law of *Atilia;* and the laws of *Julia* and *Plantia* forbid a prescription to things seized by violence. Whosoever hath knowingly sold or transferred the goods of another, upon whatever consideration, is guilty of theft." (Institutes, II, Tit. 6, Sec. 2.)

15. SLAVES CAN HAVE NO PROPERTY—ALL BELONGS TO THE MASTER.

"Section 3. Whatever your slaves have at any time acquired, whether by delivery, stipulation, donation, bequest, or any other means, is acquired by you; although you may be ignorant of or even averse to the acquisition; for he who is a slave can have no property; and if a slave be made heir, he can not otherwise take upon himself the inheritance than at the command of his master; but if commanded so to do, the inheritance is as fully acquired by the master as if he had been himself made heir, and consequently a legacy left to a slave is acquired by his master. Moreover, masters acquire by their slaves not only the property of things, but also the possession; for whatever is possessed by a slave is deemed to be possessed by his master, who may found a prescription to it by means of his slave." (Institutes, Lib. II, Tit. 9.)

"Section 4. As to slaves of whom you have the usufruct only, it hath seemed right that whatever they earn by means of your goods, or by their own work or labor, appertains to you; but whatever they earn by other means belongs to the proprietor. Therefore, if a slave be made heir, or legatee, or donee, the inheritance, legacy, or gift will not be acquired by the usufructuary master, but for the proprietor." (Id.)

"Section 5. The same rule is observed as to the *bona-fide* possessor of a slave, whether he be a freeman or the slave of another; for the same law prevails respecting a usufructuary master and a *bona-fide* possessor. Therefore, whatever is acquired otherwise than by the two causes above mentioned, either belongs to the person possessed, if he be free, or to the proprietor, if he be a slave. But a *bona-fide* possessor, who hath gained a slave by *usucaption* or prescription—inasmuch as he thus becomes the absolute proprietor—can acquire by means of such slave, by all manner of ways. But a usufructuary master can not prescribe: first, because he can not be strictly said to possess, having only the power of using; and because he knows the slave belongs to another. We nevertheless may acquire not only property, but also possession, by means of slaves whom we possess *bona fide,* or by usufruct, and even by a free person, of whom we have *bona-fide* possession. But in saying this, we adhere to the distinction before explained, and speak of those things only of which a slave may acquire the possession, either through the goods of his master or by his own industry." (Id., Sec. 4.)

16. WHO ARE WITNESSES.

"Those persons are good witnesses who can legally take by testament; but no woman, or minor under puberty, or slave, no person mad, mute, or deaf, no interdicted prodigal, nor any whom the laws have reprobated and rendered intestable, can be admitted a witness to a testament." (Institutes, Lib. II, Tit. 10, Sec. 6.)

17. OF MAKING WILLS—PECULIUM.

"The right of making a will is not granted to all. Persons under the power of others, have not this right; so that, although parents have given permission, this will not enable their children to make a valid will." (Institutes, II, 12.)

THE PECULIUM.

"By the civil law, *pecula,* or estates of those who are under power, are reckoned among the wealth of their parents, in the same manner as the *peculium* of a slave is esteemed the property of his master." (Institutes, II, 1, 2.)

18. OF HEIRS.

"A man may appoint slaves, as well as freemen, to be his heirs by testament, and may nominate the slaves of another as well as his own; yet, according to the opinion of many, no master could formally make his own slaves his heirs without freeing them; but at present, by our Constitution, masters may do this, which we have introduced not for the sake of innovation, but because it seemed most just, and because Paulus, in his commentaries upon *Sabinus* and *Glautius*, affirms that this was also the opinion of *Atilicinas*. We call a slave *proprius servus* if the testator had only a naked property in him, the usufruct being in another. But in a Constitution of the Emperors *Severus* and *Antoninus* there is a case in which a slave was not permitted to be instituted heir by his owner, although his liberty was expressly given to him. The words are, 'It is consonant to right reason that no slave, accused of adultery with his mistress, shall be allowed, before a sentence of acquittal, to be made free by that mistress, who is alleged to be a partner in the crime. Hence, if a mistress institute a slave such to be her heir, it is of no avail.' *Alienus servus* is one of whom the testator has only the usufruct." (Institutes, II, 14.)

"A slave instituted an heir by his master while he is a slave, becomes free at the death of his master, as well as his necessary heir by virtue of the will. But if he be manumitted in the lifetime of his master, he may accept or refuse the inheritance; for he does not become a necessary heir, since he does not obtain both his liberty and the inheritance by virtue of the testament. But if he should be aliened he can not enter upon the inheritance, unless at the command of his new master, who, though his slave, may become the heir of the testator. For a slave aliened can not obtain his liberty, nor take an inheritance to his own use, by virtue of the testament of the master who transferred him, although his freedom was expressly given by such testament; because a master who has aliened his slave seems to have renounced the intention of enfranchising him; and when the slave of another has been appointed heir, but remains in slavery, he can not take the inheritance but by his master's order; and if the slave be aliened in the lifetime of the testator, or even after his death, before he has actually taken the inheritance, he must accept or refuse it at the command of his new master. But if the slave be enfranchised while the testator is alive, or after his death, before he has accepted the heirship, he may enter upon the inheritance or not, at his option." (Institutes, II, Tit. 14, Sec. 1.)

"The slave of another may legally be instituted an heir after the death of his master; for slaves of an inheritance not entered upon may take by testament; for an inheritance not yet entered upon represents the person of the deceased, and not of the future heir. Thus the slave even of a child in the womb may be constituted an heir." (Id., Sec. 2.)

"If the slave of many masters, all capable of taking by testament, is instituted heir by a stranger, he acquires a part of the inheritance for each master, who commanded him to take it, according to the several proportions of property." (Id., Sec. 3.)

THE SUBSTITUTION OF HEIRS.

"A man by will may appoint many degrees of heirs, and in default of all others he may constitute a slave his necessary heir." (Institutes, II, Tit. 15.)

"If a testator constitute the slave of another his heir, supposing him free, and add, *If he does not become my heir, I substitute Mævius in his place*, then, if that *slave* should enter on the inheritance at the command of his master, Mævius, the substitute, would be admitted to a moiety." (Id., Sec. 4.)

DIVISION OF HEIRS—NECESSARY HEIRS.

"A slave, instituted an heir by his master, is a necessary heir; and he is so called because, at the death of the testator, he becomes instantly free, and is compellable to take the heirship; he, therefore, who suspects his circumstances, commonly institutes his slave to be his heir in the first, second, or some other place; so that, if he does not leave a sum equal to his debts, the goods which are seized, sold, or divided among his creditors, may rather seem to be those of his heir than his own. But a slave, in recompense of this inconvenience, is allowed whatever he hath acquired after the death of his patron; for such acquisitions are not to be sold, although the goods of the deceased should ever be so insufficient for the payment of his creditors." (Institutes, II, 19, 1.)

"If a testator bequeath his female slaves and their offspring, although the slaves die, their issue becomes due to the legatee; and so if ordinary slaves are bequeathed together with vicarial; for although the ordinary slaves die, yet the vicarial slaves will pass by virtue of the bequest. But where a slave is bequeathed with his *peculium*, and afterward dies, or is manumitted or aliened, the legacy of the *peculium* becomes extinct. The consequences will be the same if a piece of ground is bequeathed with the instruments of improving it; for if the testator aliens the ground, the legacy of the instruments of husbandry is, of course, extinguished." (Institutes, II, 20, 17.)

19. OF THE PECULIUM.

"When the *peculium* of a slave is bequeathed, it is certain that the increase or decrease of it in the life of the testator becomes the loss of the legatee; and if the *peculium* of a slave be left to him with his liberty, and he increase the *peculium* subsequent to the death of the testator, and before the inheritance is entered upon, it is the opinion of *Julian* that the increase will pass to him as a legatee; for such a legacy does not become due but from the day of the acceptance of the inheritance; but should the *peculium* of a slave be bequeathed to a stranger, an increase, acquired within the period above mentioned, will not pass under the legacy, unless the acquisition were made by means of something appertaining to the *peculium;* for the *peculium* of a slave does not belong to him after he is manumitted by testament, unless expressly given; although if a master in his life-time manumit his slave, his *peculium* will pass to him, of course, if not excepted. And such is the rescript of the Emperors *Severus* and *Antoninus,* who have also declared that when a *peculium* is bequeathed to a slave, it does not seem intended that he should have the right of demanding what he may have expended for the use of the master. The same princes have further declared that a slave seems entitled to his *peculium* if his liberty be left him, on condition that he will bring in his accounts, and supply any deficiency out of the profits of the *peculium.*" (Institutes, II, 20, Sec. 20.)

"A freed-man might formerly, with impunity, omit in his will any mention of his patron; for the law of the twelve tables called the patron to the inheritance only when the freed-man died intestate without proper heirs; but when the freed-man left only an adopted son, it was manifestly injurious that the patron should have no claim." (Institutes, III, 8.)

"The law was therefore amended by the edict of the prætor; for every freed-man who made his testament was commanded so to dispose his effects as to leave a moiety to his patron; and if the testator left nothing, or less than a moiety, then possession of half was given to the patron contrary to the will; and if a freed-man die intestate, leaving an adopted heir, the possession of a half was given to the patron; but disinherited children by no means repelled the patron." (Id., Sec. 1.)

"But afterward the rights of patrons who had wealthy freed-men were enlarged by the Paphian law, which provides that he shall have a man's share out of the effects of his freed-man, whether dying testate or intestate, who hath left a patrimony of a hundred thousand sestertii and fewer than three children; so that, when a freed-man hath left only one son or daughter, a half is due to the patron, as if the deceased had died testate without either son or daughter. But when there are two heirs, male or female, a third part only is due to the patron; and when there are three, the patron is wholly excluded." (Id., Sec. 2.)

"But our Constitution ordained that if a freed-man or freed-woman die possessed of less than one hundred *arvrei*, the patron shall not be entitled to any share in a testate succession. But where a freed-man, or woman, dies intestate and without children, we have reserved the right of patronage entire as it formerly was, according to the law of the twelve tables. But if a freed person die worth more than a hundred *arvrei*, and leave one child or many of either sex or degree as the heirs and possessors of his goods, we have permitted that such child or children shall succeed their parent to the entire exclusion of the patron and his heirs; and if any freed persons die without children and intestate, we have called their patrons or patronesses to their whole inheritances; and if any freed person, worth more than a hundred *arvrei*, hath made a testament, omitting his patron, and left no children or hath disinherited them; or if a mother or maternal grandfather, being freed persons, have omitted to mention their children in their wills, so that such wills can not be proved to be inofficious, then, by virtue of our Constitution, the patron shall succeed, not to a half, as formerly, but to a third part of the estate of the deceased, by possession *contra tabulas;* and, when freed persons leave less than the third part of their effects to their patrons, our Constitution ordains that the deficiency shall be supplied." (Id., Sec. 3.)

The foregoing relates to the more modern freed-men of Rome, who were all Roman citizens ; for previous to Justinian—or A. D. 527—the *Dedititii* and *Latini* never enjoyed any right of succession ; for though they led the lives of freed-men, at death they lost their liberties ; for their possessions, like the goods of slaves, were seized by their manumittor, who possessed them as *peculium* by virtue of the law *Junia Narbona.* But Justinian decreed that all freed-men might become freemen of Rome or Roman citizens. (Id., Sec. 4.)

OF THE ASSIGNMENT OF FREED-MEN.

"Although the goods of freed-men belonging equally to all the children of the patron who are in the same degree, yet it is lawful for a parent to assign a freed-man to any one of his children." (Institutes, III, 9.)

"Freed persons of either sex are assignable, not only to a son or grandson, but to a daughter or granddaughter." (Id., Sec. 1.)

"The power of assigning freed persons is given to him who hath two or more children unemancipated, so that a father may assign a freed-man or freed-woman to children retained under their power ; hence, if a father would assign a freed-man to his son, and afterward emancipate that son, the assignment would be good." (Id., Sec. 2.)

20. A NEW SPECIES OF SUCCESSION.

"A new species of succession hath taken its rise from the Constitution of *Marcus Aurelius;* for if those slaves to whom freedom hath been bequeathed are desirous, for the sake of obtaining it, that the inheritance which hath not been accepted by the written heir, should be adjudged for their benefit, they shall obtain their request." (Institutes, III, 13.)

By the rescript of the Emperor Marcus to Pompilius, Rufus declares, respecting Virginius Valcus, who by will bequeathed to certain persons their freedom, it was enacted,

"All those to whom freedom was directly given shall then become free, as if the inheritance had been entered upon by the written heirs; but those whom the heir was ordered to manumit shall obtain their freedom from the testator only. . . . And lest the use and emolument of this our rescript should be frustrated by any means, be it known to the officers of our revenue that whenever an exchequer lays claim to the estate of a deceased person, the cause of liberty is to be preferred to any pecuniary advantage; and the estate shall be so seized as to preserve the freedom of those who could otherwise have obtained it, and this in as full a manner as if the inheritance had been entered upon the testamentary heir." (Id., Sec. 1.)

"This rescript is introduced in favor of liberty, and also for the benefit of deceased persons, lest their effects should be seized and sold by their creditors; for it is certain that, when goods are adjudged to a particular man for the preservation of liberty, a sale by creditors can never take place; for he to whom the goods are adjudged is the protector of the deceased, and must be a person who can give security to the creditors." (Id., Sec. 2.)

"This rescript takes place whenever freedom is conferred by testament. . . . If a master die testate, and by codicil bequeath freedom, the rescript shall be in force." (Id., Sec. 3.)

"Freedom once obtained shall not afterward be revoked." (Id., Sec. 5.)

"This Constitution was made for the protection of liberty; and, therefore, when freedom is not given the Constitution has no effect." (Id., Sec. 6.)

21. THE DECREE MIRABILIS.

"If a free woman had debased herself by cohabiting with a slave, she lost her freedom by the *Claudian* decree, and, together with her freedom, her estate and substance. But this was, in our opinion, unworthy of our reign, and ought to be expunged; hence, we have not permitted it to be inserted with the digests." (Institutes, Lib. III, Tit. 13.)

22. OF A SLAVE HELD IN COMMON.

"If a slave, who is in common to several masters, stipulate, he acquires a share of each master, according to the proportion which each has in the property of him. But if such slave should stipulate at the command of any particular master, or in his name, the thing stipulated will be acquired solely for that master." (Institutes, III, 18, 3.)

"A freeman may become a slave." "*Ex libero servus fieri potest.*" (Institutes, III, 20, Sec. 2.)

"A slave is incapable not only of entering into an obligation with his master, but of binding himself to any other person." (Id., Sec. 6.)

"A promise made for a bad purpose, such as to commit murder or sacrilege, is not binding." (Institutes, III, 20, Sec. 23. See, also, Cod., VIII, Tit. 39.)

"A slave, a piece of ground, or a relic, can be paid as the price of a thing." (Institutes, III, 24, 2.)

23. OF RUNAWAY OR STOLEN SLAVES.

"If a slave who is sold should run away or be stolen, and no fraud or negligence can be imputed to the seller, it must be inquired whether the seller undertook the safe custody of the slave till delivery should be made; if he did, he is answerable; if not, he is secure." (Institutes, III, 24, 3.)

"Whoever knowingly purchases a sacred, religious, or public place, such as a forum or court of justice, it is void. But if he purchased them as profane or private, being imposed upon by the seller, then such purchaser, not being able to obtain possession, may have an action *ex empto* against the seller, and recover damage for the deceit. The law is the same if any person should mistakingly buy a freeman instead of a slave." (Id., Sec. 5.)

"Species of commerce, as that of buying and selling slaves, oil, wine, or corn." (Institutes, III, 26. See, also, Dig., XVII, Tit. 2; and Cod., Lib. IV, Tit. 37.)

24. OBLIGATIONS FROM THOSE UNDER OUR POWER, AS SLAVES OR CHILDREN.

"Whatever is acquired by our slaves is wholly our own; but what is acquired by children under our power, by means of their contracts, must be divided according to our Constitution, which gives to the father the usufruct, but reserves the property to the son." (Institutes, III, 29.)

"It is certain that a slave, who is in common between two or more, acquires for his masters in proportion to their property in him, unless he stipulate or receive in the name of them only; as, *Do you promise to give such a thing to Titius, my master?* for although it was a doubt in times past whether a slave, when commanded, could stipulate for one of his masters, yet it is now settled by our decision that a slave may acquire for him only who hath ordered the stipulation." (Id., Sec. 3.)

25. DEFINITION OF THEFT.

"Theft is the taking, using, or possessing any thing by fraud for the sake of gain; and this is prohibited by the law of nature." (Institutes, IV, 1, 1. See, also, Dig., XLVII, Tit. 2; Cod., Lib. VI, Tit. 2.)

"A theft can never be committed unless there appear to have been an intention of stealing." (Id., Sec. 7.)

"The words of the law, *Aquilia, let him who kills a slave or beast of another forfeit the greatest price which either could have been sold for that year,* mean this: If *Titius* accidentally kill a slave, who was then lame, or wanted a limb, or an eye, but had been within the space of a year perfect in all its parts, and valuable, then *Titius* shall be liable, not merely to his value on that day, but to his highest value at any time within a year preceding his death." (Institutes, IV, 3, 9.)

"It hath prevailed by construction, though not by the express word of the law, that not only the value of the slave is to be computed, as we have already mentioned, but that an estimation must be made of whatever further damage is occasioned by his death." (Id., Sec. 10.)

"The master of a slave who is killed may bring a civil action of damages founded on the law *Aquilia,* and at the same time prosecute the offender for a capital crime." (Id., Sec. 11.)

"The first chapter of the law [*Aquilia*] subjects every man to an action who, through design or negligence, kills the slave or beast of another, and that the third part gives a remedy for any other damage, so occasioned." (Id., Sec. 14.)

26. AN INJURY TO A SLAVE.

"An injury is never considered as done to a slave, but through him to the master; not, however, in the same manner as through a wife or child, as when some atrocious injury is done to the slave, manifestly in despite of the master, as if any one should cruelly beat the slave of another; but if a man should give ill language to a slave, or strike him with his fist, the master is entitled to action against him." (Institutes, IV, 4, 3.)

ON THE PECULIUM.

"The prætor hath also given actions *de peculio* against fathers and masters, who, although they were not legally bound by the contracts of their children and slaves, ought, in equality, to be bound to the extent of a peculium, which is, as it were, the patrimony and separate estate of a son, a daughter, a slave." (Institutes, IV, 6, 10.)

27. LIABILITY OF THE MASTER FOR THE SLAVE.

"For any business negotiated by a slave acting under the command of his master, the prætor will give an action against the master for the whole value of the transaction; for, whoever contracts with a slave, is presumed to have done it on a confidence in the master." (Institutes, IV, 7, 1.)

28. NOXAL ACTIONS OF SLAVES.

"Noxal actions are given on account of the offenses of slaves, as when a slave commits a theft or robbery, or does any damage or injury. And, when the master or owner of a slave is condemned upon this account, it is in his option either to pay the estimate of the damage done, or deliver up his slave as a recompense." (Institutes, IV, 8. See, also, Dig., IX, Tit. 4; and Cod., III, Tit. 41.)

"*Noxa* is the slave or the offender. *Noxia* is the offense, whether theft, damage, rapine, injury." (Id., Sec. 1.)

"It is reasonably permitted to the master to deliver up the offending slave, for it would be unjust to make the master liable beyond the body of the slave himself." (Id., Sec. 2.)

"No real actions follow the person; thus, the master is liable while the slave belongs to him. If the slave become subject to a new master, then he becomes liable; but if the slave be manumitted, he may be prosecuted by direct action; and the *noxæ deditio* is extinguished. But an action which was at first direct, may afterward become noxal; for if a freeman, guilty of malfeasance, become a slave and our first book shows in what cases this may happen—then the direct action against the slave is changed into a noxal action against the master." (Id., Sec. 5.)

"Although a slave commit a malfeasance against his master, yet no action can arise, for no obligation can arise between a master and his slave. And, although a slave hath passed out of your power, you can not sue him, neither can a slave who hath been aliened or manumitted, bring any action against his late master." (Id., Sec. 6.)

III. As we have given from the Institutes of Justinian, collated with the other parts of the civil law, all the laws on slavery in the Institutes, we will now present a brief digest of these laws, so that the reader may perceive clearly in connection their different parts, and thus be the better prepared to judge of their character.

1. The first division of persons is into freemen and slaves. (Institutes, I, 3; Dig., I, Tit. 5.) Freedom is defined to be "the natural power of acting as we please, unless prevented by force or by law." (Institutes, I,

3, 1.) Among free persons there are many differences, such as *ingenui, liberti,* and *libertini;* but among slaves there is none, as they are all reduced to the lowest level. (Institutes, I, 3, 5.) A freeman is one born of free parents. But if the mother be free, and the father a slave, the child is free. (Institutes, I, 4; Cod., VII, 14.)

2. Justinian thus defines: "Slavery is when one man is subject to the dominion of another, according to the law of nations, though contrary to natural right." (Institutes, I, 3, 2.)

The following is a condensed view of the state of slavery in Rome, as drawn by Taylor: (Elem, Civ. Law, 429, from the Roman code; Dig., Lib. L, Tit. 17, Law 32 and 209.)

"Slaves were held *pro nullis, pro mortuis, pro quadrupedibus;* nay, they were in a much worse state than any cattle whatsoever. They had no head in the state—no name, title, or register; they were not capable of being injured, nor could they take by purchase or descent; they had no heirs, and, therefore, could make no will, exclusive of what was called their *peculium;* whatever they acquired was their master's; they could not plead, nor be pleaded for, but were excluded from all civil affairs whatever; they could not claim the indulgence of absence, *reipublicæ causa;* they were not entitled to the rights and considerations of matrimony, and, therefore, had no relief in case of adultery; nor were they proper objects of cognation or affinity, but of quasi-cognation only; they could be sold, transferred, or pawned as goods or personal estate, for goods they were, and as such they were esteemed; they might be tortured for evidence, and punished at the discretion of their lord, or even put to death by his authority." The quotations we have given from the civil law sustain this picture of it drawn by Dr. Taylor.

3. As we have given the proper definition of slavery, and the picture of it as drawn from the Roman law, let us now notice the various ways by which men became slaves.

(1.) *By war.* Captives taken in war were sold. (Institutes, Lib. I, Tit. 3, L. 3. Also, Institutes, I, Tit. 23.) They were sold as belonging to the treasury, or distributed among the soldiers by lot. In reference to the practice of selling prisoners with a crown on their heads, we find the expression *sub corona venire, vendere.* (Gall., VII, 4; Liv., V, 22; Cos. Bell, Gall., III, 16.) "After the fall of the Samnites, thirty-six thousand captives were sold as slaves, for two millions, thirty-three thousand pieces of brass. Lucretius, in the Volscian war, in one town, took four thousand prisoners. The Romans in the first Punic war took twenty thousand prisoners. Augustus having taken the Salassi, sold, as slaves, thirty-six thousand, of whom eight thousand were capable of bearing arms. Cæsar, in the Gallic wars, took more than four hundred thousand prisoners."

(2.) *By kidnapping and commerce.* The slave-trade began as early as the days of Joseph. Among the Egyptians, Cyrenians, and Carthaginians, the slave-trade flourished. They were chiefly drawn from the interior, where kidnapping was carried on as now. The Grecian Isles were leaders in this course, by a regular business of commerce and piracy united, depending greatly on kidnapping as supplying the resources.

(3.) *Some were born slaves.* They were born such of bond-women. (Institutes, I, 3, 5.) It became a maxim of common law, that the child follows the condition of the mother—*Partus sequitur ventrem.*

(4.) *By selling themselves.* Free-born citizens sometimes sold themselves for the sake of sharing the price. (Institutes, I, 3, 4.) This was *permitted* by a law of Claudius, about A. D. 32, though manifestly contrary to the general rule, that no man can change his condition by his own authority. (Dig., XL, Tit. 12, Law 37.) The person selling himself was required, 1. To be at least twenty years of age. (Dig., XL, 12, 7.) 2. With a certain knowledge of his birth and condition. (Dig., XL, Tit. 14; and Dig., XL, 12, 14.) 3. The purchaser must act *bona fide*. (Ibid., Laws 7, 16.) 4. The price was completely at his disposal. (Dig., XL, Tit. 12, L. 1 and 5.) The Emperor Leo VI, Philesophus, between A. D. 886 and 908, the duration of his reign, abrogated this law of Claudius by his Novel. 59, and the reasons for the abrogation are that the law should be, in the place of a father, to protect, and the man is to be considered as insane who would change freedom for slavery, and such an act is, therefore, null and void. See the Constitution of Leo, in the 16th chapter, on the effects of Christianity on the Roman civil law.

(5.) Some, from being free, became slaves by the operation of certain laws. "A freeman may become a slave." (Institutes, III, 20, 2.)

Thieves were made slaves according to the twelve tables. "If the robbery be committed by day, and if the robber be taken in the act, let him be beaten with rods, and become the slave of him whom he robbed." (Table II, Law 2.)

A free woman who cohabited with a slave might be reduced to the same condition with the slave.

Under the empire the rule became established that persons condemned to death, to the mines, and to fight with wild beasts, lost their freedom, and their property was confiscated, so that they could make no will. (Dig., Lib. XXVIII, Tit. 1, Sec. 8.) But this was not the earlier law.

By a constitution of Claudius, a freed-man who misconducted himself toward his patron was reduced toward his former state of slavery. (Suet. Claud., 25.) But this was not the law in the time of Nero. (Tac. Arm., XIII, 27.) Criminals of various classes were doomed to servitude, and deprived of citizenship. They were then termed *servi pœnæ*, and during the commonwealth were the property of the Republic. But this mode of enslaving was abolished by Justinian.

(6.) *By diminution.* This is the change of a man's former condition, and is threefold—the greater, the less, and the least. The greater is when the man loses both the right of a citizen and his liberty, such as those who become slaves of punishment, or freed-men for ingratitude to their patrons, and such as suffer themselves to be sold for the sake of sharing the price. The right of cognation is also lost. (Institutes, I, 16, Law 1 and 6.) In many instances freed-men might still be retained in a state of servitude bordering on slavery. (Institutes, II, 19, Sec. 3 and 4.)

4. Slaves are in the power of their masters. The masters had the power of life and death over them, and whatsoever the slave acquired belonged to the master. (Institutes, I, 8, 1.) The slave had no personal rights. In the legal sense he had no *caput*, no legal rights, no legal capacity, so that he could be sold, or bartered, or pawned at the pleasure of his master. Still, positive morality in the social life had its effects in meliorating the condition of the slaves. This—the right of life and death—continued down to a late time, or to the end of the Republic. This power was gradually limited by the *Lex Petronia*, which forbade slaves to be arbitrarily punished, without the decision of a judge. By a constitution of Antoninus whoever carelessly killed his slave was punished as if he killed the slave of another. Justinian laid further restrictions on cruel treatment. (Institutes, I, 8, 2; Dig., I, 6.) A constitution of Claudius enacted, that if a man exposed

his infirm slaves, they should become free; and the constitution also declared that, if they were put to death, the act should be murder. (Suet, Claud., 25.) It was also enacted by Constantine, A. D. 334—Cod., III, Tit. 38, L. 11—that in sales of division of property, slaves, such as husband and wife, parents and children, brothers and sisters, should not be separated. This was a Christian element, unknown to the real civil code of heathen Rome.

5. Slaves can have no property. Whatever they have at any time acquired, by delivery, stipulation, donation, bequest, or by any other means, belongs to the master. (Inst., II, Tit. 9, L. 3.) The slaves, however, possessed as their private property the *peculium*, such as they acquired independently of the service they rendered to their masters. Still, even this was mostly under the control of their masters, and it could be seized by them as a matter of right, though under some restrictions, more by custom, however, than by law. (Institutes, II, 12; also II, Tit. 20, Sec. 2; and III, Tit. 29.)

6. A slave can make no contracts. The law says, "A stipulation is also void if made with one who is under your power, or if he stipulate with you; for a slave is incapable not only of entering into an obligation with his master, but of binding himself to any other person." (Institutes, III, Tit. 20, Sec. 6.)

7. Slaves had no *connubium*, or *marriage*. Their union with a person of their own rank was called *contubernium*. This name was also applied to other cases of unlawful connection. (Cod., II, 21, 4; Cod., V, 5, 3; Cod., V, 5, 9; Cod., VI, 59, 9.) Hence, there was no process for adultery in favor of a slave. (Cod., IX, 9, 23; Dig., XLVIII, 5, 6.) But though civil forms might be disregarded among slaves, the laws of nature as to incestuous commerce were held in full force, as it is said, "For although civil policy extinguish civil rights, yet over

natural rights it has no such power." (Institutes, I, 15, 3. See, also, Dig., XXIII, Tit. 2, L. 14, Sec. 2.)

Concubinage is fully described in the last title of Digest XXV. It was entered into before witnesses, otherwise it became prostitution. (Dig., XXV, 7, 3.) The parties might dissolve the contract and cohabitation at pleasure. (Dig., XXV, 7, 1.) It did not admit of adultery. (Dig., XXV, 7, 3.) As marriages were discouraged between officers of state in the provinces and the female inhabitants, they were permitted to take concubines in the provinces. (Dig., XXV, L. 5; Dig., XXIII, 2, 38 and 57.) It was regulated by Constantine—Cod., V, 26—and Justinian. (Nov., 18, 74 and 89.)

The following from Ulpiran, collated with the notes of Gothofredus Tit. 5, *de his qui in potestate sunt*—will give the exact view of marriage, according to Roman law: "Children born of lawful matrimony are in the power of their parents. It is a law of matrimony, if among those who contract the nuptials there is a marriage—*connubium*—and the male and female have the power, and each consent, if they are in their own power, or their parents, if in the power of parents. Marriage—*connubium*—is the power of lawfully taking a wife. Roman citizens can contract marriage with Roman citizens, and with Latins or strangers, if it is granted. With slaves there is no marriage—*connubium*." On the foregoing Gothofredus remarks, confirming his notes with citations from various parts of the civil law: "What is marriage—*connubium?* It is this: The male ought to be of age, the female marriageable, or more than twelve years of age. Three things are required in matrimony: First, that those who contract are Roman citizens; that they are of due age; that there is a lawful consent, either by themselves, if they have the right, or by the consent of their parents."

8. Slaves are transmitted by inheritance from parents to children, like other property. (Institutes, I, Tit. 19.)

9. A slave can not be a witness legally. (Institutes, II, Tit. 10, Sec. 6; Nov. Just., 90, C. 6; Leonis Const. 49.) But in those cases in which no other witness can be had, the testimony of a slave can be admitted—Dig., XXII, 7; Cod., IV, 20—under certain restrictions. The reason for refusing the testimony was that they could not act independently, because they were slaves.

10. A runaway slave—*fugitivus*—could not be lawfully received or harbored; for to conceal him was *furtum*—theft. The master was entitled to pursue him wherever he pleased, and it was the duty of all authorities to give him aid in recovering slaves. The rights of the master were in no wise affected by his running away. (Institutes, III, 13, 3; Dig., XI, Tit. 4, *De Fugitivis.*) He that concealed him was, by law, pronounced and treated as *fur*, or thief. *Is, qui fugitivum celavit, fur est.* The secreter of a fugitive is liable to death also. (Cod., IX, 20, 7.)

11. An injury is never considered as done to a slave, but through him to the master—Institutes, IV, 4, 3—and the master alone can seek and obtain redress.

12. The state of slavery among the Romans was terminated by manumission. It was also terminated by various positive enactments, either by way of reward to the slave or punishment to the master. The *Senatus Consultum Silanianum* is an example of the former; and various subsequent constitutions gave freedom to slaves who discovered the perpetrators of certain crimes. (Cod. Theod., Tit. 21, C. 2.) After the establishment of Christianity, liberty, under certain restrictions, could be acquired by becoming a monk or clergyman. (Novel., 5, C. 2; and Nov., 123, C. 17, 35.) Every individual master possessed the power of manumitting his slave, if he

22

chose to do so, and this manumission could be executed in several forms.

Manumission was not heard of while slavery was unknown; but when slavery, in violation of the law of nature, was introduced by unjust human laws, and invaded liberty, the benefit of manumission became then a consequence. (Institutes, I, Tit. 5.)

Manumission was effected by various ways. Cicero mentions three principal ones; namely, by the *census*, by *vindicta*, and by *will*. The civil or Roman law enumerates twelve modes of emancipation, without giving a complete list. (Cod., VII, Tit. 6 and 7.) We will select the most usual modes of manumission, as it would be unnecessary for our purpose to trace all the various forms and circumstances, as they would not instruct our readers, seeing there are many legal distinctions which are unintelligible to most readers of our times, without much discussion. We will give the leading forms and the most important circumstances of each, avoiding obscure and intricate legal distinctions.

(1.) By the *census*. A man was said to be free by the census when his name was inserted in the censor's roll, with the approbation of his master at the public census.

(2.) By the *vindicta*. This, perhaps, was the oldest form of manumission. It obtained its name from Vindicius, who made known the conspiracy of the Tarquins and was freed on that account. The form was as follows: The master, placing his hand upon the head of the slave, said in presence of the prætor, "It is my will that this man should be free." The lictor, placing his staff on the head of the slave, said, "I pronounce this man to be free." Then followed congratulations from the master and others to the newly-freed man. (Dig., XL, 2; Cod., VII, 1.)

(3.) By *will* or *testament*. The slave was freed either

directly or by an express clause of the will, and it was left to the heir to effect the emancipation. Sometimes conditions were annexed, as the payment of a certain sum to the heir, serving the heir during youth, or for a number of years, and often, to some degree, during life. (Institutes, I, 5, 1 ; Dig., XL, Tit. 4 ; Cod., VII, Tit. 2.)

(4.) By *epistle.* Slaves were also manumitted by letter, signed by the master in presence of five witnesses, or before his friends, five witnesses being present at the declaration. (Institutes, I, 5, 1.)

(5.) By *adoption.* The ancient lawyers of Rome decided that "slaves" adopted by their masters obtain freedom by their adoption ; and Justinian ordained, in pursuance, that "a slave whom any master nominates to be his son, in the presence of a magistrate, becomes free by such nomination, although it does not confer on him any filial relation." (Institutes, I, 11, 12.)

(6.) By making him *tutor.* A man, by will, may assign his own slave to be a tutor, with liberty ; or if a slave be appointed tutor by testament, without mentioning liberty, he is tacitly enfranchised, and is therefore legally constituted a tutor. (Institutes, I, 14, 1.)

(7.) A slave may be made free by being made an heir, and if he be made an heir without liberty, he becomes free of consequence. (Institutes, II, Tit. 14; also Tit. 14, Sec. 1, 2, 3.)

(8.) When Christianity prevailed, slaves could be emancipated in the face of the Church by imperial constitution. (Institutes, I, 5, 1.) By a constitution of Justinian, a master could set free both his wife who was a slave, and her children, so that they might enjoy freedom as if born free. (Novel., 78, Cap. 3 and 4.)

The foregoing comprise the principal modes of emancipation ; and yet there seems to have been great latitude given by the Roman law, and great encouragement to emancipation. If the fact of emancipation was duly tested, and the emancipation was not against the few restrictions, the mere form was a secondary matter. The twelve modes or cases given in the Codex—Lib. VII, Tit. 6 and 7—furnish the elucidation of this remark, as only few of them can be reduced to the modes mentioned above; although they are all such as to require legal causes and proper testimonials, according to Roman law.

13. There were, however, certain restrictions on emancipation. It could not take place, in fraud of creditors. (Institutes, Lib. I, Tit. 6; Dig., XL, 9; Cod., VII, 11.) A master under twenty years of age could not manumit without the approbation of his guardian or a court. (Institutes, I, 6, 4.) Augustus restrained the right of indiscriminate and unlimited manumission. A slave who was ill treated could compel the master to sell him to another. The power of life and death over slaves was first sought to be legally abolished by Adrian and Antoninus Pius. Constantine restrained the power of life and death over the slave.

The freed-man, though legally and practically free, still retained a relation of dependence on his former master. He received, however, a name which showed he was a Roman citizen. He also wore the *toga*, the dress of the free-born Roman. He was obliged to observe a respectful demeanor toward his former master, assist him in misfortune, and not sue him in law. Freed-men who had grossly violated these obligations were punished, and were sometimes again reduced to slavery.

The freed-men, in certain periods of the Roman government, were divided into the *Dedititii*, the *Latini*, and the *cives Romani*.

The *Dedititii* were those who were merely subjects of the Roman government. They were neither slaves, citizens, nor *Latini*. Their civil condition was that of a conquered people, who did not individually lose their freedom, but as a community had no political existence.

The *Latini* had not the *connubium,* and were wanting in various characteristics belonging to a Roman citizen. But he could obtain citizenship in several ways.

In considering the legal condition of the *libertini,* or *freed-men,* it is proper to remark that, though they might become *cives Romani,* their patrons had still certain rights over them. Their state did not allow them to make a will, nor take property under a will, nor of being named tutors to a will. They could take, however, by way of *fidei commissum.* The sons of *libertini* were *ingenui ;* but they were sometimes taunted with their servile origin.

Paternal power among the Romans extended to the life, death, or condition of the children and grandchildren. The father could also sell his children, and otherwise control them. (Institutes, I, Tit. 9; Cod., VIII, Tit. 47.)

The act of manumission created a new relation between the manumittor and the slave, which was analogous to that between father and son. The manumittor became, with respect to the freed-man, his patron, and the manumitted person became the *libertus,* or freed-man, of the manumittor. The word *patronus*—from *pater*—indicates the nature of the relation. The freed-man became the client of the patron. He adopted the Gentile name of the patron. Cicero's freed-man, Tyro, was called M. Tullius Tyro. The patron, too, might punish him summarily for neglect of the duties of his station. A law was prepared in the time of Nero, and passed under the later Emperors, to authorize the patron for certain crimes to re-enslave the freed-man. The *Lex Ælia Sentia* gave the patron the right of prosecuting the freed-man for ingratitude, *Ut ingratum accusare.* (Dig., XL, Tit. 9, L. 30.) An *ingratus* was called *libertus impius,* as being deficient in piety. The freed-man could not, as a general rule, institute a capital charge against his patron. The freed-man was bound to support the patron and his children in case of necessity, and the management of his property and the tutelage of his children ; and if he refused, he was called *ingratus*—ungrateful. (Dig., XXXVII, Tit. 14, L. 19.)

There are many intricate points in the Roman law in reference to the relations of patrons and freed-men. The object we have in view renders it unnecessary to pursue the subject further. (See the various parts of the civil law on this subject, and Anthon's Dictionary of Greek and Roman Antiquities, on the words, *Latinus*, *Libertus*, *Dedititii*, *Patronus*.)

The reader will perceive the vast difference between the Roman laws on emancipation and those of our slave states. In most states an especial act of the Legislature is to be had for each proposed case. In other states, expatriation is mostly exacted. So that Christian America, in the matter of emancipation, is infinitely behind heathen Rome in awarding to men the exercise of natural rights.

IV. We will now consider the actual condition of slaves as history depicts it, in connection with the legal enactments.

1. Slaves existed at Rome from the first; but they were not numerous under the kings and in the earlier ages of the Republic. The different trades were carried on chiefly by the clients of the patricians, and the small farms were cultivated by the proprietors and their children. But when new territories were conquered, and the patricians obtained large estates, slaves came into requisition. (Liv., V, C. 12.) Through wars and commerce slaves could easily be obtained at a cheap rate, and their number soon became so great that the poor freemen were thrown out of employ. Julius Cæsar endeavored, but in vain, to

enact that of those who attend cattle, one-third should be freemen. (Suet. Jul., 42.) In Sicily, the great corn region for Rome, the number of agricultural slaves was immense.

2. As to the *number* of slaves, we remark: Though large numbers were soon employed in agriculture, the number of those who served as personal attendants still continued to be small. But as luxury increased the number of slaves also increased. Athenæus states that some Romans possessed ten or twenty thousand slaves, or even more. Two hundred was no uncommon number for one person. From the time of Augustus to Justinian we may allow three slaves to one freeman. The free population of Italy was then said to be 6,944,000, and the slaves 20,832,000, making a total of 27,776,000. Gibbon says, "After weighing every circumstance which could influence the balance, it seems probable that there existed twice as many provincials as there were citizens of either sex and of every age, and that the slaves were at least equal in number to the free inhabitants of the Roman world. The total amount of this imperfect calculation would rise to about 120,000,000 of persons."

According to this the number of slaves and free persons was each 60,000,000.

3. Masters were responsible for the acts of their slaves; yet the master acquired no rights against the slave in consequence of his derelicts. Other persons might obtain rights against a slave in consequence of his wrong acts, but their right could not be prosecuted against him till he was manumitted. The slave was protected against injuries from other persons. If the slave was killed, the master might either prosecute the killer for a capital offense, or sue for damages under the *Lex Aquilia*. (Dig., IX, Tit. 2.) The master had also a *prætoria actio* to twice the amount of the estimated damage against those who

corrupted his slave, and led him into bad practices. (Dig., XI, Tit. 3, Sec. 1, where the words of the text are given.) He had also an action against a person who committed *stuprum* with his female slave. (Dig., XLVII, Tit. 10, Sec. 25.) In all these guards there was no reference to the benefit of the slave, but to the master only.

4. On the punishment of slaves we refer to the laws and the history of facts, as recorded by ancient authors. The treatment of slaves varied greatly, according to the dispositions of their masters; but they appear, on the whole, to have been treated with greater severity and cruelty than among the Athenians. Originally the master could use the slave as he pleased. Under the Republic the law does not seem to have protected the person or life of the slave at all; but the cruelty of masters was to some extent restrained under the empire. The general treatment of slaves, however, seems to have been but little affected by legislative enactments. In early times, when the number of slaves was small, they were treated with more indulgence and more like members of the family. (Hor., Ep. II, 1, 162.) But with the increase of numbers and luxury the scene was changed.

The obedience of slaves was enforced with severe discipline. The masters availed themselves of the latitude of the law in this respect to the utmost extent. One of the most easy punishments was their removal from the city to the country, where they were obliged to work in chains and fetters. (Plaut. Mort., I, 1, 18.) They were frequently beaten with sticks, or scourged with the whip; but these were so common as to create no sensation, as Chrysalus says. (Plaut. Bacchid., I, 3, 131.) Runaways, who were also called *fures*—*thieves*—were branded on the forehead with a mark, or *stigma*, and were therefore called *notati*, or *inscripti*. (Mort., VIII, 75, 9.) They were sometimes hung up by the hands with weights tied to their feet. (Plaut. Asin., II, 2, 37, 38.) A blow with the hand was a ready discipline. (Juv., 9, 5.) If a slave spoke or coughed at a forbidden time he was flogged by a severe master. (Sen., Ep. 47.) The dress of Roman ladies when not duly adjusted by the slaves, gave occasion to severe correction on the slave's back. (Mort., Lib. II, Ep. 66.) Burning alive was resorted to, and Tertullian says it was first used for slaves alone. (*Tertul. de anima,* 1.) But it were endless to go through the varied modes which a cruel ingenuity invented to torture and keep in subjection the poor slaves. (See Bibl. Repos. for 1835, Vol. VI, pp. 422–424.) The laws which abolished the master's power of life and death were obeyed with great reluctance, and virtually repealed by an increase in inferior punishments.

5. The principles of justice, however, comprised in the civil law, seem to have made their impression from time to time on the Roman mind, so as to produce enactments restraining the cruelties toward slaves. And though the remedy was not sufficient to cancel the evil, it was, at least, a pretext against the system. The first law in their favor was the *lex Cornelia de siccariis*, under the dictatorship of Tulla, about eighty years before Christ, by which the killing even of a slave became punishable. (Dig., XLVIII, Tit. 8.) The power of life and death was restrained by Claudius the successor of Caligula, about A. D. 43. (Dig., XLVIII, Tit. 8, Law 2.) Nero, in A. D. 61, by the *Lex Petronia* deprived masters of the power of sending their slaves to fight wild beasts at the public shows. The Emperor Adrian, about A. D. 120, prohibited generally cruel treatment toward slaves, and he banished Umbricia, a lady of quality, for five years, because, *for slight causes, she treated cruelly her slaves.* Antoninus Pius, about A. D. 140, applied the *lex Cornelia de*

siccariis, especially to masters of slaves; and the same law was strengthened by Severus, A. D. 195, and by Constantine. (Cod., IX, Tit. 14.) Slaves might always induce an investigation by flying to the statutes of the princes, according to the decision of Valentinian, Theodosius, and Arcadius, A. D. 386. (Cod., I, Tit. 25.) And Arcadius and Honorius, A. D. 397, ordained that all who fled to the churches were protected. (Cod., I, Tit. 12.) Nevertheless, slaveholders who were ill-disposed, had no very effectual restraint on them in consequence of these restraining laws. Yet the prevalence of Christianity greatly relieved the slaves and procured for them the cessation of many cruelties, and the mitigation of most, as we shall see, when we come to consider the discipline of the primitive Church.

6. The slave-trade of Rome was a large business. The traders called *manganes* were held in disrepute, and were distinguished from the merchants. The civil law describes them thus: "Men are not to be considered as merchandise; on this account the traders are called *manganes*, or venal persons, but not merchants." *Manganes non mercatores, sed venaliciarii appellati sunt.* (Dig., L, Tit. 16, Law 207.) The trade was lucrative, and great fortunes, then as now, were accumulated by it. The slave-dealers usually accompanied an army, and purchased the prisoners for a small sum, and sold them at advanced prices. The trader Thoranius, who lived in the time of Augustus, was well known. (Suet. Octav., 69; Macrob. Sat., II, 4.) Martial—VIII, 13—mentions another great dealer in slaves, named Gargilianus. Slaves were sold at auction at Rome, and were exposed on scaffolds, and exhibited for examination. Purchasers took care to have the slaves stripped naked in order to detect the defects which the dealers endeavored to conceal. Slaves of great beauty sold at extravagant prices. The

characters of the slaves were written on scrolls and placed on their necks.

7. The value of slaves varied with circumstances. At the camp of Lucullus slaves sold for four drachmæ each. Under the empire, or on the increase of wealth and luxury, slaves brought a very high price. Beautiful slaves always sold highest. Slaves who brought a profit to the owners brought a high price. Literary men, doctors and stage-players, brought a high price.

8. The customary allowance for a slave was a *modius* or peck of corn a week. Salt and oil were commonly allowed, and, occasionally, vinegar, salt-fish, and olives. They had daily a pint and a half of wine. Slaves near towns procured for themselves other necessaries and even luxuries.

9. They were not permitted to wear the *toga* or citizen's gown and other badges of citizenship. In most other respects they were clothed like others, till Alexander Severus appointed a certain garb for them. This was soon abandoned, because it showed to the slaves the superiority of their numbers.

10. Masters could work their slaves as many hours in the day as they saw fit, but they usually allowed them the holy days and festivals. The laborers on the great farms were shut up at night in an *egastulum*, or work-house, resembling a prison. Each slave had a separate cell. Public holidays, amounting to about thirty in a year, were allowed them.

11. There were, however, certain privileges awarded to slaves. They were permitted to follow any religion they pleased. Public slaves were employed about temples. The customary rights of burial were allowed them, because death put an end to all human distinctions. It was the duty of the master to bury the slave. (Dig., XI, Tit. 7, Sec. 31.) At the festival of Saturn special indulgen-

ces of speech and conduct were allowed them. But all such privileges and indulgences depended on the mere *will* of the master, and were never considered as a matter of right.

12. Masters were often at great pains to teach slaves various occupations, and even accomplishments; and instructors were chosen often for this purpose. The object of the education was the mere benefit of the master, and not the mental or moral culture of the slaves. There was, however, no law that prevented the instruction of slaves in any branch of learning. The employments of slaves, therefore, corresponded to all the profitable pursuits in which the master could advantageously employ him.

13. Slaves were divided into various classes. They were either public or private. Public slaves were those which belonged to the state or to public bodies, such as provinces, *municipia, collegia, decuria,* etc., or to the emperor in his sovereign capacity, and employed in public duties, and not attached to his household or private estate. These were acquired by war or purchase. Public slaves of an inferior character were employed as rowers in the fleet and in the servile public occupations. (Dig., I, Tit. 5, Sec. 1.)

A body of slaves belonging to one person were called *familia.* (Dig., L, Tit. 16, Sec. 40.) When there were many in one house they were frequently divided into *decuria,* or *tens.* But independent of this division they were divided into certain classes of a higher or lower rank, such as *Ordinarii, Vulgares, Mediastirii, Quales-Quales.* (Dig., XLVII, Tit. 10, Sec. 15.) It is doubtful whether the literary slaves, or *literati,* were comprised in any of these classes.

V. We may now take a survey of the evil nature and effects of Roman slavery. The nature of the evil is manifest from the foregoing survey, and we need not dwell on it; yet some of the evil effects may here be noticed.

1. We may consider the condition of slaves in the latter days of the republic, and during the empire previous to Constantine, as one of great hardship. Their lot was depending on the temper of their masters, not on the laws nor on humane and enlightened public opinion. Even the classical authors give mostly the fair side of their state, as they wrote mostly about household slaves, whose condition was far above those in the country. The sufferings from the *egastula* of the country are rarely noticed. Slaves were valued only as they represented money. Hortensius cared less for the health of his slaves than for that of his fish. It was a question, in time of a storm, whether slaves, horses, or other freight should be cast into the sea to save the ship.

2. The insurrections of the slaves, from time to time, were constant causes of alarm. The days of revolt were lessened from the close supervision over the slaves—from their ignorance, and the impossibility of harmony among them. As many were emancipated, and all might be, this led the more intelligent to wait their time with some degree of patience, yet there were several insurrections which greatly disturbed Rome.

As early as 458 before Christ Appius Herdonius created a revolt among the slaves. (Liv., III, C. 15.) In the year 415 before Christ it was announced that the servile bands had conspired against the city in several places. (Liv., IV, 45.) In the year 271 before Christ twenty-five slaves were crucified for a conspiracy. (Liv., XXI, 33.) In 184 B. C. a great servile commotion arose in Apulia—Liv., XXXIX, 29—in which seven thousand men were condemned. In 135 B. C. a great insurrection of slaves happened in Sicily, amounting to seventy thousand, of whom twenty thousand are said to have fallen in the defeat. The famous servile war in the time of Crassus and Pompey, occasioned the slaughter of one hundred and five thousand slaves, besides many others not enumerated. The history of the insurrections of slaves in Italy would fill a volume.

Besides these insurrectionary and political troubles, slavery was the parent of many moral and social evils. We will place this before our readers, from the pen of Mr. George Bancroft, former Secretary of the Navy:

"3. ROMAN SLAVERY IN THE RURAL DISTRICTS.

"When Tiberius Sempronius Gracchus, on his way to Spain to serve in the army, before Numantia traveled in Italy, he was led to observe the impoverishment of the great body of citizens in the rural districts. Instead of little farms, studding the country with their pleasant aspect, and nursing an independent race, he beheld nearly all the lands of Italy engrossed by large proprietors, and the plow was in the hands of the slave. In the early periods of the state, Cincinnatus at work in his field was the model of patriotism; agriculture and war had been the labor and office of freemen; but of these, the greater number had now been excluded from employment by the increase of slavery, and its tendency to confer the exclusive possession of the soil on the few. The palaces of the wealthy towered in the landscape in solitary grandeur; the plebeians hid themselves in miserable hovels. Deprived of the dignity of freeholders, they could not even hope for occupation; for the opulent land-owner preferred rather to make use of his slaves, whom he could not but maintain, and who constituted his family. Excepting the small number of the immeasurably rich, and a feeble but constantly-decreasing class of independent husbandmen, poverty was extreme. The King of Syria had reverenced the edicts of the Roman envoys, as though they had been the commands of Heaven; the rulers of Egypt had exalted the Romans above the immortal gods, and from the fertile fields of Western Africa, Masinissa had sent word that he was but a Roman overseer. Yet a great majority of the Roman citizens, now that they had become conquerors of the world, were poorer than their forefathers, who had extended their ambition only to the plains around Rome.

"4. INFLUENCE OF SLAVERY ON FREE LABOR.

"Philanthropy, when it contemplates a slaveholding country, may have its first sympathies excited for the slaves; but it is a narrow benevolence which stops there. The needy freeman is in a worse condition. The slave has his task, and also his home and his bread. He is the member of a wealthy family. The indigent freeman has neither labor, nor house, nor food; and, divided by a broad gulf from the upper class, he has neither hope nor ambition. He is so abject that even the slave despises him. For the interest of the slaveholder is diametrically opposite to that of the free laborer. The slaveholder is the competitor of the free laborer, and by the lease of slaves takes the bread from his mouth. The wealthiest man in Rome was the competitor of the poorest free carpenter. The patricians took away the business of the sandal-maker. The existence of slavery made the opulent owners of bondmen the rivals of the poor—greedy after the profits of their labor, and monopolizing those profits through their slaves. In every community where slavery is tolerated, the poor freeman will always be found complaining of hard times.

"5. INFLUENCE OF SLAVERY ON DOMESTIC LIFE.

"The great servile insurrection was designed to effect the emancipation of slaves, and both were unsuccessful.

But God is just, and his laws are invincible. The social evil next made its effects apparent on the patricians, and began with silent but sure influence to corrupt the virtue of families, and even to destroy domestic life. Slavery tends to diminish the frequency of marriages in the class of masters. In a state where emancipation is forbidden, the slave population will perpetually gain in relative numbers. We will not stop to develop the three or four leading causes of this result—pride and the habit of luxury—the facilities of licentious gratification—the circumscribed limits of productive industry—some of which causes operate exclusively and all of them principally on the free. The position is certain, and is universal; no where was it more amply exemplified than in Rome. The rich preferred the dissoluteness of indulgence to marriage; and celibacy became so general, that the aristocracy was obliged by law to favor the institution which, in a society where all are free, constitutes the solace of labor and the ornament of life. A Roman censor, in an address to the people, stigmatized matrimony as a troublesome companionship, and recommended it only as a patriotic sacrifice of private pleasure to public duty. The depopulation of the upper class was so considerable, that the waste required to be supplied by emancipation; and repeatedly there have been periods when the majority of the Romans had once been bondmen. It was this extensive celibacy and the consequent want of succession that gave a peculiar character to the Roman laws relating to adoption.

"6. INFLUENCE OF SLAVERY ON CIVIC VIRTUE.

"If a mass of slaves could, at any moment, on breaking their fetters, find themselves capable of establishing a liberal government—if they could at once, on being emancipated, or on emancipating themselves, appear possessed of civic virtue, slavery would be deprived of more tnan half its horrors. But the institution, while it binds the body, corrupts the mind. The outrages which men commit when they first regain their freedom, furnish the strongest argument against the condition which can render human nature capable of such crimes. Idleness, and treachery, and theft are the vices of slavery. The followers of Spartacus, when the pinnacles of the Alps were almost within their sight, turned aside to plunder; and the Roman army was able to gain advantage when the fugitive slave was changed from a defender of personal liberty into a plunderer.

"7. INFLUENCE OF SLAVERY ON PUBLIC MORALS.

"In like manner the effect of slavery became visible on public morals. Among the slaves, there was no such thing as the sanctity of marriage; dissoluteness was almost as general as the class. The slave was ready to assist in the corruption of his master's family. The virtues of self-denial were unknown. But the picture of Roman immorality is too gross to be exhibited. Its excess can be estimated from the extravagance of the reaction. When the Christian religion made its way through the oppressed classes of society, and gained strength by acquiring the affections of the miserable whose woes it solaced, the abandoned manner of the cities excited the reproof of fanaticism. When domestic life had almost ceased to exist, the universal lewdness could be checked only by the most exaggerated eulogies of absolute chastity. Convents and nunneries grew up at the time when more than half the world were excluded from the rites of marriage, and were condemned, by the laws of the empire, to promiscuous indulgence. Vows of virginity were the testimony which religion bore against the enormities of the age. Spotless purity could alone fitly rebuke the shamefulness of excess. As in raging diseases the most violent and unnatural remedies need to be applied for a season, so the transports of enthusiasm sometimes appear necessary to stay the infection of a moral pestilence. Thus riot produced asceticism; and monks, and monkish eloquence, and monastic vows, were the protest against the general depravity of manners."

VI. We will here adduce some of those great legal and moral principles of justice in the Roman code which are at variance with the system of Roman slavery, and with the legal principles on which it is founded. These have, or ought to have, the same weight in forming laws, that postulates and axioms have in geometry, or the fixed principles of any art or science have in discussions on the arts and sciences to which they relate.

1. Without going over the entire range of the civil law we will adduce those we find in the Institutes of Justinian, which are an abridgment of the Pandects and the Code, and contain the leading elements of the Roman law. Although these are already quoted as they occurred in the selections we have given from the Institutes, we will here place them in juxtaposition, so that we may at once see their force and meaning.

"Justice is the constant and perpetual disposition to render to every man his due." (Institutes, Lib. I, Tit. 1.)

The object of the science of law is what is "just and unjust." (Institutes, I, 1, 1.)

"The precepts of the law are, to live honestly, to hurt no one, and to give every one his due." (Institutes, I, 1, 3.)

"Liberty, from which we are denominated free, is the natural power of acting as we please, unless prevented by force or by the law." (Institutes, I, 3, 1.)

"Captivity and slavery are contrary to the law of nature; for by that law all men are born free." (Institutes, Lib. I, Tit. 2, L. 2.)

"All men, by the law of nature, are born free." (Institutes, I, 5.)

"Slavery is contrary to natural right." (Institutes, I, 3, 2.)

"Although civil policy may extinguish civil rights, yet over natural rights it has no such power." (Institutes, I, 16.)

"No length of time will be sufficient to found a prescription; as when a man holds a free person as a slave, a thing sacred or religious, or a fugitive slave." (Institutes, II, 6, 1.)

"Freedom once obtained shall not afterward be revoked." (Institutes, III, 13, 5.)

2. In connection with the foregoing, drawn from the Institutes, we will give the following *regulæ juris antiqui—rules of ancient law*—as they are found among the collection of two hundred and eleven rules at the close of the Digest or Pandects, Lib. I, Tit. 17. As these are few and short, and the Latin very expressive, we will give both the Latin and our translation of these rules, or legal maxims, or acknowledged first principles, which are in force in all courts in which justice and equity have sway.

Rule 20. "Quotiens dubia interpretatio libertatis est, secundum libertatem respondendum est." "Whenever there is a doubtful interpretation about liberty, the decision is to be in favor of liberty."

Rule 32. "Quod attinet ad jus civile, servi pro nullis habentur; non tamen et jure naturali: quia, quod ad jus naturale attinet, omnes homines æquales sunt." "Slaves are estimated *pro nullis*, [as nothing,] as it respects civil right, but not by natural right, because, as it concerns natural rights, all men are equal."

Rule 90. "In omnibus quidem, maxime tamen in jure æquitas spectanda sit." "In all things, especially those of civil right, equity is to be observed."

Rule 106. "Libertas inæstimabilis res est." "Liberty is a thing most to be esteemed."

Rule 122. "Libertas omnibus rebus favorabilior est;" or, "Favorabilis semper libertas." "Liberty in all things is more favorable than slavery;" or, "Liberty is always favorable."

Rule 146. "Quod quis, dum servus est, egit: proficere libero facto not potest." "Whatever a person has done while a slave, he can not profit by it when he becomes free."

Rule 206. "Jure naturæ æquum est, nominem cum alterius detrimento et injuria fieri locupletiorem." "By the law of nature it is just that no one, by the loss or injury of another, should become richer."

Rule 209. "Servitutem mortalitati fere comparamus." "We may almost compare slavery to death."

3. We will now show how these elementary principles of natural law, of justice, and of liberty in the Roman civil code conflict with the system of Roman slavery as established by the statutes of the Roman law.

According to the civil law, the law of nature is of supreme authority, and civil law has no power over it; yet Roman slavery is in direct conflict with the law of nature, and is in opposition to its decisions.

Slavery is contrary to the law of nature or to natural right; yet the Roman code, through the viciousness of men, has established slavery, contrary as it is to natural law and the principles of right in its own body of law.

All men are born free; yet, in opposition to this law of nature, the common law maxim obtained, that the child follows the condition of the mother; so that if the mother be a slave, the child is also a slave.

Justice renders to every man his due. Its object is whatever is just and right. Slavery deprives men of their due, such as personal liberty, personal security, and the pursuit of happiness. It also infringes on the principles of what is just and right, and introduces injustice and wrong in treating men as slaves.

The precepts of justice are to live honestly, to hurt no one, and render to all their due. But the precepts of slavery teach practices dishonorable to man, as exhibited in the slave system. It injures men in their persons, property, and good name, in making them slaves and treating them as such. It withholds from men their proper rights of liberty, security, and happiness.

"Liberty is the natural power to act as we please, unless prevented by force or law." Slavery divests of this liberty, so that its subjects can not act according to their own wills, but according to the will of others. To deprive persons of liberty there is no recurrence to justice or right, but to force or violence ; or, which is the same, by laws that are enforced with the entire power of the army, navy, and municipal power of the state, comprising also the judicial, legislative, and administrative powers of all civil officers.

"No length of time can give a prescriptive right to enjoyment of a thing unjustly acquired." This is not so with slavery. Long possession is a plea in the slave code.

In all doubtful matters about liberty, decisions are to be on the side of liberty. This is not so, at least in practice, in the slave code.

"All men are equal by natural law and right." This is the principle adopted by Jefferson in the Declaration of Independence, and it was the boast of the Roman law. Slavery in all its codes, whether Egyptian, Grecian, Roman, or American, ignores this great first truth, though it requires no argument to establish it, it being a moral and legal maxim incontrovertible in its principle.

"Liberty is always favorable in all things." This law maxim was overlooked by the civil code of Rome, first admitting and then legalizing slavery.

"A freed person can derive no benefit from what he did while a slave." The disabilities of slavery, even when a man is emancipated, follows him to the end of his life.

"Slavery may be almost compared to death." The Roman code considered slaves as *nulli, mortui, quadrupedes*—as *nothing, dead, beasts.*

The great moral, legal principles of justice and right in the Roman code condemned the system which was established under its statutes; or, in other words, the statutory laws which established slavery were at variance with the constitutional principles of justice and right in the Roman civil law. It is the same with the United States and every slave state; those laws which establish or tolerate slavery are in opposition to the great principles of justice in the Declaration of Independence, the Constitution of the United States, and the constitutions of all the states, whether free or slave states.

VII. It remains now to present a comparison between the Roman and American codes on slavery, and point out wherein they agree and wherein they differ.

1. There are several points in which the two systems agree.

(1.) In the common principles of the system they are agreed. These may comprise, as principal, depriving human beings of their natural rights, of personal liberty, personal security, and the pursuit of happiness. They agree in giving the master the complete control over the slave, so as to make him property, deprive him of marriage, and degrade him, mentally and bodily, in his social, civil, and ecclesiastical relations. In these respects there is a most perfect agreement between the slave codes of Rome and the United States.

(2.) Both codes adopt principles subversive of slavery. That all men are created free and equal is taught by both codes, and other great principles of justice in accordance with them. And some of the American principles are directly taken from the civil law, as will be seen by those who will examine the extracts we have given from the civil code. Hence, neither system can be supported without nullifying the great principles of justice and right contained in their respective codes.

2. There are also some respects in which the two codes materially differ. We will mention the following:

(1.) We have no statute or recognized custom of the Roman law by which the slave was forbidden the use of letters. Although no provision was formally made for his instruction, there was no prohibition by which he was debarred from the pursuit of any branch of knowledge which his circumstances enabled him to pursue. It was reserved for our Christian country, in nearly all the slave states, to forbid and prevent slaves from learning or from improving their minds. Here is a barbarism in a Christian country unknown in a heathen.

(2.) Our laws prohibit emancipation. In some of the states the few cases occurring must be by special legislation for the specified cases. In the border states, where emancipation is allowed by conformity to the statutes, the freed person must leave the state, and the mode of procedure is both intricate and vexatious. In heathen Rome, as we have seen, every one was at liberty to set his slaves free for any reason he saw fit, and the restrictions were so few that, in almost all cases, emancipation might be easily effected. Our slave laws pay no regard to the conscientious scruples of masters, but coerce them to retain their slaves whether they will or no ; and in endeavoring to relieve themselves from the embarrassment, good men are restrained with oppressive restraints, infringing on the sacred rights of conscience.

CHAPTER X.

THE NEW TESTAMENT.

1. When our Savior appeared, slavery reigned throughout the whole Roman empire, which then embraced the civilized world and much of the barbarous portions of it. Under the first Cæsars slavery reached its hight of enormity. No part of the empire, except Judea, was free from the evil. "The Sicilian dungeons were full. Medians, Mæsians, Bithynians, were driven in crowds to the Roman metropolis. Men-stealers were on the alert in the fastnesses of the African Troglodytes. The voice of the slave auctioneer was heard, early and late, at Corinth and Delos. From Britain to Parthia, and from the woods of Sweden to the great African desert, the cries of the bondman went up to heaven." (Biblical Repository for 1835, p. 428.) From one-half to two-thirds of the people of Rome and its provinces were slaves.

2. In Judea slavery did not exist before it came under the Roman Government; and even then it does not seem to have been introduced in any formal way. Yet that there were some slaves in possession of the civil functionaries of Rome is pretty certain. The resident Romans doubtless brought with them their slaves, as a part of their domestic arrangement. King Agrippa exhibited at one time, in Judea, seven hundred pairs of slaves as gladiators. (Joseph. Hist., 19.) We find in the history of the New Testament two centurions who had servants, or slaves, in all probability, as waiters. One is men-

tioned by our Lord—Matt. viii, 5–13—whose servant our Lord healed. The other is mentioned in Acts x, xi, who had devout soldiers, or servants, as waiters.

There was no very express mention of slavery in the Gospels, although there are allusions and references to it. The message of our Lord was first to the Jews, and as they had no slaves he did not come in contact with the system in ministering to them. Besides, as Paul was the apostle to the Gentiles at large, though Peter opened the door to them, we have in the Pauline teachings, in regard to slavery, slaves, and slaveholders, the inspired instructions that are to govern the Church. And as Paul was the apostle to the Gentiles, and a free-born Roman citizen, it was fitting that he should give to the Gentiles the Christian instructions adapted to them which he actually did, a full digest of which we will present in future pages.

The state of the question here seems to be briefly thus: 1. As slavery had never been permitted by the Jewish law in the Hebrew commonwealth, our Savior never came into contact with the system among his Jewish brethren. 2. The incidental reference to it in regard to the centurions did not bring the subject before him. 3. And the legal or Christian teaching on this was reserved for Paul, as the future history plainly shows.

It is proper, however, further to remark on this subject,

(1.) Nothing can be inferred, from our Lord's silence on the subject, in favor of slavery. Are we to infer that he approved of the sports of the amphitheater at Rome, of the conflicts of gladiators, fighting with wild beasts, the scenes of the Saturnalia, the worship of the Acropolis at Corinth, because he was silent in regard to them?

(2.) He never uttered any thing that can be construed in favor of slavery; and its advocates find no utterance of his to support the system.

(3.) There are fundamental principles in the teachings

of our Savior which are opposed to the whole system of slavery, and which are violated in perpetuating slavery, as we shall have occasion to show.

3. Both Christ and his apostles expressly condemn the practice of human slavery as a great sin.

Our Lord solemnly reaffirmed the Levitical moral law of Moses. (Matt. v, 17, 18; Luke xvi, 17.) And the moral law condemns slavery in all its constituent parts.

The apostles also pronounced the same condemnation by their similar ratification and confirmation of the moral law. (See Rom. iii, 31; vii, 12; x, 4; Gal. iii, 24; 1 Tim. i, 8–12.) The whole scope of their teaching fully shows this.

After such repeated ratifications of the moral law, there was no necessity that each of the specific crimes should be enumerated. Hence, the mode of illustration was mostly used in the New Testament, in reference to the Mosaic code, as in the case of *man-stealers*, or *slave-dealers*—1 Tim. i, 10—who are considered, morally, as in the same class with liars, perjured persons, "and if there be any other thing which is contrary to sound doctrine."

That they did not condemn slavery by *name* is most true, because, we suppose, there was no one word in the Greek language which as definitely signifies slavery as in our language. At any rate, this was not the chosen mode of Christ and his apostles, although they took a more effectual and plainer method, by forbidding all the constituent elements of slavery, and enjoining those moral observances that are destructive of it. (See Sinfulness of American Slavery, by the author of this volume, I, 310–343.)

4. The law of love is against slavery. This was given to the Hebrews in these words: "Thou shalt love thy neighbor as thyself: I am the Lord." Lev. xix, 18. This law is repeated by our Lord. (Matt. xxii, 39.) It

requires masters to render a *just equivalent* to their servants; but slavery refuses to do this. "Love worketh no ill to his neighbor." This is not true in regard to slavery. (Id., I, 275.)

5. The golden rule prohibits slavery. "Therefore, all things whatsoever ye would that men should do to you, do ye even so to them; for this is the law and the prophets." Matt. vii, 12. No one under the influence of this rule would make a slave, or continue another in that state, nor would he willingly subject himself and children to that state. (Id., I, 278–280.)

6. The *brotherhood* of man, as laid down in the New Testament, is against slavery. "One is your master, or leader, and all ye are brethren." Matt. xxiii, 8. To apply the term brethren to those who are slaves, is a perversion of language. The very word *brother* implies *father*, and *son*, and endearing, kindred relationship. Slavery confesses no father, nor brother, nor sister—not even a mother, except as a person to give the title to the property of the progeny, as a chattel. The Christian brotherhood is totally at variance with the illegitimacy of slavery, which knows no father, brother, or sister, in their proper acceptations. Cognation, agnation, or affinity, is totally disowned by slavery, as slaves are all *spurii*, or bastards, or *apatres*, without fathers.

7. There is, indeed, an *equality* in Christianity at variance with the inequality of slavery. "Neither be ye called master, [*leader*,] for one is your master, even Christ. But he that is greatest among you shall be your servant, and whosoever shall exalt himself shall be abased, and he that shall humble himself shall be exalted." Matt. xxiii, 10–12. The Declaration of Independence declares, "All men are created free and equal." The Roman law, when uttering the principles of justice, declares, "All men, from the first, were born

free;" and elsewhere, "All men are born equal." In Christianity there is neither Greek nor Jew, bond nor free; but all are one in Christ. (Col. iii, 11. See the author on Slavery, I, 307.)

8. Such distinctions of inequality as slavery includes are forbidden in the New Testament. "Ye know that the princes of the Gentiles exercise dominion over them, and they that are great exercise authority upon them. But it shall not be so among you; but whosoever will be great among you, let him be your minister; and whosoever will be chief among you, let him be your servant; even as the Son of man came not to be ministered unto, but to minister, and to give his life a ransom for many." Matthew xx, 25–28. The dominion of the Gentiles is identical with the dominion of slavery. Therefore, the domination of slavery, which reduces persons to things and to property, is at war with Christianity. While Christianity admits the official positions necessary in Church and state, it excludes from the one and the other the servility of slavery, and in its place our holy religion establishes the proper equality of the human family, both in Church and state, without interfering with the just exercise of civil and Church officers. The necessary despotism of the slave master, and the degradation of the slave, are at war with the spirit and right practice of our holy religion, which places men on the common platform of Christian equality and brotherhood.

9. The redemption of our race is antagonistic to slavery. Because the Israelites were redeemed by the power of God, slavery was prohibited forever among the Hebrews. (Lev. xxv, 42.) And Paul declares that slavery is opposed to Christ's redemption: "Ye are bought with a price, do not become the slaves of men." 1 Cor. vii, 23. Civil slavery is unbecoming the freed-man of Christ: "For ye are bought with a price; therefore,

glorify God in your body and spirit, which are God's." 1 Cor. vi, 20. The privileges of redemption elevate men to the high moral station of "kings and priests unto God." With the exercises of such stations slavery continually interferes. In this light the primitive Christians viewed the subject, and acted accordingly. Hence, Constantine the Great, in 330, made a decree that no Jew or pagan could retain a Christian as a slave. (Cod., Lib. I, Tit. *Ne Christianum.*) The three sons of Constantine, Gregory the Great, the Council of Toledo enacted similar laws.

10. The great Gospel jubilee, prophesied of by Isaiah, before Christ 698, and with which our blessed Savior opens his great mission, pronounces the final overthrow of slavery, and all other such evils, through the influence and operations of the Gospel in the salvation of men, first from sin, and then, as a result, deliverance from slavery and other evils. This glorious announcement is in the following words: "The Spirit of the Lord is upon me, because he hath anointed me to preach the Gospel to the poor; he hath sent me to bind up the broken-hearted, to preach deliverance to the captives, and recovering of sight to the blind, to set at liberty them that are bruised, to preach the acceptable year of the Lord." Luke iv, 18, 19.

Our blessed Savior here opens his ministry, and in general terms proclaims his mission. On this we make the following observations:

The great and first object in view was the salvation of the soul, by the Gospel as the means, through the redemption of Christ and the agency of the divine Spirit. Thus the *broken-hearted* sinner, enlightened by the truth, was *bound up* and saved from the darkness, guilt, power, and pollution of sin. The poor are mentioned because they composed the greater part of the human race; and as they were the most needy there was the utmost fitness in commencing with them. Thus, when they became enlightened, purified, and elevated by Christianity, the way was prepared for their deliverance from slavery, and all degrading evils and oppressions. In regard to slavery, the Gospel provides, first, by removing the *causes* of slavery; and, secondly, by removing the slavery that exists, after the usual causes of it are removed.

First. The Gospel removes the causes of slavery, and hence it is an extirpator of it, by destroying its roots or seeds, or living germs. We mention the following, and we substantiate them as matters of fact established by historical proofs that can not be denied:

Poverty, in ancient and modern times, has been one of the great sources of slavery. Because many men were poor, as they were especially in all heathen countries, they *sold themselves* and their families in order to obtain a living, or to discharge debts. The remedy of the Gospel here was indirect, yet efficient. When the masses became enlightened and moralized by the Gospel, they became industrious, intelligent, avoided wasting sins, saved their earnings, and rose above poverty, so that they were not compelled now to sell themselves to obtain a subsistence. And any poor Christians, who, by providential circumstances, were poor, were provided for by the benevolence of their fellow-Christians. It was the leading spirit of primitive Christianity. "Ye are bought with a price, do not become the slaves of men." "If thou canst, [not mayest,] or art able, or hast it in thy power to be made free, use freedom," not slavery. It was the watchword of early Christianity—Let no one bought with the blood of Christ, if possible, either become or continue a slave, if he can secure, lawfully, his freedom. This was the common sentiment and practice of the first Churches of Christ. This cut off one principal source of the slave traffic. This effect of Christianity, raising the multitudes above the pressure of poverty, cut off the principal source of slavery. Were the Africans Christians, they would not sell their children or friends for slaves, and the African trade would cease at once.

Another source of slavery in heathen lands, since wars began, was to sell the captives taken in war, and make slaves of them. Through the influence of Christian nations, imbued with Christian principles, in the place of selling the captives, the practice was established of sending them back to their own country for a redemption price; and thus, though slowly, yet surely, Christianity, in its whole range, has cut off this source of slavery. Our Lord's commission comprises this literally, "To proclaim liberty to the captives." It were useless to quote historical facts to show how literally this was fulfilled. And we can not allow that this phrase meant spiritual liberty, but civil liberty, as the *effect* of the mission of Christ. For our Lord uses here the very terms of the Roman law on slavery. "Slaves are denominated *servi*, from the practice of our generals to sell their captives, and thus preserve—*servare*—and not slay them. Slaves are also called *mancipia*, in that they are taken from the enemy by hand—*manucapti*." (Institutes, I, Tit. 3, Sec. 3.) Our holy religion proclaimed liberty—not slavery—to captives.

The religion of Christ not only struck at the very sources of slavery, but, where it was already established, it provided for its destruction. "To set at liberty them that are bound," is a phrase that means this much. This must be taken in its literal sense, for so history clearly proves. Primitive Christianity gradually set at liberty the slaves. It not only dried up the principal sources of slavery, in respect to poverty and captives, but also assailed the heathen maxim, the child follows the condition of the mother. Christianity established marriage, so that the children all became free; and those *bruised* or *downtrodden*, by the system, were set at liberty. The free states of this country are examples of this. Emancipation by Britain and other nations, furnish notable examples of the same result.

In short, our blessed Savior proclaims a general jubilee by "preaching the acceptable year of the Lord." The great design of the Gospel is the salvation of the soul. The results of this are to do away all those great moral evils that result in society from sin, and among them slavery holds a principal place. The full results of our religion will not only banish slavery, infanticide, war, etc., from our earth, but it will exclude all those moral evils which become incorporated with the social and civil institutions of man. To have preached the emancipation of slaves, by the apostles, would have been the same as to attempt an overthrow of the Roman Government. And this civil emancipation would not strike at the root of the evil. Our Lord and his apostles, therefore, went to the source of the evil, by preaching the Gospel to both slaves and masters; so that, in carrying out the moral principles of our holy religion, and a moral practice under it, the great moral evils of the world were undermined. And the process is still in motion, and will continue till our earth shall be filled with the knowledge of God, as the waters cover the face of the deep.

CHAPTER XI.

PAULINE DISCIPLINE ON SLAVERY.

In our previous chapters we have presented the principles of the Abrahamic covenant, in reference to slavery, in which it was shown that slavery under the patriarchs Abraham, Isaac, and Jacob, found no support, although a just service obtained. Subsequently, however, a system of slavery flourished in the world, as in the case of Joseph, the bondage of Egypt and other nations. It was shown, too, that the Mosaic code excluded slavery from the Hebrew commonwealth, and preserved the Jewish nation as a free people, up to the time of our Lord; and, indeed, the Jews were the only free nation then in the world. The great moral principles in the Mosaic law that excluded slavery, in common with its other moral laws, were recognized in the New Testament. Our blessed Savior proclaimed, in general terms, the great Christian jubilee for the whole world; so that his religion, just in proportion as it prevailed in its purity, would dry up the sources of slavery, and abolish the remnants of it on the earth.

In accordance with these views we might expect, that, in the development of the Christian system, we should find the principles and practice of an accurate Christian discipline on the subject of slavery. This we find laid down most exactly, yet briefly, by the apostle Paul, in his epistles to the Corinthian, Ephesian, and Colossian Churches, as well as in his epistles to Timothy and Titus.

This discipline is applied in the case of Onesimus. We call this the Pauline discipline in regard to slavery, slaveholders, and slaves. It is true that Peter adds a little; yet, on the whole, we may call it the Pauline discipline on slavery. Paul was the apostle of the Gentiles, and he was, therefore, the right apostle to teach the Gentiles the proper principles and practice in regard to slavery. He was also by birth a Roman citizen, and was well acquainted with the Roman laws on slavery, as his instructions plainly show. In treating on the Pauline discipline on slavery we shall take occasion to present,

I. The principles and rules he lays down in reference to slavery, slaveholders, and slaves.

II. The exercise of this discipline in the case of Onesimus, which became the model of the Christian Church in succeeding times.

III. That this discipline, in principles and practice, was effectually antislavery, and laid the foundation for the extirpation of slavery by the working of moral principles, and all for the good of Church and state.

I. We will first present the Pauline discipline in reference to slavery, slaveholders, and slaves, as to its principles and rules.

1. In order to present the subject clearly, we will quote all the laws, regulations, or principles, which he lays down on this topic, with direct reference to it, not incidentally, but with the express design to govern the whole subject.

1 Corinthians vii, 20–24, A. D. 59.

"20. Let every man abide in the same calling wherein he was called.	"20. Ἕκαστος ἐν τῇ κλήσει ᾗ ἐκλήθη, ἐν ταύτῃ μενέτω.
"21. Art thou called, being a servant? care not for	"21. Δοῦλος ἐκλήθης; μή σοι μελέτω· (ἀλλ' εἰ καὶ δύνασαι

it; but if thou mayest be made free, use it rather.	ἐλεύθερος γενέσθαι, μᾶλλον χρῆσαι.)
"22. For he that is called in the Lord, being a servant, is the Lord's freeman; likewise also he that is called, being free, is Christ's servant.	"22. Ὁ γὰρ ἐν Κυρίῳ κληθεὶς δοῦλος ἀπελεύθερος Κυρίου ἐστίν· ὁμοίως καὶ ὁ ἐλεύθερος κληθεὶς δοῦλός ἐστι Χριστοῦ.
"23. Ye are bought with a price; be not ye the servants of men.	"23. Τιμῆς ἠγοράσθητε· μὴ γίνεσθε δοῦλοι ἀνθρώπων.
"24. Brethren, let every man, wherein he is called, therein abide with God."	"24. Ἕκαστος ἐν ᾧ ἐκλήθη ἀδελφοὶ ἐν τούτῳ μενέτω παρὰ Θεῷ."

COLOSSIANS III, 22–25, A. D. 64.

"22. Servants, obey in all things your masters according to the flesh; not with eye-service, as men-pleasers; but in singleness of heart, fearing God:	"22. Οἱ δοῦλοι ὑπακούετε κατὰ πάντα τοῖς κατὰ σάρκα κυρίοις, μὴ ἐν ὀφθαλμοδουλείᾳ ὡς ἀνθρωπάρεσκοι, ἀλλ' ἐν ἁπλότητι καρδίας φοβούμενοι τὸν Θεόν.
"23. And whatsoever ye do, do it heartily, as to the Lord, and not unto men;	"23. Καὶ πᾶν ὅ τι ἐὰν ποιῆτε, ἐκ ψυχῆς ἐργάζεσθε, ὡς τῷ Κυρίῳ καὶ οὐκ ἀνθρώποις.
"24. Knowing that of the Lord ye shall receive the reward of the inheritance: for ye serve the Lord Christ.	"24. Εἰδότες ὅτι ἀπὸ Κυρίου ἀπολήψεσθε τὴν ἀνταπόδοσιν τῆς κληρονομίας· τῷ γὰρ Κυρίῳ Χριστῷ δουλεύετε.
"25. But he that doeth wrong, shall receive for the wrong which he hath done: and there is no respect of persons."	"25. Ὁ δὲ ἀδικῶν κομιεῖται ὃ ἠδίκησε, καί οὐκ ἔστι προσωποληψία."

COLOSSIANS IV, 1, A. D. 64.

"1. Masters, give unto your servants that which is just and right, knowing that ye also have a Master in heaven."	"1. Ὁι κύριοι, το δίκαιον [κατὰ το δικαιον] καὶ την ἰσότητα τοῖς δούλοις παρέχεσθε, ειδότες, ὅτι και ὑμεῖς ἔχετε κύριον εν οὐρανοῖς."

EPHESIANS VI, 5–9, A. D. 64.

"5. Servants, be obedient to them that are your masters according to the flesh, with fear and trembling, in singleness of your heart, as unto Christ:	"5. Οἱ δοῦλοι, ὑπακούετε τοῖς κυρίοις κατὰ σάρκα μετὰ φόβου καὶ τρόμου, ἐν ἁπλότητι τῆς καρδίας ὑμῶν, ὡς τῷ Χριστῷ.
"6. Not with eye-service, as men-pleasers; but as the servants of Christ, doing the will of God from the heart;	"6. Μὴ κατ' ὀφθαλμοδουλείαν ὡς ἀνθρωπάρεσκοι, ἀλλ', ὡς δοῦλοι τοῦ Χριστοῦ, ποιοῦντες τὸ θέλημα τοῦ Θεοῦ ἐκ ψυχῆς,
"7. With good will doing service, as to the Lord, and not to men:	"7. Μετ' εὐνοίας, δουλεύοντες ὡς τῷ Κυρίῳ καὶ οὐκ ἀνθρώποις·
"8. Knowing that whatsoever good thing any man doeth, the same shall he receive of the Lord, whether he be bond or free.	"8. Εἰδότες ὅτι ὃ ἐάν τι ἕκαστος ποιήσῃ ἀγαθὸν, τοῦτο κομιεῖται παρὰ τοῦ Κυρίου, εἴτε δοῦλος εἴτε ἐλεύθερος.
"9. And, ye masters, do the same things unto them, forbearing [*moderating*] threatening: knowing that your Master [*mar.* both your and their Master] also is in heaven; neither is there respect of persons with him."	"9. Καὶ οἱ κύριοι, τὰ αὐτὰ ποιεῖτε πρὸς αὐτούς, ἀνιέντες τὴν ἀπειλήν, εἰδοτες ὅτι καὶ ὑμῶν αὐτῶν ὁ Κύριός ἐστιν ἐν οὐρανοῖς, καὶ προσωποληψία οὐκ ἔστι παρ' αὐτῷ."

1 Timothy i, 9, 10, A. D. 65.

"9. Knowing this, that the law is not made for a righteous man, but for the lawless and disobedient, for the ungodly and for sinners, for unholy and profane, for murderers of fathers, and murderers of mothers, for manslayers,

"9. Εἰδὼς τοῦτο, ὅτι δικαίῳ νόμος οὐ κεῖται, ἀνόμοις δὲ καὶ ἀνυποτάκτοις, ἀσεβέσι καὶ ἁμαρτωλοῖς, ἀνοσίοις καὶ βεβήλοις· παραλῴαις καὶ μητραλῴαις, ἀνδροφόνοις,

"10. For whoremongers, for them that defile themselves with mankind, for men-stealers, for liars, for perjured persons, and if there be any other thing that is contrary to sound doctrine."

"10. Πόρνοις, ἀρσενοκοίταις, ἀνδραποδισταῖς, ψεύσταις, ἐπιόρκοις, καὶ, εἴ τι ἕτερον τῇ ὑγιαινούσῃ διδασκαλίᾳ ἀντίκειται."

1 Timothy vi, 1, 2, A. D. 65.

"1. Let as many servants [slaves] as are under the yoke count their own masters worthy of all honor, that the name of God and his doctrine be not blasphemed.

"1. Ὅσοι εἰσὶν ὑπὸ ζυγὸν δοῦλοι, τοὺς ἰδίους δεσπότας πάσης τιμῆς ἀξίους ἡγείσθωσαν, ἵνα μὴ τὸ ὄνομα τοῦ Θεοῦ καὶ ἡ διδασκαλία βλασφημῆται.

"2. And they that have believing masters, let them not despise them, because they are brethren; but rather do them service, because they are faithful and beloved, partakers of the benefit. These things teach and exhort."

"2. Οἱ δὲ πιστοὺς ἔχοντες δεσπότας, μὴ καταφρονείτωσαν, ὅτι ἀδελφοί εἰσιν· ἀλλὰ μᾶλλον δουλευέτωσαν, ὅτι πιστοί εἰσι καὶ ἀγαπητοὶ οἱ τῆς εὐεργεσίας ἀντιλαμβανόμενοι."

TITUS II, 9, 10, A. D. 65.

"9. Exhort servants to be obedient unto their own masters, and to please them well in all things; not answering [*mar.* gainsaying] again;	"9. Δούλους ἰδίοις δεσπόταις ὑποτάσσεσθαι, ἐν πᾶσιν εὐαρέστους εἶναι, μὴ ἀντιλέγοντας·
"10. Not purloining, but shewing all good fidelity; that they may adorn the doctrine of God our Savior in all things."	"10. Μὴ νοσφιζομένους, ἀλλὰ πίστιν πᾶσαν ἐνδεικνυμένους ἀγαθήν· ἵνα τὴν διδασκαλίαν τοῦ σωτῆρος ἡμῶν Θεοῦ κοσμῶσιν ἐν πᾶσιν."

1 PETER II, 18, A. D. 60.

"18. Servants, be subject to your masters with all fear; not only to the good and gentle, but also to the froward."	"18. Οἱ οἰκέται, ὑποτασσόμενοι ἐν παντὶ φόβῳ τοῖς δεσπόταις; οὐ μόνον τοῖς ἀγαθοῖς καὶ ἐπιεικέσιν, ἀλλὰ καὶ τοῖς σκολιοῖς."

2. We will now survey each of the foregoing passages of Scripture in order to collect from them the teachings intended to be communicated.

Corinth was long the chief slave mart of Greece, and abounded in slaves. They were distinguished by the name of *chœnix measurers*. Many of them, doubtless, embraced the Gospel when preached by Paul, Apollos, and others. It is manifest, from the language used by Paul, that many slaves were converted. On this account he gives them the instructions quoted above. (1 Cor. vii, 20–24.) From these instructions we think the following points are established:

(1.) *The renewed Christian should not anxiously desire to change the outward state in which he was when God renews or calls him, without clear direction from Providence.*

"Let every man abide in the same calling wherein he was called." Verse 20. "Brethren, let every man, wherein he is called, therein abide with God." Verse 24. This is illustrated by circumcision and uncircumcision, or the state of a Jew, or Gentile, which is set down as nothing compared with "keeping the commandments of God." Verses 18, 19. The reason is, that a man will enjoy more comfort, and can be more holy and useful, in a situation to which he is accustomed than in any other to which he is a stranger. And the apostle repeats the injunction because of its great importance; for they who are so unsettled in their minds as to be continually changing from one condition of life to another seldom make progress, or are of much use to themselves or others, in any one. But they were instructed "therein to abide with God," doing all things as unto God, and as in his immediate presence. They who thus abide with God preserve a holy indifference with regard to outward things.

L'Enfant thinks the apostle repeats the advice here "to correct some disorders among the Christian slaves in Corinth, who, agreeably to the doctrine of the false teachers, claimed their liberty, on pretense that, as brethren in Christ, they were on an equality with their Christian masters."

(2.) *Christian slaves should not be discontented with their state of slavery, nor be very anxious for obtaining liberty, on the supposition that this condition renders them unacceptable to God, or is incompatible with their being Christians.*

"Art thou called, being a servant, [δουλος, *doulos, slave,* or *bondman,*] care not for it." Verse 21. "For he that is called in the Lord, being a servant, [δουλος, *doulos, slave,*] is the Lord's [απελευθερος] *freed-man.*" Verse 22. He is now the Lord's *freed-man,* being delivered from the slavery of sin and Satan, and therefore possesses the greatest of all dignities. The apostle exhibits the small importance of human distinctions, when speaking of the most miserable lot, even that of a slave. He says, *Care not for it.* The sense is, "For the Christian slave is the Lord's freed-man; that is, in a moral and spiritual sense; and, in like manner, the Christian freeman is the slave of Christ; that is, metaphorically, by being bound to obey his precepts. Comp. Rom. vi, 20–22." (Bloomfield on 1 Cor. vii, 22.)

(3.) *The freedom of the Christian is to be prized far above the state of civil or human freedom.*

"For he that is called in the Lord, being a servant, [*doulos, slave,*] is the freed-man of the Lord. Likewise also he that is called, being free, is Christ's servant." Verse 22. The Christian, though a slave, is the freedman of Christ, is the brother of all Christians, and an heir of heaven, as well as the willing servant of Christ on earth. And even the converted freeman is no longer his own; he is bought with a price, and is Christ's servant. He is not free in this respect, nor at his own disposal, nor at liberty to do his own will, but bound to be obedient and subject to Christ.

(4.) *Every Christian slave should do his utmost to become a freeman, by using all lawful means, and embracing all proper opportunities.*

"But if thou mayest [ει και δυνασαι ελευθερος γενεσθαι, *canst*, or *art able* to] become a freeman, use it rather." Verse 21. If they can avoid it, they are commanded not to continue the slaves of men. This state of being slaves places them wholly under the dominion of another, degrades them, and places them under great disabilities. It is, therefore, a state which every Christian ought to get out of as soon as he conveniently could, though while he remains in it, he should not be excessively anxious in regard to his condition. Yet Christian slaves are bound as Christians to do their utmost to be free. "If thou mayest be free," is no adequate sense of the original; ει και δυνασαι, *if thou canst, or art able also to become a freedman*, conveys the force of the text. Every Christian slave ought to use all lawful means to become a freedman, that he might be a better Christian. The reasons for this preference are beyond number. As a slave he could not be a minister of Christ, because the services due his master would not allow him to discharge a minister's duties. If the Christian slave were a mother, and she became free, her children would be free. If the slave were single, he or she could marry, and would not be subject to the beastly *contubernium* of slavery. Free persons could go to school, could go to Church, would not be sold, nor bartered, nor given by will, nor put up on the auctioneer's block, nor parents and children separated. Hence the apostolic command to all slaves, "If it is in thy power to become a freed-man, use or enjoy freedom" in preference to slavery.

(5.) *Every free Christian is commanded, by Paul, not to become a slave by any act or will of his own.*

"Be ye not the servants of men:" much more properly, Μη γίνεσθε δοῦλοι, "Do not become the slaves of men." Wesley's translation is, "Do not become the bond-slaves of men." Freemen among the Romans could become slaves by their own will and acts, in at least two ways. Some, who were poor, sold themselves for the sake of present relief. But a Christian would be guilty for doing so, because by his industry and economy he ought not to be poor, and thus compelled, like wicked persons, to have resort to slavery for relief; and were he poor without his own fault, his fellow-Christians would aid him, so that he need not become a slave on account of his poverty. A free person, by his crimes, as for theft, could be made a slave. Hence the force of the command in the text, "Do not become the slaves of men;" as no Christian could become a slave for any of the causes mentioned without doing wrong, whether on account of poverty, which he could provide against, or for theft, or any other crime. The teaching of the apostle was, that no free person, on any account, should consent to return to slavery. And those slaves in the south who contentedly remain slaves, when their masters would set them free, exhibit specimens of ill-taught Christians, who are misled by false teaching, and overlook the instructions of Paul, "Do not become the slaves of men;" or, in other words, you refuse to become free when you have it in your power, and, therefore, you are wrong; because you ought to become free if you can. And those teachers who say the slaves are better off than if they were free, teach false doctrine; for Paul teaches slaves to become free, if they can procure their freedom lawfully, or by contract with their masters.

But Paul is especially peremptory against freemen becoming slaves; and his argument is the strongest in the world, even the argument of redemption: "Ye are bought with a price." Some paraphrase it thus: "Are ye bought with a price from slavery? Do not become the slaves of men. Never sell yourselves. Prefer and retain your liberty, now that you have obtained it." The law taught in regard to the Hebrews, "They are my servants which I have brought out of the land of Egypt; they shall not be sold with the sale of a bondman"—Lev. xxv, 42—Paul applies this to Christians: "For ye are not your own; ye are bought with a price; therefore glorify God in your body and in your spirit, which are God's." 1 Cor. iv, 20. Christians are bound to devote their bodies and all their members as instruments of righteousness, as well as their souls and all their faculties. A state of slavery, if it does not prevent this, greatly hinders it. There are many evils and snares incident to a state of slavery. The bodies of Christians are the temples of God, and are to be consecrated to him in temperance, chastity, and purity. Their spirit, too, is to be consecrated to God, by faith, hope, love, meekness, and all the graces of the Holy Spirit. The express command, therefore, of Paul is to all. If you can become free, enjoy this freedom. If you are free, never, on any account, become a slave.

(6.) The persons here called δουλοι were slaves. The word δουλος itself signifies either a hired servant or slave, according to the *usus loquendi* of the writer. That the meaning of *doulos* here is *slave* is proved from the following considerations: 1. The servants generally, if not all, at Corinth, were slaves. They were called *chœnix meas-urers*. This is plain from the very language employed by Paul in describing the social condition of the Corinthian converts, as well as the particular vices to which they were exposed: "Behold your calling, brethren, that not many wise men after the flesh, not many mighty, not many noble are called; but God hath chosen the foolish things of the world to confound the wise; and God hath chosen the weak things of the world to confound the things that are mighty. And base things of the world, and things that are despised, hath God chosen; yea, things that are not, to bring to naught the things that are." 1 Cor. i, 26–29. The terms, ignoble, unwise, weak, foolish, base things, things that are not, here expressed or implied, will apply to slaves, though inaptly to free persons. 2. The name *doulos*, meaning one in bondage, is in the passage constantly put in contrast with ελευθερος γενεσθαι, *to be made free*, as well as the whole spirit of the passage. Such is the usual style of Paul on this subject, as will appear from the following quotations: "Whether BOND or FREE." "Ειτε δουλοι, ειτε ελευθεροι." 1 Cor. xii, 13.

"There is neither BOND nor FREE." "Ουκ ενι δουλος, ουδε ελευθερος." Gal. iii, 28. "The same shall he receive from the Lord, whether he be BOND or FREE." "Ειτε δουλος, ειτε ελευθερος." Eph. vi, 8. "Where there is neither Greek nor Jew, circumcision nor uncircumcision, barbarian, Scythian, BOND nor FREE." "Δουλος ελευθερος." Col. iii, 11. The common *usus loquendi* of Paul, when treating on the subject, was to use the word δουλος in the sense of *slave*, in direct distinction from a freeman; and the above texts prove this without doubt. 3. The persons addressed are exhorted to get free from their present state, if they possibly can. This will show that their state was not one of freed-men, as we have no exhortations in Scripture that exhort men to get rid of freedom. 4. Besides, the apostle exhorts, or rather commands, the Corinthians not to become the *douloi*, or slaves, of men. Such an admonition can not apply to hired servants, as theirs is a service which has little in it in common with slavery, as to its proper state in society, except the labor performed. The state of a voluntary hired laborer is no where, as far as we can learn, presented in Scripture as one into which Christians are exhorted not to enter. 5. Bagster, in his admirable Bible, gives the following note on 1 Corinthians vii, 21: "*Being a servant;* rather a slave—δουλος—the property of another, and bought with his money."

(7.) *The instructions of Paul to the Corinthian Christian slaves gives no sanction to slavery, but, on the contrary, condemns the system.*

The reasons are the following, legitimately drawn from the passage: 1. Slaves are exhorted to obtain freedom, if it be in their power. If slavery were a good state, it would not be proper to get rid of it; and because Christians are exhorted to choose freedom and avoid slavery, the consequence is that slavery is wrong. 2. Freed persons are taught by the apostles not to become slaves, seeing they are now free. Therefore, what Christians are instructed to avoid can not be right. 3. The moral principles inculcated in the epistles to the Corinthians go to the same purpose. But the conclusion is plain from the two foregoing considerations, that because slavery is to be got rid of, if possible, by those involved in it, and to be avoided by persons free from it, that it is not of God. 4. It were easy to show that, as the Old Testament condemned the slavery of Egypt and of the other nations, and that no slavery was allowed to be established among God's ancient people, Christians could not be induced to believe that Roman slavery was right.

(8.) *Corollary* 1. *Every Christian should do his utmost to induce slaves to become Christians, and to esteem freedom from sin above civil freedom.*

This is a plain consequence from the foregoing. The freedom of Christ is of more value than freedom from slavery. Christianity is even, in an important sense, a substitute for freedom. It is even more, as it alone prepares adequately the slave to enjoy freedom to advantage. The great work of the Church and of Christians is to lead men, whether bond or free, masters or slaves, to be Christians, and then every secondary benefit, as civil freedom, and the like, will follow, provided the appropriate exertions be made.

(9.) *Corollary* 2. *Every Christian citizen is morally bound to use all proper means as a citizen to promote freedom from slavery, yet as secondary to freedom from sin.*

This is another consequence from the preceding. The first object is the salvation of the soul from the ignorance, guilt, power, and pollution of sin. The next, or secondary object, is to deliver from slavery, or degradation, that the Christian may not be impeded by slavery or any degrading condition of life. As the slave can not plead his cause, the free Christian is to plead for him. As the slave can not redeem himself, his Christian brother should do it for him. As the slave can not vote or hold any civil office, the free Christian citizen should come forward and do all this for his poor Christian brother, or for any enslaved human being, whether Jew, Gentile, Christian, or infidel.

3. Instructions for slaves and masters directed to the Church at Colosse.

Colosse was an ancient and populous city of the Greater Phrygia, an inland country in the Lesser Asia. This city and region abounded with slaves; and Philemon is said to have been the first bishop or pastor of the Church of the Colossians. The epistle was written in Rome about A. D. 64, and sent to the Colossians by Tychicus and Onesimus, and at the same time in which the epistle to Philemon was written. In the epistle to the Colossians the instructions to slaves and masters are contained, which we have quoted above, and on which we make the ensuing remarks. (Colossians iii, 22–24.) On the duties of slaves we have the following:

(1.) Obedience to their masters in all things was required. "Servants, obey in all things your masters, according to the flesh." They were required to execute all the lawful commands of their masters, but to do nothing contrary to the law of God, because the authority of God was greater than that of the master, for it controlled both master and slave. They were to obey their masters not through the fear of their masters, but through the fear of God.

(2.) The properties of this obedience from servants to masters are presented thus. 1. *Not with eye-service*—being more attentive under the eye of the master than at other times, as mere *men-pleasers*. 2. But "in singleness of heart, fearing God." They were to serve with great simplicity and sincerity of spirit, so as to eye their Master in heaven with an eye to his presence—his command—his assistance—his honor and glory. It was to be done heartily, as unto Christ, as supreme, and not to men. Thus the authority of God as over all is recognized in this obedience, so as to be influenced by his fear, and to be done as "to the Lord and not to man." Thus the commands of God were to rise superior to those of the master.

(3.) A glorious reward is held out to the slave from God, in pursuance to his obedience to his master. "Of the Lord ye shall receive the reward of the inheritance." And the service to the master in performing his daily tasks, is set down to the slave, as "serving the Lord Christ."

(4.) But the slave is not allowed to do wrong, though he may be wronged. "He that doeth wrong shall receive for the wrong that he hath done." Slaves were notable for fraud, lying, and stealing, and masters for cruelty and injustice. The instruction here shows the impartiality of the divine justice. God will avenge the wrong by whomsoever done. He will do this impartially and proportionally. "There is no respect of persons with God." So that he that doeth wrong, whether master or slave, will give an account to God for his deeds.

(5.) That the persons here called *douloi*, servants or slaves, were not hired servants but truly slaves, we justly conclude, because, 1. The Greeks and Romans had scarcely any servants but slaves. 2. The contrast between these *douloi* and their masters was great, and was such as exists between slaves and masters, and not such as exists between hired servants and masters.

The duties of masters are given in the epistle to the Colossians as follows: "Masters, give unto your servants [*douloi, slaves*] that which is just and equal;

knowing that ye also have a Master in heaven." Col. iv, 1.

First. Masters were to render to their slaves το δικαιον, *that which is just,* or as Griesbach and most others read, κατα το δικαιον, *according to that which is just.* Robinson renders το δικαιον *that which is right, just, fit,* quoting this text as an example of this meaning. St. Paul refers, we think, to the legal use of the word, or its synonym, *justitia, justice,* in the Roman law, on the subject of slavery, on which he was then formally treating, as he was giving instructions to both slaves and masters.

The Roman law defines justice thus: "*Justitia est constans et perpetua voluntas jus suum cuique tribuenti.*" "Justice is the constant and perpetual disposition to render every man his own." (Institutes Just., Lib. I, Tit. 1.) And *juris prudentia,* or the knowledge of justice, he defines to be, "*justi atque injusti scientia.*" "The science of what is just and unjust." (Id., Sec. 1.) The precepts of law or of justice, the same high authority defines, "*honeste vivere, alterum non lœdere, suum cuique tribuere.*" "To live honestly, to hurt no one, to give to every one his own." (Id., Sec. 3.) As to the origin of slavery he says, "Wars arose, and the consequences were captivity and slavery, both which are contrary to natural law; for, by natural law, all men from the beginning were born free." (Id., I, 2, 2.) "*Jure enim naturali omnes homines ab initio liberi nascebantur.*"

Justinian defines liberty thus, "Liberty is the natural power of acting as we please, unless prevented by force or by the law." (Id., I, 3, 1.) "Slavery is when one man is subject to the dominion of another, according to the law of nations, though contrary to natural right." (Id., Sec. 2.)

According to the Roman law all men were born free. Slavery is induced contrary to the law of nature, by force, so that each man has by nature a right to himself, or to personal liberty, personal security, the acquisition of property, and the pursuit of happiness. Justice renders to every man his own; and it will especially give to every one the possession of himself, comprising his liberty, security, the fruit of his own labor and skill, and all other natural and just conventional rights growing out of these. Hence the precepts of justice teach each to live honestly as to himself, to hurt no one, and to render to each his own. So that justice in the Roman sense would never allow a man to be a slave. And the law enacting slavery is contrary to natural law, to the divine law, and to just human laws. The right to a slave is an unjust right, and is founded on an unjust law—the law of mere force, or some civil law which is itself contrary to justice.

The command of Paul to masters is to render to their slaves το δικαιον, *that which is just*, or rather κατα το δικαιον, *according to that which is just*. This teaches the master to render to the slave his own, or, in other words, to give him *liberty*, and, with the least delay, to secure to him his civil liberty, and release him from the power of the slave laws, by legal process. By this the master acknowledges to the slave that he has no *just* right to him as property, or to control him, as to liberty, security, labor, or the like; and that the slave owns himself, just as much as the master owns himself. The same demand of doing that which is just on the part of the master, will require that he remove the unjust impediment of slavery from the slave, and place him in possession of himself. And the slave has the right to demand, in due time, this act of justice, as soon as may be, that neither he nor his wife and children may lie under the disability of slavery, but that they may enjoy liberty. The right of a master to a slave may be illustrated by a case or two. It may be compared to the right which a man has to an estray which he finds on his premises. He has a just right to hold this estray till he can restore it to the owner and no longer. So the master has no other right to the slave than to hold him safely till he can restore him to the owner. And every man is his own owner. The master owns and holds the slave only in trust till he can give him his liberty, and in the mean time he must render him an equivalent for his labor, as the slave is bound to render to the master an equivalent for his care and maintenance. Or the right to a slave may be illustrated by finding lost property. The finder may hold it till he can get the true owner. In the case of the slave, the true owner of him is the slave himself, so that no dispute can arise about the proper owner.

Second. The master is to render to the slave that which is *equal*, τὴν ἰσότητα, *equality*, or, rather, κατά ισότητα, according *to equality*, or *that which is equal*. For ἰσοτης means *equality*, *equity*, or *what is equitable*, and Robinson gives it this meaning in the text under consideration. And the root ισος means *equal*, *like*, *alike*. In consequence of the process of law, or the minority, or other circumstances of the slave, the master may not be able, or it might not be best, to emancipate the slave immediately. Yet he is to render no unjust act toward him, though full justice can not be now awarded. But in his treatment of him in the mean time, he is bound to render to him that which is equitable, on the principle of equality and equity. The law of strict equity is to govern here so that the master will render to the slave a full equivalent for the slave's services to him, till he can render to him the act of justice which emancipates him. The laws of the slave system can not govern here. They are null and void as to the Christian master and his legal slave. The law of reciprocal right must rule.

"Do unto all men as ye would they should do unto you," is now the standard, till the law of love shall break off the last link in the slave's chains.

Third. The duties of justice and equity to the slave are here enjoined on the master by the argument—*knowing that ye also have a Master in heaven.* God is supreme over both masters and slaves. God treats none of his creatures *as slaves,* neither should masters treat any as slaves, but as brethren—the children equally of one common Father who is in heaven, and to whom we all can pray and call him OUR FATHER. No rigorous rule is compatible with the Christian relation of master and slave. And till the justice of liberty is awarded, let the brotherhood of humanity and of Christianity treat the legal slave as a human being or Christian brother, disusing the unjust rights that the slave system may confer on the master, and using the power as master only for the protection of the slave and his final liberation.

In these instructions both to slaves and masters, we have neither sanction, support, nor durability awarded to the slave system of Rome, of America, or of any other country. This will appear fully on briefly surveying the duties of slaves, the reasons for performing them, and the duties of masters, and the reasons enjoining these duties. Christian slaves, while they are slaves, are bound to obey their masters in every thing not sinful—they were to do so not with eye-service, as men-pleasers, but in singleness of heart, doing it heartily. This service they were to render as to Christ the Lord, with the fear of God. They were to look for a great inheritance from the Lord. No wrong act was allowed to be done by the slave, however much he might be wronged himself. And he was taught that there was no respect of persons to be exercised to the sinning slave any more than to the sinning master. Such conduct on the part of the slaves, founded on such principles, would necessarily produce conviction in the mind of the slaveholder as to his duty, and to the wrongs of slavery itself.

Fourth. Thus the master was bound to do according to justice, so as to free the slave as soon as the law and the circumstances would call for. And in the mean time, the law of *equity* and reciprocal right must govern him till justice would have its demands answered. And the awful consideration hung over him that he was equally as much *subject*, or under the dominion of God, as the slave was, and both must render an account to Him.

These reciprocal duties of each would shortly lead toward placing the slave in the relation of a hired servant, to whom was rendered a just equivalent. Christian marriage, too, was to be introduced, and the parental and filial relations were to be sustained. No master could sell his brother on any account. No trading of human beings could exist under this regimen. And as the Roman laws, in almost all cases, allowed of legal emancipation, there was no difficulty, under the Pauline code, in carrying it out. This discipline was transferred to the first Christian Churches. And slavery, under this benign discipline, melted gradually away in the Roman Empire; though the remains continued for many centuries. Such is the course now for the Christian Church. This is slavery extirpation. Much of extirpation may take place before legal emancipation may take place. And, after legal emancipation, there may be much need of extirpation; so that the roots or bad effects of it may be done away, and no new forms of slavery may arise, such as the American slavery among professed Christians, after Christianity itself had done it away in former centuries.

4. We next come to the epistle to the Church at Ephesus, to which Paul addressed an epistle, A. D. 64. Ephesus was the metropolis or chief city in Asia. Paul

preached here three years—Acts xx, 31—and from hence the Gospel spread throughout the whole province. (Acts xix, 10.) In his epistle to the Ephesians, Paul's instructions to servants or slaves, as recorded in Ephesians vi, 5–9, comprise the following:

(1.) The duties enjoined. "Servants, be obedient to your masters according to the flesh." Obedience to the masters is here enjoined—*according to the flesh;* that is, in temporal things, or things pertaining to this world, leaving the soul and conscience to God only, who alone is the sovereign Lord over them. Christian liberty is not inconsistent with civil subjection, for such as are God's freemen may be the legal slaves of men, and as such obedience is their duty in all lawful things. "Even a *slave*, if a Christian, was bound to serve him faithfully by whose money he was bought, however illegal that traffic may be considered." (*Dr. A. Clarke.*) "The Gospel does not cancel the civil rights of mankind; *according to the flesh*—that is, who have the command of your bodies, but not of your souls and consciences; or, who are your masters according to the present state of things." (*Benson.*) Bengel, on this text says, "It was not proper after mention of the true Lord, in verse 4, that others should be called absolutely κυριοι, *lords*, therefore, he adds, *according to the flesh.*"

(2.) The manner of performing this obedience is pointed out. It is to be "with fear and trembling;" that is, with fear of displeasing them; yet they must act not barely out of fear, but out of love both to God and their master. It is a proverbial expression, however, implying the utmost care and diligence. They should obey, "because the law gives the master power to punish for every act of disobedience." (*Dr. A. Clarke.*)

The obedience must be, "in singleness of heart," in great simplicity and sincerity of spirit, without guile, hypocrisy, or dissimulation. Not from mere fear, but from a principle of uprightness, serving them as you would serve Christ. "Not with eye-service," in serving their masters when present, but neglecting it when they are absent. They should not be "men-pleasers," who have no regard to pleasing God, but as the "servants of Christ," who do "the will of God from the heart."

The service must come from the *heart*, and with *good will* or *cheerfulness*.

(3.) The authority and will of God are to control the slave in his service to his master. The "will of God" is to govern the slave, and overrides all commands of the master which would enjoin any thing morally wrong, or forbid doing right. But as the slave is in a state of servitude, it is the will of God that the slave should act conscientiously in that state. The service should be as *unto Christ*, with sincerity and honesty of heart, with regard to the honor and cause of Christ. It should be *as to the Lord and not to men*—regarding God more than men, and obeying him beyond any master, when God's will or command so require it. "The authority of Christ ought to control and govern all men, even those in external slavery." (*Bengel.*)

(4.) A glorious reward is secured to slaves in the performance of their duties. "Knowing that whatsoever good thing any man doth, the same shall he receive of the Lord, whether he be bond or free." Verse 8. The service of slaves to their masters, for the time being, is a *good work* on their part. Any good thing done, by bond or free, will meet with a reward from God. He is the universal guardian and protector of all his people. According to the Roman and all slave codes, the slave could claim no wages as reward for his work. All he could have was his *peculium*, or little earnings arising from his extra work done beyond his exacted task. And this, too, could be taken by the master, as far as the *law* of slavery was concerned. God here secures to the slave the full *reward*, through grace, of all the good he will do, in *common* with the freeman. And this indirectly teaches the master, in its principle, in doing *justice* to the slave, to give him wages for his work, and even *liberty* also, without any unnecessary delay. And in this kind and *indirect* yet plain way, the master is instructed to take the yoke from off the neck of the slave.

(5.) That the *douloi*, or servants mentioned here, were slaves we maintain, because, 1. The names δουλος, *bond*, and ἐλεύθερος, free, are placed in contrast. 2. Both masters and servants are placed here correlatively, so as to show that the service is not that of freemen, but of slaves, as the absence of temporal remuneration in the relation is noticed, though introduced by spiritual reward, so as clearly to convert, in the issue, the state of slavery into that of equitable service. 3. The temper of the service, as *with fear and trembling*, though it may be accommodated to hired servants, does not comport with them as it does to slaves. Their servile state allows of this temper, as a natural moral disease of slavery, and, for the time, unavoidable, till, by Christianity, a more elevated feeling comes in, as it must, when the slave shall have passed fully from slavery to a state of freedom. 4. Wages or reward is supposed to be absent from the relation here regulated; though it is to be introduced through the spiritual teaching, and ultimately to prevail, and, therefore, do away the state of slavery in the end. 5. This is confirmed by the constant reference to God, and Christ, as governing and controlling, so that this high motive is put in as more than a substitute for the present servile condition. And the hopes of a glorious future held out, are here dwelt on in a manner to suit slavery, but not to suit a state of complete freedom.

In the instructions to masters of the Ephesian Church we have the following: "And, ye masters, do the same things unto them, forbearing threatening; knowing that your Master also is in heaven; neither is there respect of persons with him." On this we observe, *First.* That the masters are required to "do the same things unto them." This does not mean to render the servants the same *kind* of service, but the manner of treating them; that is, in obedience to the same command of God, with an eye to the same glory of God, with the same singleness of heart, with the same love and good will. On the words τὰ αυτὰ, *eadem, the same things*, Bengel remarks, in his Gnomon, "Compensate them with those things that benevolence enjoins. *Love* should moderate the duties of slaves and masters, as one and the same light does the various colors. Equality of nature and of faith is superior to the difference in states of life."

This is a *reciprocal* demand on the master, and it must imply just and equitable returns to slaves for their service, or an equivalent answering to wages. The master, too, is not to be the *sole judge* here according to the slave system, as the slave, or his chosen arbiter, is to decide the reciprocal duties of the master to the slave. Here will come in, in good place, the injunction to the masters at Colosse, in which the masters were to render to the slave according to justice, and according to the rule of an *equivalent* from them to the slaves. This rule, as we have shown, would sooner or later secure freedom, and in the mean time either wages or an equivalent to the slave for his services to his master.

Second. Masters should "forbear threatening." The words ανιεντες την απειλην mean rather to *mitigate, relax,* or *not exact threatening;* that is, the threatened punishment. Masters were not to exercise their authority by cruelty or severity; but they should govern with mildness and moderation. Masters were not allowed by the apostle to exercise cruelty to their slaves, nor even threats. They were to govern, says a Lapide, "with the same humanity, benignity, love, sincerity, and fidelity to the servants as the servants were required to serve them." We take it that the master was neither to inflict nor even threaten corporeal punishments to his slaves, because both were now under the teachings of the Gospel, and supposed to be governed by its spirit. Of course, the corporeal punishments of the slave system must cease, and the Christian spirit of love must govern, which does not comport with the use of the whip, stocks, and the like. And this is enforced by the consideration that the God of heaven was Lord both of the master and slave.

Third. Besides, "God is no respecter of persons." The rich master and poor servant stand before him on the same level, and both shall be rewarded according to their works; yet God will especially remember the oppressed, and will hear their cry.

Fourth. That the masters here spoken of were slaveholders we can not doubt. As the servants were slaves, the masters were slaveholders; for the terms here are correlative, the one corresponding to the other. They were masters *according to the flesh*, or according to the Roman law under which they lived, and at the time the masters were generally slaveholders and the servants were generally slaves.

The instructions of Paul to the Church of Ephesus gave no sanction or support to slavery; but, on the other hand, they were subversive of it. The instructions to both slaves and masters were moral and religious, and every thing wrong was forbidden. The slaves must not steal, or lie, or commit any wrong act. The masters were also forbidden to do wrong, and required to do right. The spirit of love and reciprocal good to each other was enjoined. No person was to be sold, or beaten, or injured, or deprived of just rights. By this discipline, founded on brotherhood and love, slavery must die, and die it did.

We do not find, however, that immediate emancipation was enjoined, though in most, or many cases, emancipation followed. 1. All the subjects of the Roman empire were completely under the power of the Emperor and other subordinate tyrants, so that the state of slaves and free persons was very much alike in many respects. Yet there was always, as there is now, an essential difference between freedom and slavery. 2. The apostle knew well the obstacles in the way of general emancipation under the Roman law. Therefore, Paul more immediately enjoined on masters and slaves the moral and social duties rather than emancipation. And the performance of these reciprocal duties, more speedily than emancipation, were beneficial to both parties, and hastened the time for a safer and more advantageous liberty. 3. The instructions to masters and slaves are mostly connected with instructions to parents and children, to husbands and wives. The moral duties enjoined on these relations were designed to secure the proper duties belonging to each. The prohibitions and commands to slaveholders and slaves were manifestly designed to restore and establish the relation of hired or remunerated servants, and do away the *abuse* of just service ; and slavery was that *abuse* or *perversion* of it. Slavery is such a perversion of service as concubinage, or *contubernium*, is of lawful marriage. Hence, most, if not all, the instructions concerning the slave-master and the slave will apply to the Scriptural relation of master and servant. There is, too, a total absence of the principal elements of the slave system in these instructions respecting slaves and masters, and this goes to say that slavery is disowned by Paul as an institution that could not be regulated, but must be destroyed. Therefore, the want of instructions, by Paul, as to the support of it in its leading elements, is the death-warrant of the whole system. 4. Besides, the instructions to parents and children, husbands and wives, are subversive of slavery, if observed. Children are required to obey their parents; but in the slave code they must obey their masters. Wives are required to obey their husbands; but by the laws of slavery they must obey their masters. Wives and husbands are to be married; but slavery ignores marriage, and substitutes *contubernium.*

5. We have two passages which concern the subject of slavery in Paul's instructions to Timothy. The first is as follows: "Knowing this, that the law is not made for a righteous man, but for the lawless and disobedient, for the ungodly and for sinners, for unholy and profane, for murderers of fathers, and murderers of mothers, for manslayers, for whoremongers, for them that defile themselves with mankind, for men-stealers, for liars, for perjured persons, and if there be any other thing that is contrary to sound doctrine." 1 Tim. i, 9, 10.

The Greek word ανδραποδιστης is, according to Robinson and all the lexicons, *a slave-dealer, a man-stealer.* Bengel says of such, that they are "those who, by force, make men slaves. They are not unlike those who enlist soldiers by fraud, cheats, and force, or press them." They are those who abduct the slaves of another, or who reduce or retain free men in slavery. The word is derived from ανδραποδον, a *slave,* which is from ανηρ, a *man,* and πους, a *foot,* or, in other words, a *downtrodden man.* The postfix ιστημι, to *stand,* forming ανδραποδιστης, is, therefore, one who *stands on the trampled man,* and disposes of him as he will, by force, fraud, law, or any other means, so as to have him under his dominion, and make him a *slave,* or *andrapodon,* a *downtrodden man.* These slave-dealers, or man-stealers, are those who carry on a traffic in human beings, by purchase, sale, or use, either in reducing freemen to slaves, or continuing slaves as slaves, except so far as is necessary to free them. The nations or states that legalize slavery, or connive at it, are also to be classed among *slave-dealers*, or *man-stealers*, in the strict moral sense of the term.

And this is the Scriptural view of the slave-dealer, "And he that stealeth a man, and selleth him, or if he be found in his hand, shall surely be put to death." Exod. xxi, 16. "If a man be found stealing any of his brethren of the children of Israel, and maketh merchandise of him, or selleth him, then that thief shall die, and thou shalt put evil away from among you." Deut. xxiv, 7. Thus the merchant in human beings is condemned, whether the stealer, the seller, or user of a man as property, excepting always, as far as is necessary, to pursue a legal course in order to restore the man to liberty.

The Latin Vulgate translates the Greek word by *Plagiarii.* And the Roman lawyers and law applied this name to slave-dealers, and denominated their theft *plagium,* because the law pronounced those worthy of death who were guilty of dealing in slaves.

And these *slave-dealers* are classed with the worst sinners. They are ranked morally with the lawless, disobedient, ungodly, sinners, profane, murderers, liars, perjured persons, and the like. "*Man-stealers*—the worst of all thieves, in comparison of whom highwaymen and house-breakers are innocent. What, then, are most traders in negroes, procurers of servants for America, and all who enlist soldiers by lies, tricks, or enticements?" (Wesley.)

Observe, too, here, that the *masters* of slaves, who, as above, retain them only so far as is necessary to free them, whether these masters are κυριοι or δεσποται, are not to be classed with slave-dealers, and Paul does not place them without distinction on the same list. The mere *master*, or owner, may have obtained his slaves by inheritance, and is contemplating their freedom, or he may have purchased slaves with the same view; namely, freedom; and, hence, such may be brethren *beloved*, *faithful*, *good*. Hence, also, instructions are given to such slaveholders or masters, the observance of which would preserve them from being on the list of slave-dealers, or mercenary slaveholders. But Paul gives no instructions how these latter classes should conduct themselves in their profession, or business, any more than he does to liars, murderers, and the like, with whom he associates them. But if the *master*, whether *kurios* or *despotes*, it matters not, is a *slave-dealer*, or becomes such, he is then to be classed with the liars and murderers, and to be treated as such, and the law is *against him*.

There is another passage in the first Epistle of Timothy which teaches the duties of slaves to their masters, and incidentally presents the character of Christian masters, whose duties are clearly defined in the Epistles to the Colossians and Ephesians. It reads as follows: "Let as many servants [δοῦλοι, *slaves*] as are under the yoke count their own masters worthy of all honor, that the name of God and his doctrine be not blasphemed. And they that have believing masters, let them not despise them, because they are brethren; but rather do them service, because they are faithful and beloved, partakers of the benefit. These things teach and exhort." 1 Tim. vi, 1, 2.

(1.) The servants, or slaves, were enjoined to be obedient to their unbelieving masters. They were to "count them worthy of all honor"—all the honor due from a servant to a master—and show it by obedience and respectful behavior. The reason for this was, that the name of God, or God himself, and his doctrine, or Christianity, be not blasphemed, or spoken evil of, as tending to destroy the political rights of mankind. "Civil rights are never abolished by any communications from God's Spirit. The civil state in which a man was before his conversion is not altered by that of his conversion; nor does the grace of God absolve him from any claims which either the state or his neighbor may have on him. All these outward things continue unaltered." (Dr. A. Clarke.) The service is not enjoined on the score that the masters had a right in justice to the services, but that God and Christianity might not be evil spoken of. The obedience and services of slaves have often been influential in the conversion of their masters and the promotion of religion. The conduct of stubborn and disobedient slaves would have a very different effect. The honor of the Gospel was concerned in the rendering, on the part of the slave, a prompt obedience to the commands of his master.

(2.) Servants, or slaves, are also instructed to obey their believing or Christian masters; that is, those who hold them for the slaves' own good, and with a view to their freedom. These are not to despise their masters, because they are brethren in Christ, and on that account on a level with them. Christian brotherhood consists with inequality of place and relation, and with subjection of one to another; but they ought to do them service because they are faithful and beloved, and partakers jointly of the common salvation.

(3.) The servants, or δουλοι, mentioned in this passage, were slaves. In the first verse they are said to be υπο ξυγον δουλοι, *servants under the yoke*. A servant *under the yoke* is a slave, or a servant in a state of slavery. When the Romans and others intended to deprive men of their liberty, they made them pass under the yoke. "The yoke is formed of three spears, two being fixed upright in the ground, and the other tied across between the upper end of them. Under this yoke the Dictator sent the Æquani." (Tit. Liv., Lib. III, C. 8.) Slavery in Scripture is called a yoke. (Lev. xxvi, 13; Isaiah ix, 4, and x, 27.)

(4.) It follows that some, holding the legal relation of masters, were Christians and members of the Church. Thus they were πιστοι, *faithful*, or *believers*. They were *brethren* in the Christian sense of the term, and brethren to their Christian slaves; they were αγαπητοι, *beloved* of God, and his followers; they were "partakers of the benefit," or, according to Wesley on the place, they were "joint *partakers of the great benefit* of salvation." These believing masters had slaves when they became believers; yet it should be carefully understood that their Christianity taught them to give full civil liberty to the slaves as soon as it could be done to the best advantage of the slave, the master retaining the legal tenure only till that could be accomplished. In the mean time, the slave was a *brother*, and treated as such. This is the true state of the question, as both the apostolic discipline and the workings of it in the primitive Church fully show.

(5.) Hence, the instructions of Paul to Timothy give no support to the system of slavery; because, 1. He condemns the *man-stealer*, or, rather, *slave-dealer*, whether the seller, purchaser, or user of the slave, *andrapodon*, or downtrodden man, classing him with the worst sinners. And this character embraces all who make merchandise of men, in any sense, except to free them. 2. The injunction to slaves to honor unbelieving masters gives no countenance to the system as good, as it enjoins honor or obedience because God and Christianity would be evil spoken of. 3. The obedience to believing masters considers Christian slaves as *brethren*—a condition at war with slavery and utterly subversive of it. 4. The Christian masters were believers, beloved, brethren to the slaves, partners in the same Christian cause. Such, therefore, could not hate but love their servants, who were their brethren, and, being Ephesians, observing the instructions given by Paul to that Church, in which he required masters to treat the slaves with reciprocal kindness, to avoid threatening, that the Master of both was in heaven, and there is no respect of persons with God. 5. And though emancipation is not mentioned in terms, it was to follow as soon as justice and equity could accomplish it; but till that point of time the slave was to be treated as a brother. 6. The subsequent history of the Church shows that such was the true position of master and slave in the time of the apostles and in the Churches organized and governed by them, as the Churches of Corinth, Colosse, Ephesus, and Crete.

6. Titus was left by Paul in the island of Crete "to set in order the things that were wanting, and ordain elders in every city." Chapter i, 5. Crete was a large island, two hundred and fifty miles long and about fifty wide. It became a Roman province and abounded in slaves, as the greater part of the world then did. In it there were many churches, and as Titus was the chief pastor, Paul instructs him in the difficult matter connected with slavery in exercising Church discipline.

The following is the Pauline teaching to the Churches in Crete: "Exhort servants to be obedient to their own masters, and to please them well in all things; not answering again; not purloining; but showing all good fidelity; that they may adorn the doctrine of God our Savior in all things." Titus ii, 9, 10. On the foregoing passage we remark:

(1.) The general duty enjoined on servants, or slaves, "obedience to their own masters." This extends to all honest and lawful things, whether their masters be pagans or Christians; if pagans, not assuming that Christianity freed them from their ordinary commands; if Christian masters, not thinking that they had a greater liberty to be disobedient. They were, therefore, to please their masters well in all things lawful, or wherein it can be done without sin.

(2.) The particular duties enjoined on servants are the following: Not answering again, or not contradicting or gainsaying the master's just commands, or even when blamed unjustly. The state of the servant calls for great moderation.

Servants should be *honest, not purloining;* that is, not stealing the least thing, nor taking any thing that is their master's, which is not allowed by their consent, but showing all honesty in every thing. Among the heathen slaves theft was so common, that *fur*, a thief, was commonly used to signify a servant, because slaves were generally thieves. Paul teaches that slaves should be strictly honest in all things, both as it respects their masters and others.

Fidelity was enjoined on slaves. They were to show "all good fidelity" in every trust reposed in them, so as to speak the truth, and discharge all their duties punctually and advantageously to their masters.

(3.) The reason for this conscientious discharge of their duties was, that they might "adorn the doctrine of God their Savior in all things." This would render their religion amiable and honorable in the eyes of their heathen masters and others, when they would see its influence on its professors, especially on those in the lower walks of life. The history of Christianity furnishes many illustrious examples of the conversion of multitudes by the Christian walk and conversation of slaves.

(4.) That the relation of master and slave is the one

here intended, is manifest from the very instructions given to the slaves. The duties enjoined were designed to correct evils inherent in slavery, such as insubordination, stubbornness, impertinence, theft, and perfidy. These were leading vices of the system of slavery, and not of services done for wages. Such, at least, were not the prominent vices of hired servants, as they were of slaves. The conclusion is, that the masters and servants spoken of here were slaveholders and slaves.

7. Although we have given the entire of the Pauline instructions respecting slaves and their masters, with the exception of the Epistle to Philemon, we may also embrace, in connection with the teachings of the missionary to the Gentiles, those given by the missionary of the circumcision.

Peter says, "Servants, [οἱ οικεται, *house-slaves*,] be subject to your masters [δεσποταις, *despots*] with all fear; not only to the good and gentle, but also to the froward [σκολιοις, *perverse*;] for this is thank-worthy, if a man for conscience toward God endure grief, suffering wrongfully." 1 Peter ii, 18, 19. This is the same in substance that Paul gives to Timothy, chapter vi, 1, 2.

(1.) The slave is bound to obey his master while under his authority, not because of any just right the master has to hold him in bondage, but because of the benefits he receives from him. The master is all the civil magistrate the slave has to protect him, to feed and clothe him. For this cause the slave is as much bound to obey his master as the subjects of a tyrant are while they enjoy his protection. And till Providence presents some way of relief, there is no essential difference between the relation of a slave to his despotic master, and that of a subject to a despotic king. Hence, Peter commands subjects to submit themselves to every ordinance of man for the Lord's sake. (Verse 13.) After continuing the exhortation to some length, he presently recognizes the duties of servants, or slaves, to their masters.

Obedience was enjoined not only to the good and gentle, but also to the froward or perverse master. Submission is not enjoined on the ground that the institution was right, but for conscience' sake. The obligation to relative duties does not depend on the character of the persons to whom they are rendered, or on the performance of the duties they owe to us, but on the unalterable relations of things as established by God. It was praiseworthy for a person to suffer wrongfully, after the manner of Christ, "who, when he was reviled, reviled not again." Verse 23. The apostle refers to those punishments suffered by slaves as contrary to justice and mercy, while they are exhorted to endure them, and suffer patiently, though suffering wrongfully.

(2.) That the servants mentioned here were slaves, we have full proof. 1. The epistle was addressed to persons scattered throughout Pontus, Gallatia, Cappadocia, Asia, Bythinia, provinces in Asia Minor, where the Grecian and Roman systems of slavery prevailed. The word οικετης here means any one under the authority of another, particularly household slaves, or servants, as *verna, familia, domestici, famuli*. It is used but four times in the New Testament—here, and in Luke xvi, 13, Acts x, 7, Rom. xiv, 4. The strong presumption is that, in all these places, slaves were intended, as they generally performed the duties now performed by hired servants among us. 2. In this passage the house servant must have been a slave, because he is instructed to obey with *all fear*, for *conscience toward God*, to *endure it as a grief*, and *suffering wrongfully*, after the example of Christ. Surely these accidents can not apply to hired servants, who served by contract for wages.

(3.) The masters, also, or *despotai*, must have been

slave-owners or slaveholders, as *master* is the corresponding relation to *slave*, or one under the power of another, whether he is called *doulos, oiketes,* or *andrapodon,* as among the Greeks, or *servus, mancipium, ancilia, verna, famulus,* as among the Latins, or slave, or servant, among us, when the servant is the property of a master.

There were two classes of masters here mentioned; the one class comprised the good and gentle, who were Christians, who treated their slaves well, held them in trust till they could safely emancipate them in conformity to *justice* and rendering them an equivalent for their services till that point of time, according to the Pauline discipline to the Colossians. (Col. iv, 1.) The other class of *despotai* were the *froward*—the σκολιοι, the *perverse, severe,* and *unjust* masters, who treated their slaves according to the laws of slavery, with little regard to justice. The "good and gentle" class of slaveholders might be called *masters,* but not *andrapodistai, slave-dealers.* The bad men might be called *andrapodistai, slave-dealers,* properly and characteristically, as well as slaveholders, masters, or slave-owners. The master might be a Christian, the slave-dealer, or the mercenary slaveholder, never, as Paul ranks him with murderers and liars. But he never places the mere master—him who sustains that relation with the simple view of the slave's good, and his freedom—in this category.

(4.) Surely the apostle Peter gives no support here to slavery. The slave is represented as suffering *wrongfully,* and he is exhorted, by the example of Christ, to endure this as a *wrong,* and not that which is just, or according to justice. Can any language more directly than that of Peter express the injustice of slavery? We think not.

CHAPTER XII.

PAULINE DISCIPLINE—CASE OF ONESIMUS.

THE case of Onesimus will furnish us with an example in which the instructions laid down by Paul were applied, and which became the model for the Christian Church in after times.

The Epistle to Philemon was not addressed to Philemon alone, but also to Apphia, supposed to be his wife, and to Archippus, who is supposed to be his son, and to the Church in his house. (Verse 1.) It was written from Rome, and sent by Paul to Philemon, his family, and the Church in his house at Colosse. It appears, from verses 1, 10, 13, 23, that it was written when Paul was a prisoner, and when he had hopes of obtaining his liberty. (Verse 22.) It was written at the same time with the Epistle to the Colossians, or about the end of A. D. 63, or beginning of 64. For Timothy joins him in both epistles. And in both the epistles, Epaphroditus, Mark, Demas, and Luke join in the salutations. And Onesimus, who carried this Epistle, was one of the messengers by whom the Epistle to the Colossians was sent. (Col. iv, 9.) The general instructions, therefore, respecting masters and slaves in the Epistle to the Colossians, must be taken into the account with the particular teachings given in the one sent to Philemon, to his wife, son, and the Church in his house.

Philemon appears to have been a person of consideration in the Church at Colosse, and was converted by the ministry of Paul—verse 19—about the time when he exercised his ministry at Ephesus. (Acts xix, 10.) He had a Church in his house—verse 2—and was so opulent as to be extensive in works of charity, and in entertaining those Christians who had occasion to visit Colosse. (Verses 5–7.) He was a man of influence in the Church, and the historians place him as bishop or chief pastor of the Church at Colosse.

The *occasion* of writing this letter was the following: Onesimus, the servant of Philemon, had, on some pretense, run away from his master and come to Rome, where Paul was then a prisoner. It is likely he was led to visit Paul, from having seen him in Colosse at his master's house. He became a genuine convert to Christianity, and was sedulous to serve Paul in promoting his comfort.

1. The circumstances of this case seem to show that, at the date of this Epistle, Onesimus was the legal slave of Philemon. As such Paul resolved to send him back to his master; and, to remove all difficulties, wrote to the latter this special Epistle.

2. Let us now examine how Philemon was, by Paul's instruction, required to receive and treat this slave on his return to his master.

(1.) Philemon was to receive him in the following manner: "Not now as a servant, [δουλος, a *slave*,] but above a servant, a brother beloved, especially to me, but how much more unto thee, both in the flesh, and in the Lord? If thou count me therefore a partner, receive him as myself. . . . I wrote unto thee, knowing that thou wilt also do more than I say." Verses 16, 17, 21.

Although Philemon could receive him as his legal slave, yet he was *besought* by Paul to receive him "not now as a slave, but above a slave." Formerly, when neither of them were Christians, Philemon might receive him *as a slave;* but he could not do that *now,* as both were Christians, as he must be received above a slave. He must receive him—ουκετι ως δουλον—*not now, no more, no farther, no longer, as a slave;* that is, he was now to be elevated above the condition of a slave. A slave was in the lowest condition in which a human being could be placed, and so low were slaves in the eye of the law that they could be placed no lower nor no higher, and among them there was nothing like grade, or higher or lower, but one dead level of the lowest possible position. So says the Roman law. "In the condition of slaves there is no difference; but among free persons there are many diversities. Thus some are *ingenui,* or freemen, others *libertini,* or freed-men." (Institutes, Lib. I, Tit. 3, Sec. 5.) Thus the first step was taken to rescue a man from slavery when he was to be considered *above a slave.* Thus the destruction of slavery commenced when the man was only one step raised above this condition, however small. All the rest was to follow. He was to be a *brother,* and a brother *beloved,* both to Paul the apostle and to Philemon the master. He was to be such in the flesh, or while his legal service existed, but especially in the Lord, or as a Christian. He was to be received as Paul was received, and this was the forerunner of liberty, not by constraint, but willingly; for Philemon was expected to do more than Paul said he should do. Let us look at the Christian state of brotherhood to which the Christian slave was elevated, as a first-fruit of religion.

(2.) Onesimus is now the *brother* of his master, the brother of Paul, Christ being the elder brother of the family. God is the common Father, to whom they are all to pray, Our Father. All are redeemed by Jesus Christ; all are sanctified by the same Spirit. Onesimus, the slave of Philemon according to the flesh, or Roman law, now worships with him in the Church in his house, and he is considered as much a Christian and a beloved brother as Paul himself. The term *brother* is a new term to be introduced between slave and master. It gives the death-blow to slavery, and it is a relation never known or used in the slave system.

(3.) As Philemon was a member of the Church at Colosse, and from the Epistle conveyed to that Church by Onesimus and Tychicus—Col. iv, 7, 10—he learned the instructions given to slaves and masters, he there found his own duty laid down in these words, "Masters, give to your servants [slaves] that which is just and equal, knowing that ye also have a Master in heaven." Col. iv, 1. Justice, according to its demands, would require that he should dissolve his relation as master; and equity required that, till this act of justice could take place, reciprocal duties and relations should control the matter. And the Church, to whom the Epistle was sent, was bound to see that this healthy discipline was carried out in reference to slaves and masters.

3. Let us see here the leading points in Paul's argument in favor of Onesimus. Paul had given *command* on the subject of slavery in his Epistle to the Colossians, and which was addressed to Philemon as well as other members of the Church at Colosse. He was, therefore, in possession of this special law, command, or injunction, in regard to the matter, which required *justice* and *equity* on his part toward Onesimus. Paul, in his letter to Philemon, omits the injunction as unnecessary to be repeated, and proceeds to *entreaty*: "I rather BESEECH thee." He brings to view the Christian character and privileges of Philemon, and calls him dearly-beloved and fellow-laborer. He congratulates him for the "Church in his house," for his love and fidelity to Christ and all saints, and that the bowels of the saints were refreshed by his bounty. He represents himself as prisoner of Jesus

Christ, and Paul the aged. Onesimus is his son, who was converted by his ministry, who was once unprofitable as a servant, but now may be relied on for honesty, veracity, and fidelity, that he is now a Christian and a beloved brother. He then pleads that Onesimus should be received as Paul himself, and treated with brotherly regard. He promises to pay for any wrong done by Onesimus, or had he improperly, in his days of sin, squandered his *peculium*, that he would repay all. He expresses his confidence that Philemon would do more than he requested him to do; and, to enlist him fully, he requests him further to provide a lodging for him, as he trusted that, through the prayers of Philemon, he would be permitted to pay him the intended visit. It was with such addresses as this that the primitive Christians made their pleas in behalf of those who were in bonds, as bound with them; and all know how admirably they succeeded in promoting freedom and the elevation of their race.

4. Now what was the effect of the instructions of Paul in this case, in reference to the freedom of Onesimus? The result was his emancipation from slavery. Of this we have sufficient historical data to assure us of it as a matter of fact. This is attested by the apostolical constitutions, and apostolical canons, which we have already quoted. And this is the concurrent testimony of antiquity on the subject. This is delicately hinted at by Paul, where he says, "Knowing that thou wilt also do more than I say." Verse 21. He did not in terms enjoin emancipation, but he knew, that this result would follow, and he therefore leaves it to be wrought out from the moral and religious principles which he inculcated on the subject, and the spirit of Christianity; for as there was a *will*, there would be found a *way*, to execute it. This the history of Christianity attests.

5. The disciplinary example of the case of Philemon and Onesimus, gives no support to slavery, but on the other hand is subversive of it. If those who are slaves would become Christians, and their masters would treat them *not now*, or *no more* as slaves, but brethren beloved, as *above slaves*, the result would be freedom. And though the slaves, under the teachings of Christianity, would be more faithful slaves while they were slaves, the treatment of them as brothers would soon lead to freedom. This, too, is history.

What would we think of Philemon, had he neglected Paul's instructions and entreaty, and treated Onesimus according to the slave laws? For example, had he whipped him first for running away, and then sold him to a slave-dealer, and sold his wife and children to the highest bidder, would he be tolerated in the Christian Church, after selling his brother and putting the money in his pocket? By no means. The primitive Church had no such custom among them, and no such conduct would be tolerated. And can our Christians who reject the discipline and principles laid down by Paul, be considered as any other than wicked, who buy and sell their fellow-men, and live on their labor without remuneration? Every Christian is bound to do like Philemon, to treat the slave as a brother, while he is a slave, and grant him his freedom with as little delay as the law will allow, or the circumstances of the case require. Nothing short of this is Christianity. How can any Christian come to his dying pillow, and leave slaves to others to inherit them, when emancipation is within his reach, even though it would be necessary to remove them to another country or state? Even this is not too much to do for freedom.

CHAPTER XIII.

PAULINE DISCIPLINE—GENERAL SURVEY.

It is time now to take a general survey of the principles and discipline of the Pauline instructions to masters and servants.

1. The apostle acknowledged some masters to be true Christians—such masters as sustained the legal relation, not for gain, but with a view to the good of the slave, and his ultimate freedom.

2. It appears evident that such masters were admitted to Church membership in the Churches founded and governed by the apostles.

3. The great endeavor of the apostolic preaching, as relating to slavery, seems to have been to bring slaves and masters to an intellectual, experimental, and practical knowledge of the truth—to assign to each their respective duties, and lay down those great principles of right and wrong, which would inevitably issue in emancipation, and meanwhile correct, so far as possible, the moral evils of the system in reference to slaves and masters, respectively.

If, in their preaching, the apostles seem not to dwell largely on the evils of slavery itself, this may, in part at least, be accounted for from the fact that these evils were evident to all persons taught in the principles of the Gospel. The influence of the perfect love of God and man—the comprehensive beneficence begotten by Christianity—the union in one common brotherhood—having one God—one Savior and Sanctifier—one common inheritance of grace here, and of glory hereafter—all conspired to bring about one result—the civil freedom of the slave, and the elevation of both slave and master to the higher freedom of the sons of God.

4. Paul enjoined duties to masters and slaves while both remained *in* this relation of master and slave to each other. The passages quoted, at a preceding page, from Paul, show that certain duties were required from masters and slaves while in that relation, or while it continued. Masters are enjoined—Ephesians vi, 9—to do the "same things" to their slaves which had been enjoined on them; that is, they were to exhibit the same kindness, fidelity, and regard to the will of God. They were to "forbear threatening," or to "disuse threatening," and not govern by terror, but by love and kindness. They were urged by the consideration that they had a Master in heaven, who had no respect of persons.

Masters were required to "give unto their servants that which is just and equal, remembering that they had also a Master in heaven." Colossians iv, 1.

Philemon was entreated by Paul to receive his slave Onesimus not now, or *ουκετι, no more, no longer*, as a slave, but above a slave, a brother beloved, the brother of himself and Paul—as Paul himself. As a member of the Colossian Church he was commanded to render to him according to justice and equity. He was entreated to receive him as a beloved Christian brother, with the command to render to him afterward that which was just and equal. (Philemon 16.)

5. The duties of slaves to their masters show that these duties were enjoined on them while in a state of slavery, to be performed to their legal masters, whether Christians or heathen. The texts enforcing those duties have been quoted. *Obedience* or all honor to the masters is enjoined

in all things. This is limited to the will of God, or the precepts of morality. *Service* is a labor to be rendered to the master, with the same restraint as it is to be unto Christ, as unto the Lord. *Fidelity* or *trustworthiness* for the interests of the master is required, so as to be *honest* and *faithful* to all trusts reposed in them.

Besides, these slaves were slaves properly so called, and though they became brethren to their masters, they still continued to be legal slaves till emancipation took place.

6. In the list of duties of slaves and their masters in reference to each other, we have certain *privileges* belonging to each in this relation. The master was privileged with *obedience*, *service*, and *fidelity* from the slave, in conformity to the moral laws of God and Christianity; and the slave had his *privileges* also. He looked for *justice*, *equity*, and *love*, or brotherhood, from the master, and the cessation of threatening, or the use of the whip.

But these mutual duties and privileges would reduce slavery gradually to lawful service, which was certainly the intention of Paul in his code, as was the intention in the Abrahamic administration. Emancipation would come in, as a consequence.

As Paul, in giving his instructions to masters and slaves, does it in connection with his instructions to husbands and wives, parents and children, it is inferred by some, that he therefore sanctions slavery. But the contrary will appear on careful examination. It is true that he gives the instructions to slaves and masters in connection with the relations of husbands and wives, parents and children, in the following places, namely: In his Epistle to the Corinthians, Ephesians, and Colossians. It is confessed on all hands that the parental and filial relations were established by almighty God. And if the instructions and laws of these relations are subversive of slavery, the latter can not be of God. Now this is the case. Marriage is appointed of God, or the union of one man and one woman till death. Wherever legal marriage is there is no slavery, properly so called, at least no Roman slavery. This cuts up by the roots the *contubernium*, or polygamy, of slavery. Besides, children are to obey their parents in preference to their masters. They can not obey both; therefore, they must obey their parents. Parents, too, are to bring up their children in the nurture and admonition, or in the instruction and discipline, of the Lord. This takes them away from the hands of all others. So that the establishment of marriage and the parental and filial relations are at irreconcilable variance with slavery. And as God has established these he never established nor sanctioned slavery, which is a perversion of just service, as polygamy, concubinage, and *contubernium* are perversions of lawful marriage; and lawful marriage being established, the others necessarily are annihilated or entirely superseded, as enormities that can not be tolerated by the morals of the Gospel.

7. Hence, the legislation of Paul in reference to slavery would restore service to its original and just condition, by removing those abuses which slavery introduced. This was done, as we have seen, by the Mosaic code. The instructions of Paul to masters and slaves would apply substantially to employers and hired servants; and, indeed, most theologians have applied the instructions, with great propriety, to masters and hired servants in countries where slavery does not exist. All employers are bound to render to persons in their employ according to justice and equity, as well as to forbear or disuse threatening, and treat them as brethren, fellow-men, with civility and love. They are privileged, too, to have their commands about their business executed as they wish, and they ought to have the proportion of labor

or service agreed on performed. All servants or persons in employ are also bound to *obey* these commands, to do the amount of work, and to do it honestly and with fidelity. They are privileged, too, to receive their wages and civil and respectful treatment.

Besides, the apostle Paul lays down no laws or rules to institute or maintain slavery proper. He lays down no rules about buying and selling men, and the endless moral wrongs of the slave system. And while he *omits* all such rules and enjoins only what is just and right, he neither sanctions, supports, nor sustains slavery by any instructions he has given to slaves and masters. Does Paul give instructions to man-stealers or slave-dealers to prosecute their business? Certainly not, as these were willful transgressors. But some masters, or owners of slaves, may have no act whatever or no will, in becoming slaveholders; and such, *so far*, can not be guilty of any willful, wrong act. Their future course is to decide this question of right and wrong on their part.

Paul made laws for the master, as responsible to God, and not for slavery. He made laws for the slave as a redeemed man and a sufferer, but not for the perpetuity of the system which oppressed him. This does not prove that Paul approved of the system. Paul made a law respecting the relation between Nero and his subjects—Romans xiii, 1–7—yet he certainly did not teach by this that his government and laws were good and just. Paul considered slavery as a hard condition, from which he exhorts all who can to be free, and that none who are free from it should willingly enter on it. So he exhorted Christians to bear persecution; but certainly he did not approve of persecution.

8. Paul, in his instructions to slaves and masters, gives no sanction or approval to the system of slavery.

(1.) In order to present the subject clearly, let us select

some of the leading elements of the slave system that then prevailed, which was Roman slavery, seeing Rome then governed the civilized world, comprising all the territory in which Churches were formed, and, of course, those Churches which Paul instructs on this subject. In our chapter on Roman slavery we gave a pretty full outline of the system. We may select the leading points. The principal modes by which persons became slaves were, by war in selling the captives, by kidnapping and commerce; some were born slaves; some sold themselves for slaves; others became slaves in consequence of their crimes.

As to the state of the slaves, they were held *pro nullis, pro mortuis, pro quadrupedibus.* They were entirely under the power of their masters, who could put them to death, torture, correct them, or dispose of them at pleasure. They were property, and could be sold, bartered, leased, given by will, or otherwise disposed of. They could have no property, and could not take by will, purchase, or descent. They were not entitled to the rights of matrimony, had no relief in case of adultery, nor were they proper objects of cognation, so as to stand in the relation of parent and child, husband and wife. They could not be witnesses. The master might or might not manumit, so that the slave could not secure freedom without the consent of his master. Such are some of the leading elements of Roman slavery.

(2.) Now, we ask, where did Paul, in treating on this subject, expressly say any thing to support this system? Certainly no where. He does not, it is true, single out these points, as all such were clearly, in many places, denounced by the word of God. And yet, in classing the slave-dealer with the worst of men, he condemns the whole system in which he traffics. The instructions of Paul, without exception, give no countenance to the leading elements of slavery—where does he sanction any one of the modes of enslaving men?—while his teachings to masters and slaves would do away the essential parts of slavery, and would, by this means, transform it into a just service, and thus supersede slavery by that which slavery had perverted from its just and original condition.

(3.) The instructions to masters give no countenance to slavery.

The duties of masters are given in two short texts—Eph. vi, 9; Col. iv, 1—which require that masters should treat slaves as they would be treated, that they should not threaten or whip, that they would render justice and equity to the slave; and the reasons for their course were, that they had a Master in heaven over them, whose laws must be obeyed, and with whom there was no respect of persons, so as to distinguish between master and slave. None of these precepts teach or tolerate that masters should consider their legal slaves as nothing, as dead persons, as beasts; that they had any moral right to hold them in bondage; to annul marriage, and break up the parental and filial relation; to put them to death, torture, and whip them; to sell, give, barter, or will them; to receive the profits of their unrequited labors; to make all their religious privileges to depend on his will, etc. The teachings of Paul grant no such rights to masters; and though, while the relation must exist, the master has the power to *govern* and to require *service*, according to the rule of reciprocal right only, yet Paul's laws of privileges and duties to the master give him not one of those as rights which go to constitute slavery proper. And the lessons given the masters will, in due time, lead to emancipation, as an inevitable result, by the application of the principles and duties laid down. It is preposterous to think that Paul's instructions to masters would *tolerate* them in treating a brother Christian, or a brother man, as property, or a thing, so as to sell his brother, or treat him as the slave system of Rome allowed him to be treated.

(4.) No argument in favor of slavery can be drawn from the instructions of Paul to slaves themselves. The passages have all been already quoted, and are the following: 1 Corinthians vii, 20–24; Ephesians vi, 5–8; Colossians iii, 22–25; 1 Timothy vi, 1–5; Titus ii, 9, 10. In the first passage the slaves are taught to obtain their freedom, if they lawfully can, and if they are free not to consent to be slaves. In the other passages they are taught to be obedient to the lawful commands of their masters, to render service to them with fidelity. The main duties are patience, meekness, fidelity, kindness, truth, and honesty—duties obligatory to all men. There were vices which they were to avoid, such as pilfering, lying, and eye-service; and the apostle enjoins on them, as Christians, to avoid these. They were to do all this in obedience to God, or "as unto Christ," "as the servants of Christ," "as to the Lord," "fearing God." They were to do right—to do no wrong. They, too, had the privileges from their Christian masters, to be treated as brethren, according to the law of love, with justice, equal rights, etc.

(5.) Surely these duties enjoined on slaves, and the privileges growing out of the instructions of Paul, never could recognize the claim that these slaves should still be considered and treated as things—as property—as beasts, as having no right to marriage, or that their children must not obey them—that they may be sold, bartered, killed, tortured, whipped, work for nothing, etc. All this is simply preposterous. Indeed, the right of the master to slaves is never conceded or even referred to. The obligation of obedience is never based on the ground that slavery is right, but, on the other hand, that it is wrong, being unjust and unequal.

9. The principles and duties prescribed by Paul, in reference to masters and slaves, are opposed to slavery, and, if carried out, would secure its abolition.

The supreme sovereignty of God over all human beings, and the laws he has given to govern mankind, present a direct antagonism to slavery. The instructions of Paul very clearly bring this to view. He addresses masters thus: "Knowing that your Master also is in heaven;" or as some copies read, "Knowing that both your and their Master is in heaven." Ephesians vi, 9. Servants are to be "obedient, as unto Christ." Verse 5. They are to serve, but it is "as the servants of Christ." Verse 6. They are to serve and "do the will of God from the heart." Verse 6. The servant is represented as "called in the Lord;" is the "Lord's freed-man," απελευθερος; is "Christ's *doulos*, or slave." 1 Corinthians vii, 22. In his service he is "therein to abide with God." Verse 24. To the Colossians Paul says, in referring to the obedience of slaves, "Servants, obey—fearing God." Colossians iii, 22. "Do it heartily as to the Lord and not to man." Verse 23. They will "receive the inheritance from the Lord;" and they "serve the Lord Christ." Verse 24. They are exhorted to honor their masters, "that the name of God and his doctrine be not blamed." 1 Tim. vi, 1. They are exhorted to obey for the sake of religion, or that "they may adorn the doctrine of God our Savior in all things." Titus ii, 10. Onesimus was "a brother beloved in the Lord." Philemon 16. Paul beseeches Philemon, in regard to his slave Onesimus, "let me have joy of thee in the Lord," and "refresh my bowels in the Lord." Verse 20. And Peter exhorts slaves to endure their hard lot, "for conscience toward God, enduring grief, suffering wrongfully." 1 Peter ii, 19.

From the foregoing it will be seen that the obedience and service of the slave must be referred to the sovereign authority of God, with no reference to any rights of the master other than as governed by the will of God, in honor of him, for the sake of religion, as a matter of conscience. And all this in reference to those things which comprise moral or social acts, as of obedience to just commands, and rendering a reasonable service. And all this, too, only for a time, or till freedom could intervene. The leading elements of slavery are here necessarily omitted, such as unequaled toil, rejection of marriage and filial or parental obligations, sale and purchase of the slaves, that they are *pro nullis, pro mortuis, pro quadrupedibus*, and the like.

Chrysostom, on 1 Corinthians vii, 23, has a very appropriate remark on this point. "There are limits set to slaves by God himself; and up to what point one ought to keep them, this is also exacted, and to transgress them is wrong; namely, when your master commands nothing which is unpleasing to God, it is right to follow and obey, but no further. For thus the slave becomes free. But, if you go further, even though you are free, you are become a slave."

10. Doing good is enjoined on all, both slaves and masters, as part of the system of instructions given on the subject. "Knowing that whatsoever good thing any man doeth, the same shall he receive of the Lord." Ephesians vi, 8. Our blessed Lord went about doing good. Christians are to be employed in well-doing. We might simply ask, if only good acts were to be performed, how could slavery ever have existed? Or, how long would it last in the performance of that which is good on the part of masters and slaves? It was a lawful act, under Roman slavery, to kill the slave. Surely this was not good. And if well-doing were applied to

the system of Roman slavery, nothing of it would be left, but that of which it was a perversion; namely, legitimate, honest, free labor. The same text applied to American slavery, would issue in the same result entirely. "Cleave to that which is good," is a command that would annihilate the system in short order.

11. The apostle of the Gentiles, the Roman citizen, too, in his official teaching concerning slavery, masters, and slaves, declares that no one, whether slave or master, can do wrong without suffering the penalty inflicted on sinners. "But he that doeth wrong shall suffer for the wrong; and there is no respect of persons." Colossians iii, 25. Or, 'Ο δὲ αδικων, κόμιεῖται ὅ ηδικησε. "He that doeth unjustly, shall suffer for the injustice." Doing wrong, or acting unjustly, is condemned, whether to masters or slaves. Slavery is contrary to natural law, or to justice, which "renders to every man his due." The precepts of justice are, "to live honestly, to hurt no one, to give every one his due." (Institutes, I, 1, 1.) Now, injustice, or wrong, is the opposite of justice, or right. Slavery does not give every one his own, as it deprives the slave of his liberty, his personal security, and the fruit of his labors. It furthermore *hurts* the slave, by stripes, severe labor, degradation, and dishonor. It hurts him in his good name, his property, and his person. The slaveholder does not live honorably, as he lives by injuring others, and by their labor, skill, and sufferings. Hence he is said to be ὁ αδικων, one who *doeth wrong*, or who *acts unjustly*, from α, not, and δικω, to be just. Or he acts αντι δικην, *contrary to justice*, or αντι το δικαιον, *contrary to that which is just*. The voluntary slaveholder acts contrary to justice, and Paul requires all slaveholders to act *according to justice*, or *according to that which is just*. And slavery is contrary to *jus naturale*, *natural right* or *justice*, and is therefore unjust. All men

are born free. He that makes slaves of children, as soon as they are born, whether by the help of law, or by theft, or force, is unjust.

Now, it is God's law, that "he who does wrong will suffer for the wrong," and as a confirmation of it there is "no respect of persons." Slaves are poor, and God will punish those who make or keep them poor by enslaving them. Especially will God avenge the *contubernium* of slavery, the ignoring the paternal and filial relations, selling men, women, and children, like beasts, and all the other wrongs of the system of slavery, which is properly a *malum in se.* Now, separate *doing wrong* from the system of slavery, and the system is destroyed by the process.

12. The equality of the human race, or the common nature of man, is taught by Paul in his instructions to slaves and masters. In regard to slaves he says, when teaching that he who does wrong shall receive for the wrong, that "there is no respect of persons." Colossians ii, 25. In enjoining on masters reciprocal acts of justice to the slaves, he says, "Neither is there respect of persons with him." Ephesians vi, 9. Human nature is one, and it is a common possession. Hence, according to natural law, all men are born equal, and have equal rights. Hence, all men are entitled to their natural rights of personal liberty, personal security, and the right of holding property. With God there is no such respect of persons as slavery induces. All have one common father—all are partakers of the same nature—all are equally redeemed—all partake of a common salvation, and all are heirs to the same inheritance. The teaching of Paul to slaves and masters, in declaring, in reference to this very point, that there is no respect of persons, shows plainly, though in general terms, that slavery does respect persons in an unjust way, and is therefore wrong.

13. Paul strictly enjoins the brotherhood of man, in reference to slavery. "And they that have believing masters, let them not despise them, because they are brethren." 1 Timothy vi, 2. Paul teaches Philemon to *receive* or treat his slave Onesimus, not now, *ουκετι, not any more,* "as a slave, but as a brother." Philemon verse 16. All Christians are to be regarded as *brethren.* "One is your master [*καθηγητης, leader,*] and all ye are brethren." Matthew xxiii, 8. This is the uniform language of the New Testament. To apply the terms brethren and sisters to slaves, initiates a new element into the subject unknown to all slave laws, and all slavery principles. In the West Indies the pro-slavery men, during the controversy there from 1808 to 1833, ridiculed the idea of brothers and sisters among the missionary Churches. They asked, "Can you make your negroes Christians, and use the words *dear brother* or sister, to those you hold in bondage? They would conceive themselves, by possibility, put on a level with yourselves, and the chains of slavery would be broken." It would be strange work in a Christian Church to see Christians killing, beating severely, selling, giving away to prostitution, their slaves, as the Roman laws authorized. Indeed, the exercise of the slavery code of any law is at variance with the brotherhood of man and of Christianity. And so Paul teaches, when he says, receive him no longer as a slave, but above a slave, a brother beloved.

14. Paul introduces redemption as a reason why no freed-man, or freeman, should agree to become a slave. He says, "Ye are bought with a price; do not become the slaves of men." 1 Corinthians vii, 23. The reasons for this are obvious. Slavery sits very uneasily on the freed-man of Christ, as it brings with it many evils, snares, dangers, and disabilities. Because Christians are bought with a price they are bound to "glorify God in

their body and spirit, which are God's." Their bodies are represented to be the "temple of God;" "the temple of the Holy Ghost;" which show they are bodily consecrated to God. It is hard to approve of a Christian, redeemed by Christ, as holding his brother in bondage, regarding him as property, and proceed to prostrate in the dust the relation of husband, father, son, and Christian. In connection with slavery Paul says, "The grace of God that bringeth salvation hath appeared to all men, or all conditions of men." Titus ii, 11. The following addresses to Philemon do not well comport with the exercise of slave laws: "I beseech thee for my son Onesimus, whom I have begotten in my bonds;" "Receive him as myself;" "He is my bowels."

15. If we examine the instructions given by Paul to masters, we shall find nothing in them that would either establish or continue any length of time the system of slavery, but on the other hand, that which would gradually destroy it as a system, and in the mean time would commence and carry on the good work of emancipation. We arrange here, as follows, the instructions given to slaveholders: 1. They were to render to their slaves according to justice. 2. They were to render to them equity, or reciprocal rights. 3. They were to disuse threatening, or the use of the whip. 4. And the *privileges* due them growing out of the duties enjoined on slaves.

(1.) Masters are taught to render to their slaves, το δικαιον, that *which is just*, or rather κατα το δικαιον, *according to that which is just*. The δικαιος, *just*, *upright*, is one who *does right;* while ὁ αγαθος, the *good*, is one who *does good*, a *benefactor*. Cicero defines justice thus, "Justice, from which virtue alone men are called good"—"*justitia, ex qua una virtute boni viri appellantur.*" (Cicero Off., 2, 10.) "Justice, to which belong piety, goodness, liberality, benignity, comity, and others of the like sort"—

"*justitia . . . cui adjuncta sunt pietas, bonitas, liberalitas, benignitas, comitas, quaque sunt genus ejusdem.*" (De Fin., 5, 23.) Justice, according to the Roman law, as we have seen, is the "constant and perpetual disposition to render to every man his due." It has respect to "what is just and unjust." Its precepts are "to live honestly, to hurt no one, to give every one his due." The slaveholder is required to render to the slave his due, not to hurt him, and to live honorably in respect to him.

Besides, all are instructed, in regard to slavery, to do no wrong, or no injustice. For ὁ αδικων, he that doeth unjustly, shall receive or bear the sin of doing unjustly.

Hence, in regard to slaveholders, they are required to do justly toward their slaves, and to do them no wrong. In the last verse of chapter iii, to the Colossians, all αδικια, *injustice*, or *wrong*, is expressly forbidden. And then in the following verse—chapter iv, 1—the slaveholder is instructed to render to the slave *that which is just*, or *according to that which is just*. Justice secures to all *life, liberty, personal security, the right of property, the pursuit of happiness*. To these we may add the rights of marriage, of parents and children, of husbands and wives, of worship, of education, etc.

According to justice the life of man is sacred and inviolable. The Roman master could kill the slave when, and as he chose. He could throw him to the fishes—make him fight with wild beasts—convert him into a gladiator—expose him, on an island of the Tiber, to starve, or kill or maim him in any other way. This was the Roman law in Paul's day. In after times this power was restrained, although the restraint was inefficient. Was this murder of God? Personal liberty is the right of all men, and required by justice. All men are born free and equal, according to the Roman law, and according to the Bible, and the Declaration of Independence, and the Constitution of the United States. The slaveholder is bound to give liberty to the slave, as his detention is an act of injustice, a wrong; and he that doeth wrong shall receive for the wrong.

The slave, according to justice, is entitled to *personal security*. Slavery assaults his person often with stripes, hunger, cold, degradation, and exposure. Justice forbids this; therefore, the slaveholder is bound to restore and secure to the slave his security from the insults of the overseer, himself, or any other in his name.

According to justice, a man who earns property by his skill, his labor, his self-denial, and economy is entitled to own that property. But slavery allows no property to belong to the slave, as a matter of right, or justice, although it is earned by his industry or skill. As to the *peculium* of Roman slavery, it was allowed by *indulgence*, and not by right, and was always liable to be seized by the master. Justice gives to the slave his own earnings, and this being granted, the master must relinquish all right to the slave's earnings beyond an equivalent for what he gives him.

All men have the right of marriage, by the law of God. The master must grant this in justice, and do away with servile *contubernium*. Then husbands and wives must remain united, performing the duties of each. Children must obey their parents, and parents must govern their children. All this is according to justice, and it grants this to all men. This undermines completely the power of the master, and restores it to the original owners. The master must not separate man and wife by sale, or otherwise. The parents must teach and govern their children, which overthrows greatly the power of the master. Indeed, slavery, whether Roman or American, knows no father, no marriage, no husband, no wife, no child of any father; and as justice secures these relations, and masters are bound to render it, slavery perishes under the administration of justice, in following out the precepts of the marriage relation in regard to husbands and wives, parents and children.

Now, as the exercise of justice secures to slaves life, liberty, security, property, marriage, and what belong to them, it is plain that it is against slavery. And as it is wrong, or unjust, to deprive any one of these, the requirements of justice are against slavery.

(2.) The master is taught to observe the golden rule in regard to any slave he may by law possess: 'All things whatsoever ye would that men should do to you, do ye even so to them." Matt. vii, 12. This law is enjoined on the slaveholder. He is bound to render to the slave that which is equal—ισοτητα, *equality*, or *an equivalent*, from ισος, *equal, the same.* Masters are required to render their slaves a *just equivalent* for their services. This is further confirmed by the command to masters, "Do the same things to them." Eph. vi, 9. No one under the influence of the law of love or the law of reciprocal right would ever make a man a slave, or continue him as a slave, or treat him as a slave, except just so far as to release him from slavery. The relation itself, if voluntarily assumed, and with recognition of property in the slave, is sinful, and this relation is always to be dissolved with the least possible delay, and can not be sustained except to destroy it.

(3.) Masters are required to "forbear [or moderate] threatening." Eph. vi, 9. Robinson renders the phrase, ανιεντες την απειλην, *leaving off*, or *ceasing from threatening*. Dr. Clarke says the words "signify to mitigate, relax, or not exact threatening; that is, the threatened punishment." This teaches the disuse of threats and punishments, and calls for the substitution of love and remuneration. The whip, stocks, screws, hand-cuffs, chains, prisons, patrols, are the necessary accompaniments of slavery. Paul commands the disuse of these among Christians, and in doing so, he commands the disuse of slavery, practically, immediately, and legally, as soon as the nature of the case will allow, and the interests of the slave demand.

(4.) As to the *privilege* of the masters corresponding to the *obedience* enjoined on slaves, and the *services* of labor to the masters, we observe that the system of slavery can find no support from these privileges; because the master is not allowed to command any thing wrong, false, immoral, oppressive, or at variance with justice; and the servant must obey God rather than man in all these things. And as to *services* rendered, they must be also tempered with justice, and a *just remuneration* must be given to the slave. This would reduce slavery to lawful and just service in its practical operation.

On the part, therefore, of the master, he is to *render*, *give*, to his slaves, according to the demand of justice, which renders to each his own, and hurts no one. This secures to the slave the rights of life, liberty, personal security, the ownership of the property secured by his skill and labor, the rights of marriage, of husbands and wives, of parents and children, and the rights of education and religion. It is *unjust* to withhold or wrest away any of these rights, according to Paul's teaching to masters and slaves. So the right to hold a slave is an *unjust*, *usurped* right, though established by law. The master is bound to relinquish at once the justice of his claim, and, till it is in his power to free him, render to the slave a *just equivalent* for his labors as to a hired servant, and never attempt by gift, will, sale, or otherwise, to transfer the servant, bound in chains, to any human being, whether son, daughter, or other person. Such is the amount of Paul's instructions to slaveholders.

16. If we consider the instructions given to slaves by Paul, we shall find nothing in them that would originate or continue slavery any longer than to dissolve its bonds in the manner best calculated to set at liberty the captives. This will appear if we consider, 1. The obedience enjoined; 2. The service or work to be rendered; 3. The vices they are to shun; 4. And their privileges, arising from the injunctions to their masters.

(1.) The duty of obedience or submission to the commands of their masters is enjoined on slaves in the following lessons of teaching: "Servants, be obedient to your masters according to the flesh," Eph. vi, 5; "Servants, obey your masters in all things according to the flesh," Col. iii, 22; "Count your masters worthy of all honor. . . . Let them not despise believing masters;" 1 Tim. vi, 1, 2; "Exhort servants to be obedient to their own masters," Titus iii, 9; "Servants, be subject to your own masters with all fear; not only to the good and gentle, but also to the froward," 1 Peter ii, 18.

Now, look at the *motives* or *reasons* for this obedience to the commands of masters. They were to consider themselves as the "servants of Christ;" that they were "bought with a price;" were "heirs of an inheritance;" they were to do the "will of God," to obey as "unto Christ," and "to the Lord;" they were to obey, that the "name of God and his doctrine be not blasphemed," and that they might adorn the doctrine of "God their Savior in all things."

Obviously, here is no *right* of the master recognized in all this; but the supreme law of God is to govern in all things; and the *interests* of religion, and not the mere commands of the master, are the controlling reasons. God's *laws* of right and wrong must govern the slave as well as the master. No *wrong* or injustice is to rule. The motives are all moral and religious ones, such as are incumbent even on persons suffering persecution, or living under unjust laws.

(2.) The duty of *service*, or laboring for the master, is pointed out in the following language: "With good will doing service," Eph. vi, 7; "Not with eye-service," Col. iii, 22; "Rather do them service," 1 Tim. vi, 2; "To please them well in all things," Titus ii, 9. The *motives* or reasons connected with this service are of the religious and moral sort. There is nothing like a *debt* or moral *obligation* to serve their masters, other than the reciprocal obligations of justice and remuneration demand.

(3.) Honesty, fidelity, and honor were enjoined on the slaves. These are enjoined on all relations. And as theft, treachery, and insubordination are the vices inseparable from slavery, the slaves are commanded to shun these because they are wrong in themselves; they are contrary to the rule of reciprocal retribution to the masters for food, clothing, protection, etc., and it is necessary for them to shun these vices, as they disqualify them for freedom, to which they were now on the way, through the influence of their religion.

(4.) As to the *privileges* of slaves, growing out of the duties of masters toward them, they were entitled to *justice*, as we have seen, to kindness, remuneration, brotherhood, and other benefits, as well as the disuse of the lash and all bodily punishments.

17. As to emancipation, some observations may be given here on that subject. It is worthy of remark that, among the direct instructions given to masters, there is no injunction requiring, in terms, the civil emancipation, although the duties of masters, as enjoined by Paul in requiring justice, equity, the disuse of cruelty, the requirement of what is right, and the absence of what is wrong, would end in civil freedom, as far as it was in the master's power. On this point we offer a few remarks.

As we have seen, in quoting the Roman law on slavery, there were few obstacles in the way of legal emancipation, as any master could set his slaves free, with some exceptions. We refer to what is given in a preceding chapter on this point.

Yet there were some cases in which the owner could not set the slave free. Emancipation could not take place in fraud of creditors. (Institutes, I, Tit. 6; Dig., XL, 9.) A master under twenty years of age could not manumit without the leave of his guardian. (Institutes, I, 6, 4.) Augustus restrained the right of indiscriminate manumission, so that no one could set free more than a certain proportion of his slaves at any one time.

At the first, under the Republic, emancipation was complete whenever effected. But under the emperors there were great differences existing as to the degrees of freedom. In the time when Paul wrote, the state of the Roman law was as follows: The freed-man, though legally and practically free on the whole, still depended on his former master. He could wear the toga and have a name, mostly of his master. He was compelled to honor his master, assist him in misfortune, and not sue him in law. Freed-men who violated these obligations were punished, and were sometimes reduced to slavery, as these requirements were the conditions on which they were freed.

Freed-men, in Paul's time, were divided into *Dedititii*, *Latini*, and *cives Romani*. The first were *subjects* or tributaries of the Roman Government, and were neither slaves, citizens, nor Latins. The Latins could not enjoy the legal rights of the *connubium*, and they were otherwise disabled as to rights of citizens, because they were not citizens. But they could obtain citizenship in several ways.

Although the freed-men might become Roman citizens,

their patrons had certain rights over them. They could not make a will, nor take property under a will, nor be named tutors to a will. They could take, however, by way of *fidei commissum*. Yet the sons of freed-men were *ingenui*, or freemen, but often taunted on account of their servile origin.

The act of manumission created a new relation, similar to that between father and son. The manumittor became the patron of the freed-man, and the latter was the *libertus*, or freed-man, of the former. The freed-man adopted the Gentile name of the patron, was his client, must respect him, and render him aid, if necessary. The patron claimed a right to all these. There are many intricate points in the Roman law in reference to the relations of patrons and freed-men. The further pursuit of them would not be relevant to our purpose. (See Dig., XL, Tit. 9, L. 30; and XXXVII, Tit. 14, L. 19; and other parts of the civil law connected with these. Compare Anthon's Dictionary on *Latinus*, *Libertus*, *Dedititii*, *Patronus*, etc., with Roman historians, philosophers, etc.)

The state of the question, in reference to the Church, was the following: In some cases, legal freedom could not be given, though in most cases it could. When given, the freed-men were still subject to their patrons, and owed them such services as tributes to their former relation, and this remained till death. Besides, the moral reasons were also in the way of Christians, such as the case of minors, of aged and disabled persons, the ties of marriage which bound Christians, of parents and children. On these accounts no law of emancipation, especially immediate, could apply as a general law. Hence the absence of such a law in the Pauline code. Yet the principles laid down by Paul would lead to emancipation in all those cases that were practicable and just; and, in the mean time, the Pauline code, by instituting the law of love, of justice, of remuneration, and discarding all injustice and wrong, inducing the CHRISTIAN BROTHERHOOD, was a noble substitute for freedom, as well as a guarantee for it in the future as soon as it could be conferred.

18. Furthermore, all Christians had the history of God's providence before them in reference to freedom and slavery. They found slavery condemned in the case of Joseph, and in the bondage of the Hebrews in Egypt, as well as by the principles of right and wrong in the Old Testament. They found freedom approved and maintained in the families of Abraham, Isaac, and Jacob, under whose administration it gradually disappeared, so that, on the descent to Egypt, it ceased to exist. In the Mosaic code the laws on bond-service rooted out the elements of slavery from among the Hebrews, and inherent, too, in depraved human nature, and established freedom. Hence, the Jews could say, as a nation, in our Lord's time, "We were never in bondage to any man." Our Lord's great commission in general terms proclaimed liberty, not slavery, to the captives, and freedom to all whom it found to be slaves, by its holy influences and heavenly brotherhood. And Paul, the apostle of the Gentiles, the Roman citizen, gave such instruction to masters and slaves as would gradually undermine the system, so as to establish in all Christian lands, in the issue, full civil freedom, as well as freedom from the service of sin.

THE END.

www.ingramcontent.com/pod-product-compliance
Lightning Source LLC
LaVergne TN
LVHW010200110826
845151LV00002B/564
* 9 7 8 1 4 2 5 5 3 6 7 2 5 *